HOW WE OUTWITTED AND SURVIVED THE NAZIS

The True Story of the Holocaust Rescuers, Zofia Sterner and Her Family

HOW WE OUTWITTED AND SURVIVED THE NAZIS

The True Story of the Holocaust Rescuers, Zofia Sterner and Her Family

ROMAN
DZIARSKI

With a foreword by
Eva Fogelman

BOSTON
2023

Library of Congress Cataloging-in-Publication Data

Names: Dziarski, Roman, 1949- author.
Title: How we outwitted and survived the Nazis : the true story of the Holocaust rescuers, Zofia Sterner and her family / Roman Dziarski.
Other titles: True story of the Holocaust rescuers, Zofia Sterner and her family
Description: Boston : Cherry Orchard Books, [2023] | Includes bibliographical references and index.
Identifiers: LCCN 2023025141 (print) | LCCN 2023025142 (ebook) | ISBN 9798887191973 (hardback) | ISBN 9798887191980 (paperback) | ISBN 9798887191997 (adobe pdf) | ISBN 9798887192000 (epub)
Subjects: LCSH: Sterner, Zofia, 1908-2006. | Sterner, Wacław, 1908-1979. | Kosman, Zofia, 1910?-1994. | World War, 1939-1945--Underground movements--Poland. | Holocaust, Jewish (1939-1945)--Poland. | World War, 1939-1945--Jews--Rescue--Poland. | Warsaw (Poland)--History--Uprising, 1944. | Warsaw (Poland)--Biography.
Classification: LCC D765.2.W3 .S7642 (print) | LCC D765.2.W3 (ebook) | DDC 940.53/1835--dc23/eng/20230609
LC record available at https://lccn.loc.gov/2023025141
LC ebook record available at https://lccn.loc.gov/2023025142

ISBN 9798887191973 (hardback)
ISBN 9798887191980 (paperback)
ISBN 9798887191997 (adobe pdf)
ISBN 9798887192000 (epub)

Book design by Lapiz Digital Services.
Cover design by Ivan Grave.

Published by Cherry Orchard Books, an imprint of Academic Studies Press
1577 Beacon Street
Brookline, MA 02446, USA
press@academicstudiespress.com
www.academicstudiespress.com

Contents

Foreword

During World War II, Poland was the only German-occupied country in which anyone caught helping a Jew was sentenced to death. At times, the whole family was killed and hanged in the town square in order to scare others, preventing them from saving the life of a Jew. And yet, in Warsaw alone twenty-eight thousand Jews were hidden, and of those, 11,500 survived. To save one Jew required more than one person to procure food, to obtain false identification papers, to transport them to a safe hideout, to stand vigil, and sometimes to get medication, or find a trustworthy doctor. But also, for a pound of sugar, a bottle of vodka, a pair of boots—valuable commodities in wartime Poland—some Poles would denounce a neighbor who they suspected of harboring a Jew.

The moral dilemmas that an individual confronted in deciding to save a Jew were emotionally consuming. Do you risk the life of your child to save the life of a total stranger? Do you endanger the health of your elderly parents? Do you bring into your home people with contagious diseases? Do you bring into your house additional mouths to feed if you barely have enough food to feed your own family? Do you risk being killed and leave your family without a bread winner in order to transport a Jew to safety? With all these dilemmas—impossible choices all—it is a miracle that there were any rescuers at all!

The official number of rescuers that have been honored as Righteous Among the Nations of the World by Yad Vashem, the World Holocaust Remembrance Center in Israel, does not represent the actual number of Christians and Muslims who risked life and limb to save Jews. Some Poles and Jews were caught and killed. Others were part of the network of rescuers and their true names were not known. Jews did not necessarily know the names of the people who forged false documents for them, or the priests who baptized them, or those who found refuge for them. Children most certainly did not know the names of the nuns or priests in convents, monasteries, and boarding schools in which they were hidden. If Jews were moved from one safe house to another, chances are that they did not know all the individuals involved in their rescue. In some instances, when the war ended, rescuers told their charges to not tell anyone their names for fear of retaliation. In small villages, rescuers were afraid to receive mail from other countries lest their neighbors suspect that they helped Jews during the war. Rescuers were also modest; they felt that what they did was the right thing to do, and they did not want any recognition.

In the case of Poland, 7,177 Poles have been honored by Yad Vashem (as of January 1, 2021). Clearly, thousands of others have not received recognition for the reasons discussed above. Those honored by Yad Vashem did not have ulterior motives for their activities, such as saving a life for Jesus, procuring a child to be their own, financial reward, or obtaining a business. At times, motivations changed. For example, there are cases of hiding a baby and then not wanting to give the child back to the parents who returned after the war. In such, instances, the rescuer was not honored by Yad Vashem.

What is interesting to consider is that even though the goal of rescue was the same in all cases—to save Jews from certain death—the rescuers were not a monolithic group. I interviewed hundreds of rescuers in order to study what they had in common in socialization in their formative years, in personality, and in their situation at the time of their initial decision to rescue. To my surprise, I discovered that rescuers came from all social classes, educational levels, political persuasions, religious beliefs, ages, and genders. Among them were rich people, aristocrats, and poor peasants. They ran the gamut from those with higher academic degrees to men and women who did not know how to read and write. Some were devoutly religious, while others were determined atheists. Still others believed in communism and socialism as their religion.

It is common knowledge that many of the priests in the churches in Poland continued to preach that the Jews killed Christ. Were the values that rescuers learned as children different from those around them? Not surprisingly, the values that a child acquires at home are more significant that those taught by religious leaders or teachers. And indeed, rescuers were imbued with the worldview that all people are people under one God. They were taught to respect and accept a tolerance of people who were different. Familial acceptance of the dynamic of "difference" was at the heart of many of the rescuers' childhoods. Of course, there was a small percentage of those who became rescuers who were antisemitic. They were, however, able to transcend their negative feelings towards Jews when they saw a child in distress or an adult who would soon be killed.

Mothers and fathers were described by rescuers as nurturing, loving, and not punitive. Their parents used explanation to teach what a child did wrong, rather than resort to what was the norm in European countries—corporal punishment. This method set the stage for children to think for themselves, to be independent, and not to fear authority.

One additional factor in the socialization of rescuers is that many of the rescuers grew up during World War I, when fathers were at war, food was limited, and everyone had to help one another. Children experienced loss and had family members and strangers care for them. Rescuers witnessed a central adult in their family perform altruistic acts of kindness. At times, they too were asked to engage in such behavior.

Rescuers shared therefore a heightened sense of empathy and a certain competence. Other qualities, such as resourcefulness, levelheadedness, a facility with role-play, and an ability to withstand anxiety and terror made it possible to continue engaging in rescuing activities for months and years.

Whereas the rescuers had socialization experiences and personality traits in common, their motivations for helping Jews during the German occupation vary. It is important to note that the men, women, and children who risked their lives were not on a suicide mission. Rescuers had some confidence that they would succeed in their risky efforts. I will set out the five types of motivation.

I describe the largest percentage as "moral rescuers." These individuals were either asked to help or they chose help to those they realized were in imminent danger of being killed. These rescuers felt they could not live with themselves if they knowingly let a person die. Their morality stemmed from different sources. Some were more cognitively oriented: "It is the right thing to do." Others were inspired out of pity and compassion for a human being in distress. A third morality stemmed from religious values. Morally motivated rescuers, then, aided people they knew and did not know.

The "Judeophile rescuers" began their helping behavior with people they knew—a lover, spouse, or relative; a colleague, boss, or friend; a caretaker, schoolmate, doctor, or patient. Most of these relational rescuers went on to risk their lives for Jews they did not necessarily know.

Each rescue story is unique. The saga of Zofia Sterner in *How We Outwitted and Survived the Nazis* is that of a relational rescuer. Sterner's initial rescue efforts were undertaken to help her Jewish husband. Despite being in danger herself for being married to a Jew and being pregnant, Sterner was relentless in saving dozens of others. Many of those Jews whom she helped knew neither her name nor the risks she took to save their lives. Sterner did not just hide people in her apartment. Being a rescuer became her full-time occupation. She got Jews out of the Warsaw Ghetto, procured false identification papers for them, found safe hiding places, role-played when necessary, and provided people with food. For much of the war Sterner did not know if her husband was alive or dead; and throughout the war she had to raise her daughter in the grimmest of circumstances.

The "ideological network rescuers" were motivated by their anti-Nazi ideology. They often began by rescuing anti-Nazi resisters. When Jews became endangered, all the systems set in place to help anti-Nazis were used for saving Jews. Network rescuers developed mechanisms to print false identification papers, baptismal certificates, and ration cards; they had hiding places, access to good intelligence, and could communicate by code. Some of the networks were religious—congregants who had Jews living in their homes and rotated the risk among them. The conditions of the occupation necessitated that rescuers work with others where possible. For Sterner to help as many people as she did, she too depended on network rescuers.

"Concerned detached professionals" were teachers, doctors, nurses, clergy, lawyers, social workers, and mental health professionals who risked their livelihoods to save lives. During the occupation these people employed clandestine means to prevent Jews from going to the slaughter.

Diplomats constituted a special category of concerned detached professionals. They could not keep their rescue activities secret or the fact that they wrote visas for thousands of people to escape to neutral countries. They lost their diplomatic status and lived a life of poverty after the war. Since many of those who received visas did not know the name of the diplomat, these diplomats were honored by Yad Vashem posthumously.

The "child rescuers" were youngsters who began their rescue activities at the request of their parents. They went into the ghetto with food and messages or to sneak Jews out. The children would travel with Jews to a hideout. The rationale was that if a man or woman was sitting with a child on a train or bus, the Germans would not think that a Jew was escaping. Sometimes these youngsters stood vigil outside a house to give warning if Nazis approached. As the war in Poland lasted six years, some of the children became teenage rescuers.

How We Outwitted and Survived the Nazis reads like a thriller. It is a page-turner. What makes it unique is that the story conveys the precarious lives of Poles under the German occupation and after liberation without whitewashing the antisemitism that existed. If, like Roman Dziarski, Poles and Jews can acknowledge the suffering of each group, perhaps these groups can transcend the argument about "who suffered most" and work together to teach the history of World War II and its aftermath.

—Eva Fogelman
New York, April 25, 2023

Eva Fogelman is the author of Pulitzer Prize-nominated *Conscience & Courage: Rescuers of Jews During the Holocaust*, a social psychologist, psychotherapist, filmmaker, and founding director of the Jewish Foundation for the Righteous.

Preface

> I hate war as only a soldier who has lived it can, only as one who has seen its brutality, its futility, its stupidity.
> —*Dwight D. Eisenhower*

> Nothing will end wars unless the people themselves refuse to go to war.
> —*Albert Einstein*

War is often portrayed through epic battles that decide winners and losers. But for both civilians and soldiers, war is just trying to survive, hour by hour, day by day. This was even more true in World War II, which was not an ordinary war. It was an unprecedented, orchestrated genocide. It brought out, in sharp contrast, the worst and the best in people. Through their willingness—without hesitation—to risk everything and help others, ordinary people revealed their true humanity and heroism.

This story describes the daily struggles of ordinary people, Zofia Sterner and her family, not only to survive WWII and the Holocaust, but also to live their lives and help to rescue Jews from the Nazis. This story is about remaining human in the most inhumane conditions.

Marek Halter in his book *La force du Bien* (*Stories of Deliverance: Speaking with Men and Women Who Rescued Jews from the Holocaust*) writes of Zofia Sterner:

> [T]here is such a confidence . . ., such a gift, such an excess of Good! I was greatly struck by Zofia Sterner's account of how she led her charges out of the Ghetto . . . . For the entire occupation, the Sterners devoted their hearts and souls to the cause which they had voluntarily chosen: to save Jews, give them comfort, and help them leave for more secure places, with passes in their pockets.[1]

But what exactly happened? How did the Sterners do it? How did they themselves survive and avoid capture and extermination by the murderous Nazi regime? I have written this book to answer these questions.

The story is set in Poland during WWII (figs. 1 and 2) and is entirely true, as remembered by Zofia Sterner and her family (figs. 3–12). It is based on Zofia's diary notes,[2] transcripts of her recollections,[3] my conversations with her and her family,[4] the testimonies of her husband Wacek at the Warsaw war crimes trials in 1946 and 1947,[5–7] Wacek's book about his capture and internment,[8] and Zofia and Edward Kosman's letters. All the names and events are real, as the people in the story recalled and recorded them. To preserve historical accuracy, I have not added any fictional or imagined characters, events, dialog, or dramatization. I have written the story in the present tense, as though events are unfolding before Zofia's eyes.

In order to provide the reader with a better understanding of what the people in Zofia's "memoir" were facing at the time, I have included a few brief descriptions of the broader historical events as she knew them during or after the war. I have also included a few photographs from those dark days. These images are very disturbing. They show the callous brutality of the Nazi genocide that the people in this book were fighting against. I have also added some easily accessible references for further reading and additional historical details in the postface.

Abbreviations and Glossary

AK	Armia Krajowa—Home Army (the largest Polish resistance organization)
AL	Armia Ludowa—People's Army (Polish communist resistance organization)
Bund	Ogólno-Żydowski Związek Robotniczy Bund—General Jewish Labor Bund (Jewish socialist party in Poland)
Endecja	Narodowa Demokracja—National Democracy (Polish right-wing nationalist political movement)
NKVD	Naródnyy komissariát vnútrennikh del—People's Commissariat for Internal Affairs (Soviet political secret service police)
NSZ	Narodowe Siły Zbrojne—National Armed Forces (Polish right-wing resistance organization)
ONR	Obóz Narodowo-Radykalny—National Radical Camp (Polish fascist, far-right, ultra-nationalist organization)

PAL	Polska Armia Ludowa—Polish People's Army (Polish socialist resistance organization)
SS	Schutzstaffel—Protection Squadron (the foremost German security, surveillance, and terror agency). It included the Allgemeine SS (the main branch of the agency), the Waffen-SS (the combat section of the SS), the SS-Totenkopfverbände (SS-TV, the "Death's Head" units, which ran the concentration and extermination camps), and other groups, such as the Einsatzgruppen (Deployment Groups, which were SS paramilitary death squads)
UB	Urząd Bezpieczeństwa—Department of Security (Polish communist political secret service police)
ZWZ	Związek Walki Zbrojnej—Union of Armed Struggle (Polish resistance organization that in February 1942 became Armia Krajowa, AK, the Home Army)
Żegota	Rada Pomocy Żydom przy Delegaturze Rządu RP na Kraj—Council to Aid Jews with the Government Delegation for Poland (Polish resistance organization established to save Jews)
ŻOB	Żydowska Organizacja Bojowa—Jewish Fighting Organization
ŻZW	Żydowski Związek Wojskowy—Jewish Military Organization

The Main Characters

The Narrator (figs. 3, 4, 6–8)—Zofia (Zochna) Sterner (nee Domańska, November 5, 1908–August 24, 2006) was married to Wacław (Wacek) Sterner. Before WWII, she worked as a clerk in a bank in Warsaw, from which she was fired for organizing a worker's union and a strike. Later, she worked in the Ministry of Industry and Trade in Warsaw. After WWII, she worked for an export and import trade company in Warsaw. She was ethnically Polish, but because she was married to a Jew, the Nazi regime treated her as Jewish, which meant that she was supposed to live in the ghetto and eventually face extermination. This rule was enforced in Poland, but not in Germany and most other Nazi-occupied European countries. She did not comply with this rule and never lived in the ghetto.

Wacek (figs. 3, 4, 7)—Wacław Sterner (November 28, 1908–January 24, 1979) was Zofia Sterner's husband and a civil engineer. During WWII, he was a member of the underground Polish Union of Armed Struggle (Związek Walki Zbrojnej, ZWZ) and Polish People's Army (Polska Armia Ludowa, PAL); during the Warsaw Uprising, he was a lieutenant in the Polish Home Army (Armia Krajowa, AK). His pseudonyms were "Boss" and "Adolf." After WWII, he was in charge of the displaced persons camps in Buchhorst, Krümmel, and Spackenberg in Germany; and in Poland, he was the deputy director of the Warsaw Reconstruction Directorate. He was decorated with the Cross of Valor. Wacek's father was of German ancestry and his mother was Jewish. During the German occupation, the Nazi regime's rules classified him as Jewish, and thus he was supposed to live in the ghetto and face extermination. But he lived outside the ghetto, passing as an ethnic Pole.

Basia (fig. 5)—Barbara Sterner (later Kaczarowska, November 21, 1940–June 11, 2020) was a daughter of Zofia and Wacław Sterner. During the German occupation, the Nazi regime's rules classified her as Jewish because her father was Jewish, and thus she was supposed to live in the ghetto and face extermination. But she lived with her parents outside the ghetto. After WWII, she graduated from the University of Warsaw with a master's degree in Polish language and literature and became an editor at the Iskry Publishing House in Warsaw. She was the mother of Małgorzata (Małgosia) Kaczarowska.

Tadeusz (figs. 6–8)—Tadeusz Domański (July 16, 1913–September 14, 1981) was Zofia Sterner's brother. During WWII, he was a second lieutenant in the underground Polish People's Army (Polska Armia Ludowa, PAL) and had the pseudonym "Żuk." After WWII, he was in charge of the displaced persons camp in Krümmel, Germany; afterwards, in Poland, he was a foreign trade representative for the Polish government. He was decorated with the Golden Cross of Merit.

Niusia (figs. 8–10)—Janina Dziarska (nee Domańska, June 24, 1910–March 17, 2003) was Zofia Sterner's sister. She was a dentist and, during the Warsaw Uprising, was a nurse in the Polish Home Army.

Kazio (figs. 9–11)—Kazimierz Dziarski (November 27, 1907–December 29, 1986) was Janina Dziarska's husband. He was a dentist. During WWII, he was an officer in the Polish army in France (General Bronisław Prugar-Ketling's Second Infantry Fusiliers Division) and later in the Polish First Armored Division in Scotland.

Zofia (Zosia) Kosman (fig. 13) (c. 1910–January 11, 1994) was Edward (Edek) Kosman's wife. She was a biologist. Because she was Jewish, she was forced to live in the Warsaw Ghetto during the German occupation. She escaped and was helped to survive by the Sterner and Dziarski families. After WWII, she emigrated to Australia.

Ezra Edward (Edek) Kosman (fig. 13) (August 26, 1910–June 10, 1997) was Zofia (Zosia) Kosman's husband. He was born in Warsaw, graduated from medical school in 1933, and specialized in internal medicine. Because he was Jewish, during the German occupation he was forced to live in the Warsaw

Ghetto (on 12 Zamenhofa Street), where he worked as the chief physician in a Jewish hospital. He escaped from the ghetto and was helped to survive by the Sterner and Dziarski families. During the Warsaw Uprising, he served as a physician in the Polish Home Army. After the war, he emigrated to Australia and worked as a physician.

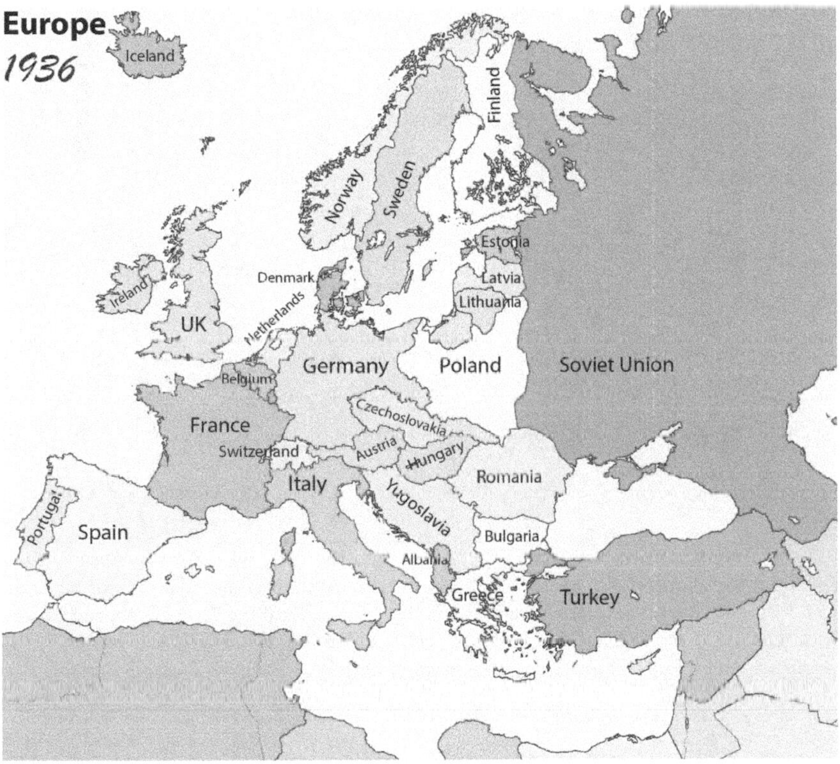

FIGURE 1. Pre-World War II Europe.

FIGURE 2. Pre-World War II Poland. The cities, towns, and villages featured in the story are indicated with black triangles; the border between the German and the Soviet occupation zones from October 1939 to June 1941 is shown by black dots. After the German invasion of the Soviet Union on June 22, 1941, the entire territory of Poland fell under German occupation.

FIGURE 3. The narrator, Zofia (Zochna) Sterner (1943), and Wacław (Wacek) Sterner (1930s), Zofia's husband.

FIGURE 4. Zofia and Wacek Sterner on vacation in the Carpathian Mountains in Poland before WWII, late 1930s.

FIGURE 5. Basia—Barbara Sterner, daughter of Zofia and Wacek Sterner—in Warsaw, 1943.

FIGURE 6. Tadeusz Domański, Zofia Sterner's brother, with Zofia in Warsaw, early 1940s.

FIGURE 7. Tadeusz, Zofia, and Wacek (from left to right) in Warsaw, 1933.

FIGURE 8. The Domański family in Warsaw, c. 1916: Anna (née Szczerek, June 23, 1877–December 26, 1957) and Józef (1863–April 5, 1941) with children (from left to right): Zofia (Zochna), Janina (Niusia, later Dziarska), and Tadeusz.

FIGURE 9. Niusia (Janina Dziarska) and Kazio (Kazimierz Dziarski), her husband, c. 1939.

FIGURE 10. Niusia and Kazio on vacation in the Mazovia region in Poland before WWII, late 1930s.

Figure 11. Kazio (top, the first on the left, middle row) with other Polish officers in his unit in Wiesendangen on November 28, 1941; and on a street in the Zürich area in 1942 (bottom, Kazio in the middle).

FIGURE 12. The Dziarski family in Warsaw in 1906: Wiktoria (nee Kacprzak, died February 7, 1943) and Michał Andrzej Dziarski (c. 1873–March 5, 1924) with their children (from left to right: Maria [Mancia, February 1, 1906–Feb 1945]; Anna [later Barczewska, c. 1892–July 12, 1930]; Jadwiga [Jadzia, c. 1903–c. 1908]; Janina [Janka, later Urbańska, c. 1894–c.1965]; and Eugeniusz [Gienio, December 17, 1896–December 4, 1972]). Kazio and Zofia [later Winiarska] were not born yet.

FIGURE 13. Zosia and Edek Kosman in Vaucluse, Australia, November 1988.

Chapter 1

Fleeing

> There are no extraordinary men and women . . . just extraordinary circumstances that ordinary men and women are forced to deal with.
> —*William Halsey*

We are moving slowly on a narrow road packed with fleeing people, on foot, in horse-drawn wagons, and occasionally in cars. We've been on the road for three hours. It is already afternoon, and we are not even halfway to Kielce. Suddenly, our car engine starts to sputter and then dies. Steam or smoke is coming out from under the hood. "Darn it! The engine overheated," my chauffeur mutters. We get out of the car and other people help us push it off the road.

There are fields on both sides of the road and a few houses in the distance, which we have already passed. "Where are we?" I ask my chauffeur.

"Maybe three kilometers away from Pińczów. We just passed Michałów." He opens the hood, shakes his head, and says, "I'll go to the village and look for help. Madam, please wait in the car and watch the luggage."

He is gone for a long time, which is not surprising, as everything is in a disarray. I have a lot of time to think. It is Monday, September 4, 1939. The news that the war had broken out came over the radio early in the morning on Friday, September 1. The next day, we saw scores of bombers flying low, in formation, dropping bombs on the railroad station and the city hall. The noise from the engines and the explosions was unbearable, and everything was covered with dust and smoke.

For weeks before it began, people were saying that war was imminent and that we had to get ready. There were ominous signs. Germany withdrew from the German-Polish nonaggression pact at the end of April and Hitler demanded the Free City of Danzig (Gdańsk) and the Polish Corridor (with its access to the Baltic Sea).[9, i] But then, most people did not want to believe that a new war would start and hoped that Hitler was just posturing in order to pressure Europe into making concessions. Besides, Poland still had mutual defense treaties with France and Great Britain. Mere days before the war started, many still did not believe it would happen. After all, mobilization orders for the Polish military had been issued twice and then immediately canceled.

At the beginning of the war, Wacek and I were living with my parents in Miechów, near Kraków. They had moved there a few years earlier from Warsaw (Warszawa) when my father retired. We have been constantly on the move since we got married in 1935 because Wacek is supervising the construction of a highway from Warsaw to Kraków.

Wacek must report to the provincial government office and a mobilization point in Kielce, some one hundred kilometers away. We decided to go together, hoping that we can stay in Kielce. But I left my parents in Miechów with a heavy heart, as I am worried about them staying alone now just as the war has started. They assured me, though, that the hostilities will soon be over and that they are not in any danger. They told me that in World War I the armies fought between themselves and civilians were left alone.

Wacek went ahead to Kielce on a motorcycle to beat the traffic, and I am following in the car with our luggage. We planned to meet later today in front of the City Hall. He kept telling me, "My dear, don't worry about anything.

---

i Gdańsk (the Free City of Danzig) was a semi-autonomous city-state created in 1920 after World War I in accordance with the Treaty of Versailles. Most of its citizens were ethnic Germans, but Germany did not govern it and Poland had certain rights to the use of its railways and port facilities. The Polish Corridor, established as Polish territory by the treaty, gave Poland access to the Baltic Sea. It was located west of Gdańsk and East Prussia, which was part of Germany but had no land connection with the rest of that country (fig. 2). After the German annexation of Austria and the Sudetenland portion of Czechoslovakia in 1938, and occupation of the rest of Czechoslovakia in 1939, Hitler demanded Gdańsk and the Polish Corridor.

The most important thing is that we'll be together, and we'll support each other." So if I can get the car fixed, I will still make it there tonight or tomorrow.

We do not know what Wacek's assignment in Kielce will be. He could be an officer in the army, as he was a cadet in the military academy when we first met. I begin to worry that he may be killed in the fighting. But as a civil engineer, maybe he can continue supervising the construction of the bridges and the highway from Warsaw to Kraków. They will need a lot of repairs after all the bombings. This gives me hope that we can stay together.

Finally, my chauffeur comes back with a local mechanic and some spare parts and tools. They will work on the car. But because it is almost evening, my chauffeur has found us a room in the village for tonight. He gives me the address and I walk back to the village and find the house. It is a small cottage, but the room is clean and the hostess is pleasant. She offers me some milk, bread, butter, and cheese for supper. The chauffeur and the mechanic come back late with good news—they have managed to fix the car.

We spend the night in the village, and at 5:00 am the next morning we set out for Kielce. We only get to nearby Pińczów, and as we are driving through the market square the military police stop us. They demand the gas from our car. They explain that all the gas from all civilian vehicles is being confiscated for the use by the military. Obviously, there is no gas available anywhere at any price. This makes our car useless. I decide to leave the car in Pińczów and walk to Kielce, some forty or fifty kilometers away. I hope that because I did not meet Wacek in Kielce yesterday evening, he will come back on the motorcycle to pick me up.

I set out from Pińczów at around 8:00 am with my chauffeur, who kindly carries my suitcases, even though he does not have to. After walking for over three hours, we find out that the road north to Kielce through Kije is already under artillery fire. Now we can only get to Kielce by a longer way—going back southeast to Busko and then north through Chmielnik. We take this route and walk towards Busko on narrow local roads. There is a lot of confusion and people are fleeing in every direction. Exhausted, we finally arrive in Busko at around 3:00 pm, but find the situation there quite desperate. There are lots of soldiers getting ready to march and there is nothing to eat, not even bread. To make matters worse, the route to Kielce from Busko is also impossible now because the Germans have already invaded Chmielnik, which is on the way. I immediately realize that my hopes of meeting Wacek are completely dashed, as neither of us will be able to get through the enemy lines.

We have not eaten since the morning and even water is hard to find, but we can pump some from occasional public wells. My chauffeur leaves me, as he has also realized that he cannot reach Kielce. So I am now on my own and my only option is to go back to my parents in Miechów. But how? I am also running low on cash. I only have twenty złotys after paying for the expensive car repair. I desperately go around Busko and finally find a carter with a horse-drawn wagon who is returning to Pińczów and then Wodzisław, and who could possibly take me from there back to Miechów. I immediately take this opportunity. I buy a couple of biscuits for twenty groszy (0.2 złotys) and a bit of chocolate for another twenty groszy, the only food available. Also, a stranger, seeing my distress, gives me an apple. This is all my food for the entire trip, and I must manage it wisely.

We get back to Pińczów around 6:00 pm. There is a huge panic in the city. Everyone is fleeing and talking about the executions of large numbers of captured civilians by the Wehrmacht soldiers. But we decide to continue to try to get home to Miechów, despite the danger of being captured by the advancing Wehrmacht. It is hard for me to believe all these stories about executions of civilians. After all, Germans are such law-abiding and highly cultured people. Nevertheless, these stories make me now even more determined to get back and try to protect my parents.

Soon, we will find out how true these stories were. On August 22, 1939, a week before invading Poland, Adolf Hitler gave the following instructions to his military commanders: "Kill without pity or mercy all men, women, and children of Polish descent or language."[9] This order was the beginning of ethnic cleansing in Poland—Operation Tannenberg.[10] Hitler named the operation after the First Battle of Tannenberg,[ii] which took place in 1410 (fig. 14)[11] and was still remembered by the Third Reich's leaders centuries later. In this battle, the Kingdom of Poland and Lithuania defeated the Order of Teutonic

---

ii The First Battle of Tannenberg, also known as the Battle of Grunwald, took place on July 15, 1410 (fig. 14). The battle was a decisive victory for the Kingdom of Poland and Lithuania, led by King Władysław II Jagiełło, and a total defeat of the Order of Teutonic Knights of German/Prussian origin, who were expanding eastward into Poland and Lithuania. Most of the Teutonic Knights' leadership was killed or taken prisoner, which stopped the eastward expansion of the order and cemented the domination of the Kingdom of Poland and Lithuania in Eastern Europe. Teutonic Prussia was transformed into the Duchy of Prussia in the sixteenth century, but remained a Polish-Lithuanian fiefdom until 1660, when it was liberated and became a part of Prussia. In 1871, the Duchy of Prussia became a part of unified Germany as East Prussia, and after WWI it became an exclave of Germany (fig. 2). After WWII, East Prussia was divided between Poland and the Soviet Union.

Knights of German/Prussian origin, and cemented the domination of the Kingdom of Poland and Lithuania over Eastern Europe until the end of the eighteenth century. Thus, by invading and subjugating Poland, Hitler wanted to reverse this history.

But we are still unaware of all the destruction that awaits us, and we leave Busko for Miechów. Soon, a group of fleeing men attacks our wagon and pushes the carter out of the driving seat. They turn the horses around and start racing back to Busko. We are still in the wagon, but our protests are ignored. They say that German tanks are advancing towards us and that we have to flee. Late in the evening, we are in Busko once more.

I have no place to spend the night, and my only option is to stay on the wagon and continue to go east with the rest of the people. But a new hope emerges: I may be able to stop at any of the county offices in the towns on our way and look for a county engineer, who is bound to know Wacek, the province's chief engineer, and may offer some help or a way to contact him.

I do not get off the wagon for two days and three nights, except for during air raids, when we have to jump down, run into the fields, and lie on the ground, hoping that the bullets from the machine guns from low-flying planes do not hit us. This happens every few kilometers and is most terrifying. Luckily, they do not hit us or our horses.

I ate all my food a long time ago, but fortunately my travelling companions on the wagon kindly share their food with me. We continue east on small local roads through Stopnica and Staszów, together with other people who are also fleeing east. All the county offices on our way have already evacuated and are closed. My hopes are now on Sandomierz, the largest town further east.

I cling onto the wagon. It is my only means of transportation. But in Bogoria, despite their previous kindness, the men who took it over throw me and my suitcases over the side. They have decided not to go to Sandomierz. It is difficult to make any rational decisions about what to do and where to go because the situation is changing so rapidly, there is so much confusion, and there are no reliable sources of information. I become desperate and start crying and pleading with the men to continue going to Sandomierz, which is my only hope for getting help and finding out where Wacek is. Eventually, my tears persuade them to let me back on and continue the journey to Sandomierz, which is some forty kilometers away by this time.

We arrive in the middle of the night. I stay on the wagon till the morning, only to find out again that all the offices are closed in Sandomierz as well and that the county engineer has left in an unknown direction. My hopes are dashed again; I do not know where to go next. As I have not slept for three days and four nights, I would like to stop and find a place to rest, but I do not want to spend what remains of my money to pay for a room. I will need it to buy food. And most of all, we have to continue going east to stay ahead of the Wehrmacht which is fast advancing behind us. Unfortunately, our horses are exhausted and cannot continue without getting some food, which is nowhere to be found. So we have to abandon our wagon, and I decide to continue on foot to Rozwadów, the next town some thirty kilometers east. I still have my two heavy suitcases. Two men from the wagon join me and offer to carry one of them; I carry the other. We cannot find any food, and although we are hungry we continue walking.

Luckily, we come across another horse-drawn wagon that is also travelling east, and the carter allows us to get on. The road is still full of people, mostly on foot, carrying packages or suitcases. Some push carts or baby strollers loaded with their belongings, often with babies or children strapped on top. There are a few horse-drawn wagons, but no cars, as gas is not available. On the way, we pick up a lieutenant. This is very fortunate because his uniform garners a lot of respect and he gets some oats for our horses in the village. The oats give the horses enough nourishment for them to continue pulling the wagon. Without food, they would soon collapse.

There are two air raids, and we have to stop and run into the fields. The airplanes with noisily rattling engines and machine guns mainly target the nearby village and the road. Three houses are on fire, people are fleeing from the village, and some fall. I do not know if they have been hit or are trying to evade the bullets. Then the airplanes turn around and, flying low, some sixty meters overhead, direct their machine gun fire at us and at the carts and wagons on the road. We are terrified and barely avoid getting hit. When the raid is over, we return to the road and see several horses lying on the ground in pools of blood, some still jerking their legs. But fortunately, our horses have not been hit, and we get back on the wagon and continue our journey.

The lieutenant is very kind and encouraging. He promises to take me to Rozwadów, from where we can take a train to Lublin and then another to Warsaw, where my sister and brother live. That lifts my spirits, as I hope Wacek will also try to go back to Warsaw. But I am still very weak from the lack of food and sleep for several days. Fortunately, a schoolteacher in one of the roadside villages generously gives us some hot milk and a piece of bread—now our only remaining sustenance.

We arrive in Rozwadów around noon, but it turns out that the rail connection with Lublin is blocked because of the bombed rail tracks, stations, and trains. The Rozwadów station master suggests going to Warsaw via Lwów, Rawa Ruska, and Lublin. This is a very long, roundabout way, but we agree because there is no other option. The train is in the evening, so we go into the town, which is still relatively unaffected by the war. We finally find a restaurant that is open and eat our first meal in many days. We also buy several rolls and sausages for the journey.

At 6:00 pm, we finally get on the train, which is overcrowded and cold. We are heading southeast to Przemyśl, some 130 kilometers away from Rozwadów. Then we will have to go to Lwów, another 110 kilometers to the east. I meet a young lad, Jóźko. He turns out to be a released detainee from Lwów and is also heading to Warsaw. I have nothing warm to wear, and Jóźko covers me with his blanket. We spend a lot of time talking about our pasts and discussing our views. He is a communist or a communist sympathizer and was held for organizing or participating in some communist activities. I am a socialist and I believe in workers' rights and equality for everyone, but I am wary of a Soviet-style communist regime.

The further we go, the more I am horrified by the devastation of the towns and villages. There are many destroyed or burning buildings and train stations. They must have been bombed very recently because the air is still thick with smoke and dust from the collapsed buildings. We flee as fast as we can, but the German bombers are faster and destroy everything ahead of us. The train constantly stops because the tracks are damaged and must be repaired. And all the time, we worry that the German tanks and troops will soon catch up with us.

During the frequent air raids, we jump off the train and run into the fields. The bombs target the trains, tracks, train stations, and other buildings. But then the low-flying planes chase after the people from our train, who scatter into the fields, and spray them with machine gun fire. Some people fall down. I have never seen people being shot at and killed. I am nauseated and my head is spinning. When the raid is over, the passengers carry the wounded back onto the train. I do not know how to help the wounded or who will take care of the dead. The bodies are abandoned in the fields (fig. 15) because we must get back on the train and not be left behind.

Our train gets stuck behind other trains stopped ahead of us several times, and we have to move to these ones. Unfortunately, in Przeworsk, our lieutenant, who has been my guide, decides to go somewhere else and leaves us.

We ate all our food a long time ago and there is nothing available at the devastated, bombed-out stations we are passing. But when the train stops, Jóźko jumps out, runs into the fields, pulls up beets from the ground, and we eat them raw.

As we continue moving east, the destruction is getting increasingly worse. We pass more burning railway stations, right after bombardment. Often the dust from the destroyed buildings is still in the air; it smells strongly of smoke and breathing is hard. The signals do not work, but miraculously we avoid disastrous collisions with other trains. There is no railway service anywhere at the stations and passengers themselves carry water, coal, and wood for the steam locomotive. In Jarosław, we must do it under the fire of machine guns from low-flying airplanes. Destruction and danger are everywhere, but I have no more energy to process it all. I have become numb to my surroundings, and I can only think that I have to get through to the next point of my journey. I cannot even think about what I will do next. I cannot even remember what day it is anymore. Someone says that it is already September 9.

Late at night, we arrive in Żurawica, nine kilometers away from Przemyśl, but we learn that the railway tracks are completely destroyed and blocked. Nobody knows when the trains will start running. Luckily, bedsides Jóźko, I have two other very kind and caring travel companions—Stefan Guzik and Władysław Skalski. We discuss our options. Since the roads to Przemyśl may also be blocked, we decide to walk on local roads east to Medyka, ten kilometers away, bypassing Przemyśl. Early in the morning, Stefan brings some food from the village, which is a miracle, as no food is available anywhere. We leave the train and start walking. I still have my suitcases with me—I carry one and Jóźko carries the other, as Stefan and Władysław have their own luggage to carry. They are all very helpful and cordial and try to cheer me up; I am still using Jóźko's blanket because it is cold.

We get to Medyka on September 10 at around noon. I am exhausted and decide to get rid of my suitcases because I cannot carry even one suitcase anymore. With a heavy heart, I hand out all Wacek's things and manage to sell his new suit for fifteen złotys. I keep some of my clothes, and Stefan and Władysław graciously agree to put them into their suitcases and carry them for me.

Medyka is a small village, but has a train station. And we get a pleasant surprise there: an evacuation train is leaving eastward for Lwów. A large crowd is waiting, and when the train arrives, everyone rushes to get on. Stefan and I squeeze into the train car with difficulty. But in the commotion, we lose sight of Władysław and Jóźko. Unfortunately, in his suitcase Władysław has my purse—containing my national identification card and medical insurance booklet—and my clothing. There is nothing I can do about it now and I am just happy that I got on the train. Driven by some instinct, I put my second identification card from the province and my money into my skirt pocket.

The train does not leave for several hours because there are multiple air raids. However, nobody leaves and we all take a chance on the train not being hit and blown up. We do not want to lose our cramped seats on the overcrowded train, which could be easily taken by the many people left on the platform. Eventually, at 9:00 pm, the train leaves Medyka for Lwów. The direction is still eastward, further and further away from Warsaw, but we have no other option, as we have to keep fleeing from the advancing Germans.

The train crawls all night, somehow avoiding being hit in several air raids. The raids are usually very accurate and do a lot of damage to the tracks, which have to be constantly repaired. Although Lwów is only eighty-five kilometers from Medyka, it takes us until 3:00 pm on September 11 to arrive. The train station is destroyed. The station warehouses are on fire and so are many train cars. The thick smoke makes the air difficult to breathe and stings the eyes. The train trucks are damaged, and the train cars are piled up. There is no way to get through; the trains are not running. My hopes of going to Warsaw are dashed again. I am weighed down by the thought that I cannot go there and by not knowing how long I will be travelling or what to do next.

Chapter 2

Getting Help

We have not eaten in more than a day and there is no food available at the bombed-out Lwów train station. We leave the train and start walking to the city. The streets are littered with debris from the collapsed buildings. There is smoke and dust in the air, many bomb craters, and we have to avoid buildings that are still on fire and may collapse any minute. In the city, we cannot find anything to eat either. The stores are closed or empty.

I part with Stefan and my other travelling companions and look for the provincial government office. I hope to get some information there and find a district engineer, who may know Wacek and may be able to help me. Only a few people are still in the building. They do not know anything and send me to the county office. When I get there I am so weak that I can barely stand and talk. Again, the clerk tells me he does not know anything. At this point, my vision becomes blurred, the room spins, I lose my balance, and everything goes black.

I wake up lying down on a couch in a room that looks like an office, and a gentleman I do not recognize is kneeling beside me. He introduces himself as Mr. Biliński, the mayor of Lwów, and he tells me I am in his office. He gives me some water to drink, and I lie on his couch for several minutes simply thinking that I am still alive—apparently it was not yet my time to die. Then, another gentleman enters the room and introduces himself as Mr. Władysław

Dziadosz, the governor (voivode) of Kielce Province. I gather all my energy, jump to my feet, present my entire situation to him, and ask if he can help me, as Wacek, the chief province engineer, is his employee. The governor is very polite, even cordial, and tells me to come the next day to the Provincial Office, where I will be able to obtain some money. He also tells me that the Kielce Provincial Office has been moved to Horochów; but he does not know, of course, whether Wacek is there, as all the communication lines are broken.

I already feel much better, my heart is lighter, and I have regained hope that I will find my dear Wacek. Mr. Biliński is also very kind and cordial and takes me to a restaurant for dinner. I have not eaten in two days, and I have not had a proper meal in many days. I order a pork schnitzel with roasted potatoes and stewed cabbage. It is delicious, but soon after dinner I get sick and vomit, since my empty stomach cannot take such a rich meal. Weak again, I return to the county office, which is still open. They allow me to lie down on the couch and spend the night there.

For the first time in many days, I sleep all night; and best of all, in the morning I wash myself and change my clothing for the first time in more than a week. I can finally clear my head and think about what to do next. It is already September 12. Going back west to Warsaw is now out of the question, as Mr. Biliński told me he heard on the radio that the city is under heavy aerial bombardment and artillery fire. The Wehrmacht troops are already on the outskirts. I think that my best option would be to wait somewhere here in the countryside until the hostilities are over. Then I remember that my high school friend, Janka Schwarzenberg-Czerny, lives somewhere east of Lwów with her husband, Tadek. I must find her, but I do not have her address.

I go back to the Provincial Office and find the lieutenant governor, Mr. Lutowski, there. I refer to the conversation I had yesterday with the governor, and ask how I can get the money I was promised. Mr. Lutowski says that he knows nothing about the arrangement and refuses to help. Fortunately, at that moment, Mr. Dziadosz comes in and orders him to pay me two hundred złotys in the form of a loan given to Wacek. He hands me a receipt to sign, which to my surprise, says that the loan to Wacek Sterner comes "from the fund for the construction of the monument of Marshal Piłsudski." Obviously, the governor has realized that there are more important things to do with the fund now.

Having some money in my pocket greatly lifts my spirits, and I buy a toothbrush, toothpaste, soap, and some other essentials. All day long I walk around Lwów, asking for Janka's address. Finally, I come to the Agricultural Chamber of Commerce. They tell me that she has a farm in Zuchorzyce and give me her address and directions. They do not know if she is there now, but I decide to look, as I do not have anywhere else to go. There is a train scheduled to leave from Lwów at 2:00 am. However, another heavy bombing starts in the afternoon. It is not safe to stay in the city any longer or travel by train, if any are even available.

Thus again, at 7:00 pm I set out on foot all by myself from Lwów to Zuchorzyce, some twenty-five kilometers east. I do not know the way, but someone tells me to walk first towards Łyczaków, and then towards Kurowice. The road is full of people, civilians and soldiers, all fleeing towards the Romanian border. I still have some luggage with me, but after a while it becomes too heavy to carry and I throw things out of my suitcase one by one. Finally, I come across a horse-drawn wagon that is carrying ammunition, and the carter allows me to get on and sit on the munition boxes. I keep hoping that they do not explode when we hit a bump on the road or encounter another air raid. Every few kilometers, the carter throws me off the wagon and demands a payment of two złotys to let me get on again.

At 2:00 am, I get down from the wagon in Kurowice and set out on foot to Zuchorzyce, ten kilometers away. It is dark and there is nobody on this side road. I have nothing to eat or drink, and all the water wells I pass are empty. Thankfully, I come across a hut by the road and knock on the door. After a while, a woman opens the door and I ask for some water. She promptly comes back with a cup of water, a jar of *kompot* (fruit stew), and a piece of bread. She also shows me a shortcut to Janka's farm in Zuchorzyce. Finally, at 6:00 am, exhausted, I am knocking on the door of a large manor house.

Janka opens the door with a look of disbelief on her face, and we fall into each other's arms, crying. She takes my suitcase, leads me inside, shows me where to wash and change, and serves a delicious breakfast of hot coffee with milk, bread, butter, eggs, sausage, and cheese. She still cannot believe that I am here—but I do not have enough energy to explain anything. I drink and eat a little and collapse into a bed with clean, soft, white pillows and sheets. I just lie there, too tired to fall asleep or to get up, but eventually sleep wins over. It is September 13.

Chapter 3

A Mob and Loss

When I wake up, it is late afternoon or early evening and I finally have enough strength to tell Janka about my harrowing journey. Janka and Tadek live on a large dairy farm with eighty cows, which produce milk that they deliver to Lwów; and they also make cream, butter, and cheese. Obviously, she has heard about the war and bombing raids on Warsaw and Lwów on the radio, but it is still very peaceful here on the farm, with no signs of any hostilities. She is horrified when I tell her about all the destruction and killing that I have seen.

The next few days are relaxing and quiet, and I begin to recover from my physical hardships. There are fields around us and a forest in the distance. The sun is warm; the birds are chirping; the trees are still lush and dark green; and the tall grass in the meadows has turned golden. The tranquility of my surroundings brings back my childhood memories of our summer vacations. To escape the heat in Warsaw, we always spent the summers in the countryside. We often went to the farm of our friends, the Marchwińskis, in Kamionek near Warsaw, which was situated on the vast lands of Count Łączyński, on the east bank of Vistula (Wisła) River. We lived in their large manor near Lake Kamionkowskie. Their daughter Jania Marchwińska was my best friend. I remember running through the grassy meadows, picking flowers and wild strawberries, swimming in the lake, holding newly hatched chicks or newly born piglets, and riding in horse-drawn carriages, as if it was yesterday.

But my pleasant memories soon give way to psychological torments. I worry about my parents in Miechów, my sister and my brother in Warsaw, and above all about Wacek, who must be completely without money, as he did not get his paycheck on September 1 when the war broke out. He is also without any fresh clothes, as I had all his luggage. He could be in the army fighting now, or captured and taken prisoner; he may not be alive. I cannot find out anything because all communications with the rest of the country have been cut. My mental suffering seems worse than all the physical hardships of my journey to Zuchorzyce. I try to keep myself busy and cling to anything I can do or help with in the house and around the farm. I even help them make butter from cream and load it into large barrels. I do all this work to distract myself from my dark, unbearable thoughts.

To make matters worse, a few days later, on September 17, the news comes over the radio that the Red Army has invaded Poland from the east. Janka tells me that the border is some 150 kilometers east from Zuchorzyce; but we immediately realize that with most of the Polish troops fighting the Germans advancing from the west, the Red Army could be in Zuchorzyce and then Lwów within days. There will be no place to flee. And indeed, by September 19, the Red Army has reached the outskirts of Lwów. The fighting bypasses Zuchorzyce, but we are devastated and apprehensive about what will happen to us. Later, we found out that the Soviet invasion of Poland was arranged between the Third Reich and the Soviet Union. According to the infamous Molotov-Ribbentrop Pact of August 23, 1939, Hitler's army was to invade Poland from the west on September 1, 1939, and the Soviet Red Army from the east.[12, 13]

On September 19, a Soviet commissioner from the nearby village visits the manor. He looks around the entire farm and the house and talks to Janka and her husband, Tadek. The commissioner says that he came to assure them they are safe and have nothing to worry about, as the new Soviet authorities will protect them. We are not sure what to make out of his visit and whether we can trust him. We know the Soviets have annexed the entire eastern region of Poland, and we worry that they want to take the land and everything else from landowners and introduce the communist system here. Most of the landowners in this region are Polish, but over 60% of the villagers are Ukrainians or Belarusians. These peasants often hate the landowners, because the landowners usually take advantage of the peasants. We do not know what will happen to Janka's farm under Soviet rule.

The next morning, Janka bursts into my room and tells me to dress quickly and put on as many layers of my clothes as I can. While I dress, I look out the window and see that a mob of peasants has surrounded the manor. The crowd stands there quietly; it slightly undulates from side to side for what seems to be a very long time, but is probably only a couple of minutes. Then suddenly, as though on command, the mob storms the manor and begins looting. The peasants do not attack us and pay really very little attention to us; it is like we are not there. But they grab everything in the house that they can carry. It is the worst thing I have ever seen. They take all of the house and kitchen appliances, pots, crockery, silverware, food, clothes, linens, pictures, window curtains, carpets, and furniture. They remove all the door handles, yank the stove out of the kitchen, and rip the metal portions of the fireplaces out of the walls. They even take the shoes from Janka's little daughters' feet and steal the dolls the little girls are hugging. When it is all over, there is absolutely nothing left in the house—just bare walls. We sit on the floor speechless, looking at the destruction and each other in total disbelief. Eventually, we gather ourselves and go outside, only to discover that the entire farm has been looted, too.

In the evening, two village women who used to work on the farm come to the manor. They tell Janka that they pretended to take two of her cows, a sewing machine, some linens, and a few other possessions. But they have hidden and saved them in their village huts. When it gets dark, we go and retrieve the cows and the items. The women also give us some food for supper.

There is not much I can do to help Janka, besides trying to cheer her up. I know now that I will only be a burden to her and that I need to leave. She gives me the address of her distant cousin in Lwów, but I have no way of getting there. The only things I have are the clothes I am wearing and a pair of very fancy dress shoes that I hid from the looters. I do not know why I kept these shoes and did not throw them away when I was getting rid of my luggage, or why I hid them from the looters—I have no use for them. But now they are my prized possessions. So, I go to the village to sell them. They garner a lot of attention, but because I am petite, they are too small for all the peasant women who try them on. However, one woman likes the shoes so much that, even though she cannot squeeze her feet into them, she exchanges several eggs, a loaf of bread, and a headscarf for them.

I also find out that the Red Army took Lwów on September 22 and that the entire province is now under Soviet rule. This means that travel is restricted; to go from one town to another, travel documents approved by the Soviet authorities are required. I look for someone who is going to Lwów. By chance, I meet a Jewish man, Mr. Löwi, who lives in the city, has a pass to travel, and is going back home in his horse-drawn wagon. He is very kind and agrees to take me with him, which is obviously risky, because I do not have travel papers.

We set out the next day, on September 24. I dress in my peasant's headscarf and pretend to be Mr. Löwi's sister. When we enter Lwów late at night, two Soviet soldiers stop us to check our documents. I am very frightened, but they are satisfied with Mr. Löwi's travel pass and our explanation that I am his sister and allow us to proceed. Mr. and Mrs. Löwi are very well-off and have a large, elegant house in the city. Because it is late and I have no place to go, they invite me to spend the night at their house. Mr. Löwi makes his poor brother move out of his room in the middle of the night and gives it to me. Although everything is spotlessly clean, I cannot sleep in this still-warm bed of a stranger, with all the unfamiliar smells and surroundings. But of course, I cannot refuse this generous offer. In the morning, they serve me a scrumptious breakfast and then I set out for the city. I pass several buildings destroyed by bombs or artillery fire and see Soviet soldiers patrolling the streets; fortunately they do not stop me.

I find the house of Janka's distant cousin, Dr. Obmiński, and his wife. I do not know them and they, of course, do not know that I am coming. They turn out to be very hospitable and caring and invite me to stay. I spend a few restful and pleasant days there, but I am still worried about Wacek and my family, and now also about my health.

Throughout the entire journey, I have been trying to put out of my mind that I am pregnant. I did not tell Wacek before we left because I wanted to wait two more weeks to be certain that everything was going well. But I am having frequent pains in my lower abdomen, and I worry that all the hunger and the physical and mental strains of the last three weeks are taking their toll. The next day, September 28, which is Wacek's name day, I have more severe cramps in the evening, and I go to lie down. Soon my bedsheets become heavily stained with unusually dark-brown watery blood containing clots and debris. I call Mrs. Obmiński and she quickly summons her husband. He confirms my worst fears—miscarriage. It is already late at night, and because of the curfew we cannot seek help or go anywhere. I feel weak and confused. The next morning, Dr. Obmiński takes me to his hospital. They confirm his diagnosis and check me in for further observation.

My worries are now amplified by grief and guilt. Why didn't I tell Wacek? Why did I go on this trip? What could I have done to protect my unborn baby? I keep telling myself that the trip to Kielce was supposed to be short and nobody could have predicted how badly it would turn out. But all the time, I am tormented by these dark thoughts and guilt.

Chapter 4

Reunion and Fleeing Again

After three days in the hospital, I feel better. It is October 2, and I will remember this day for the rest of my life, because suddenly and totally unexpectedly, Wacek and Mrs. Obmiński enter my hospital room. With disbelief and indescribable joy, I jump out of bed and fall into Wacek's arms! He is alive and well; he has miraculously found me and he is taking me out of the hospital!

After we separated on September 4, 1939, Wacek joined the Polish army in Kielce and defended Kielce and Dęblin. Then, he travelled throughout the whole of Poland looking for me. He first went to Warsaw and then to all other towns and cities where we have family or friends— and that is how he eventually got to Zuchorzyce, from where Janka directed him to Lwów.

As Lwów is under Soviet occupation, we have nowhere to go. Dr. and Mrs. Obmiński are very generous to allow both of us to stay at their house for several days while we weigh our options as to what to do next. Because going back to Warsaw is still dangerous due to the continuing hostilities, we decide to look for work and to live somewhere in Lwów. Another gracious couple, Mr. and Mrs. Waranka, invite us to stay with them until Wacek gets a job and we can get ourselves established. We move into their house on October 15, but by now we are almost out of money. We register at the local employment office and, luckily, Wacek gets a job as a street sweeper. I also sell my watch to a Russian soldier. And we find our old friends from Warsaw, Sławek Tarnowski and his wife, who fled to Lwów. They help us a lot. They buy a winter coat for me and lend Wacek one hundred złotys.

Finally, on October 26, Wacek gets a very good job offer from the occupying Soviets and goes to Werba, 160 kilometers east, to finalize it. Starting November 1, he will be employed as a manager of the Krzemieniec quarries. Thanks to his civil engineering education and asphalt and concrete road building skills, he will supervise the quarries and the construction and widening of the road from Lwów to Kijów. Apparently, the Soviets are getting ready for the continuation of the war and want an easy route for their tanks and trucks. For now, I am relieved that we will have a steady income and can stay away from the hostilities.

On November 15, Wacek comes back to Lwów by car to pick me up, and the next day we drive to Krzemieniec, a town about 170 kilometers east of Lwów. Wacek already has an apartment for us with basic necessities. As Lwów is severely overcrowded with refugees, there are constant shortages of everything and long lines, which are very tiring. In Krzemieniec, the economic situation is much better; at last, we have enough money to support ourselves and save for the return trip to Warsaw, when the time comes. Of course, provisions are still hard to find, but Wacek is very resourceful and always brings food home—so I do not have to stand in long lines and we have enough to eat. We are short on clothes, though, which are hard to get. While our situation seems stable, there are still plenty of reasons to worry. All communications with the rest of Poland are broken, and I do not know how my family is doing. And we constantly hear about the arrests of enormous numbers of people and deportations of Polish citizens from the Soviet-occupied part of Poland to labor camps in Siberia. This worries us the most.

Soon enough, such a disaster hits us. Despite Wacek's job, at the beginning of February 1940 we end up on the Soviet secret service list for deportation to Siberia. But we are warned about it by our Jewish friend who has some connections in the Soviet secret service office. Right away, Wacek goes to his employer and asks if they can do anything to protect him. But they say they know nothing about it. The NKVD (the Soviet secret service) handles arrests and deportations; his employers cannot protect him, as anyone who opposes the NKVD becomes their next target.

Wacek immediately quits his job. We sell everything we have and move out of our apartment. We stay with different friends every night and desperately look for a way to get out of Krzemieniec. The winter is extremely hard; the temperature is so low and there is so much snow that the trains have stopped running. At the train station, covered with paper, lie the corpses of entire families, including women and children, that were loaded onto trains for deportation to Siberia and froze to death. I shiver at this horrific sight, which makes us even more determined to flee as soon as possible. Finally, Wacek manages to find a trustworthy peasant with a sleigh drawn by two horses, who is willing to take us to another town fifty kilometers away for a hefty payment. We set out at once.

The journey is through a totally barren landscape covered with snow, which is so deep that we cannot even see the road. But our carter somehow finds his way and delivers us to the railroad station in the next town, as promised. However, a pass is required for any travel and to get on the train, and we obviously do not have it. Moreover, passenger trains are not running. We wait at the empty station pondering what to do, when a military train with Soviet soldiers heading west pulls in for a short stop. Wacek speaks some Russian and somehow persuades the soldiers to allow us to board the train's cargo car. I cannot believe our luck and admire his persuasion skills! We climb onto the train, which carries us all the way to Lwów. We are cold and uncomfortable, but we huddle together, and I am so relieved and happy that I have Wacek with me! I know that this has saved us from certain death in the labor camps in Siberia.

I am back in Lwów—fortunately this time with Wacek—and we are staying with our friend, Lucek Kamiński, whom we know from Warsaw. There are Soviet soldiers everywhere, and we try to keep a low profile and go out only when absolutely necessary. Wacek is feverishly looking for a way to get around all the travel restrictions to escape from the Soviet-occupied territory and go back to Warsaw. We want to be there together with our entire family, so we can support each other, although we feel that life under the German occupation will be equally bad or worse. Tragically, our host, Lucek, is arrested and deported to Siberia. But by some stroke of luck, we were not home at the time of his arrest and, again, we narrowly avoid deportation. His arrest has shaken us terribly, and now it is even more dangerous to stay here. We must make a move as soon as possible. Wacek finds a smuggling operation that issues us with false travel documents and he buys train tickets to Brześć, some three hundred kilometers north, on the border with the German-occupied Polish territory.

The train to Brześć is overcrowded and cold, and we stand in the hallway packed with other fleeing people for the entire journey, which takes all night. Brześć is a large city, and the border is heavily guarded and impossible to cross. Wacek's plan is to go another one hundred kilometers northwest to Drohiczyn, a small town on the Bug River, and cross the border somewhere there. There is no train that goes to Drohiczyn, so we go on local roads, sometimes walking or sometimes getting rides from local people on horse-drawn sleighs.

We arrive in Drohiczyn late at night. Everywhere on the streets there are posters saying that anyone who harbors refugees or helps them to cross the border will be executed. Wacek prearranged for us to meet a guide, a teenage boy, who is supposed to take us across the border. We have already paid for this service, but the guide is not at the address we were given, and we do not know anybody else here. We knock on the doors of a few other houses, but none opens.

As we have no place to go or to stay, we decide to cross the border on our own. We walk back southeast out of town looking for a remote area to cross the border, which is guarded on our side by the Soviets and on the other side by the Germans. The border is on the Bug, a large river, which is luckily completely frozen and snow-covered; we can cross it on foot. We are now far away from any roads or houses and there is no one in sight. The air is still and quiet. Although it is the middle of the night, it is quite bright with the full moon and snow; anyone could easily see us from a distance. We have no choice but to take a chance and make a mad dash across the frozen river. At the very last minute, we spot two border guards, so we hide in the snow behind the steep bank of the river. After ten minutes, which seems like eternity, we run across the river as fast as the deep snow allows. We are relieved that we made it across safely, but we are still wary of the German border guards and patrols, and we hope that by the morning the blowing wind will cover our footsteps in the snow.

We walk for another three hours until we reach Platertów, a small village. It is almost dawn, and we are hungry, cold, and exhausted. We come across a small building that looks like a village school and we knock on door of the house beside it. It opens, and we are welcomed into the warmth. By now, we are only about 150 kilometers away from Warsaw, but I know that getting there will not be easy, as we do not have the proper identification papers.

We are relieved that we managed to avoid arrest by the Soviet secret service and deportation to Siberia. Later, we discovered how good our decision to escape from the Soviet-occupied territory was. The Soviets took between 230,000 and 450,000 Polish prisoners—soldiers and civilians—and, rarely honoring the Geneva convention and the terms of the surrender, killed tens of thousands of them. They sent most of the remaining prisoners to labor camps in Siberia, where many of them perished from hunger, cold, and disease.[13]

We are now in the part of Poland that is under German occupation, and we know that our life here will also be hard. To our horror, our hosts, the local schoolteachers, tell us that during just the first month of the war the invading Germans killed tens of thousands of Polish civilians and that the killings have continued. No one expected such brutality, and I cannot stop thinking about whether my parents, my sister, my brother, and the rest of my family and friends have survived this onslaught.

Soon we find out the whole truth. In the first month of the occupation, Wehrmacht and SS (Schutzstaffel) soldiers systematically killed some 150,000 to 200,000 Polish civilians.[9] Moreover, these massacres were not random, but a part of Hitler's meticulously planned Operation Tannenberg. These were targeted killings, based on previously prepared lists identifying sixty-one thousand members of the Polish elite (activists, intelligentsia, scholars, scientists, clergy, artists, and actors).[10] Many of these people were shot at hundreds of mass execution sites by special SS death squads—Einsatzgruppen—or just gunned down by Wehrmacht and SS soldiers (figs. 16–19).[9, 14]

Chapter 5

Back with the Family

It is March 21, 1940, and I am walking on the streets of Warsaw again—but they look different from the beautiful and vibrant city that I remember from before the war. Everything is gray and dark, covered with soot and dust. We pass several bomb craters and collapsed or burned down buildings, especially in the center of the city. There are very few people on the streets. They walk quickly without stopping to talk or look in the store windows; many stores are closed anyway.

But when I see familiar streets and buildings, they bring back memories of growing up here, our elegant life, meeting Wacek, and our happiness together. In my mind's eye, I see my family apartment on 45b Tamka Street, where I grew up, the white marble stairs, the mahogany elevator, our spacious, beautiful rooms, our stylish bathroom with its large porcelain bathtub . . . Then I see Wacek in his black tailcoat, white vest, and white gloves, and me in a black French taffeta dress, fitted on the top and flowing on the bottom, with matching black silk dancing shoes, white handbag, and matching white long silk gloves and white fan made of ostrich feathers . . . We are dancing in the stylish Swiss Valley ballroom on a soft cork floor . . . I try to hold on to this sweet vision, but it disappears and is replaced by the grim reality of my miserable surroundings.

I am now dirty, exhausted, and hungry. Wacek does not look any better either, although, as always, he is in good spirits. We have nothing left except the tattered clothes we are wearing. It is already evening when we finally reach the corner of Puławska and Dworkowa Streets, where my beloved little sister, Niusia, lives. I ring the doorbell and Marysia, her housekeeper, opens the door. The look of disbelief on her face changes into a big grin. She quickly and quietly ushers us inside and runs to get Niusia. We fall into each other's arms, crying and laughing. My parents and my brother, Tadeusz, all appear and there is no end to embracing, kissing, and tears of joy. I cannot believe that they are all here, and safe, although my parents look older and more frail than when I left them in Miechów. After a while, I hesitantly ask Niusia, "Where is Kazio?" immediately regretting that I may get an answer I do not want to hear. She casually says, "He went to a village to get some meat for Easter," but I detect a note of anxiety in her voice.

We wash, they give us clean clothing, and we sit down at the kitchen table to eat. Since we have not had a proper meal in a long time, the potatoes, scrambled eggs, black bread with a bit of lard and salt, and hot black ersatz coffee taste delicious. There is a lot to talk about, and we do not even know where to start. Marysia is hustling about to arrange a place for us to lie down and rest. The apartment has three spacious rooms, but one is taken up by Niusia's and Kazio's dental office. They find a spare mattress and, for now, put it on the floor in the dental office. We will sleep there and move it out before patients start arriving in the morning.

The next day, we begin thinking about what to do. We have spent all our money on the journey, and we have to start from scratch. But finding work is next to impossible because bank accounts have been frozen and many businesses have gone out of business, including the bank where I used to work and Tadeusz's insurance company. The Germans have confiscated many factories and firms, the ministry where I worked before the war is also closed, and the provincial government for which Wacek worked does not exist anymore. At the moment, Niusia and Kazio are supporting the entire household.

In the evening, Kazio comes back. He proudly presents the pork that is wrapped up and tied to his body under his clothing. He managed to buy the meat in a village near Warsaw from a farmer who had secretly slaughtered a pig. Everyone is relieved that Kazio got back—smuggling food is illegal and, if he'd been caught, the Germans would have sent him to a labor or concentration camp. All nutritious food, such as meat, cheese, butter, and eggs, has to be delivered to the occupiers and is not available for us, although it can still be bought at high prices on the black market. In the stores, we only get miserable food rations that provide little nourishment, such as dry bread and poor-quality potatoes, groats, turnips, and sometimes cabbage. So everyone is looking forward to this feast.

I talk to Kazio and Niusia. Kazio is very restless and full of ideas. Not only is working out how to get around all the restrictions and food shortages, he is also heavily involved with his friends in organizing a resistance to the German occupation. He is amassing carloads of weapons and hiding them in the cellar. I have no idea where he gets them; probably they were stashed away somewhere by the defeated Polish army. Niusia supports and admires his activities, but she is terribly worried about his safety, knowing how dangerous all of this is.

Right after Easter, Kazio leaves for Zakopane to meet with other resistance organizers. He is supposed to return in a few days, but he doesn't. Finally, after two weeks, we get a message from one of the resistance organizers that Kazio has had to flee the country. We do not know what happened, and Niusia and all of us are distressed and worried; we do not even know if he is still alive. And now the entire extended family depends on Niusia, who works in her dental office for twelve hours every day, while the rest of us are desperately trying to find jobs.

Chapter 6

Evading

The Germans now control all aspects of the Polish economy and life, and we have lost all our legal rights and protection. In October 1939, they passed a decree requiring Poles over the age of fourteen to perform forced labor. They confiscated all major factories and businesses and subjugated food production. They set up multiple labor camps and concentration camps in occupied Poland, and they are also sending thousands of Polish citizens to labor camps in Germany. To our horror, we also read in the underground press that the Germans even have set up labor camps for children (fig. 20).[14]

The total suppression of Polish culture and education is very depressing. The Germans have destroyed Polish libraries, museums, scientific institutes, laboratories, and national monuments. They've closed universities, high schools, and cultural institutions, and allow only primary school education.[15] Polish theaters, radio stations, newspapers, and publishing houses have also been closed down. Even possessing a radio is a crime. There are, though, already many underground newspapers, cultural events, schools, and universities operating in secret, despite all the associated dangers. If detected, all participants are arrested and sent to concentration camps.

Wacek and I have to register at our local city office; everyone has to carry an identification card that bears their address. This makes it easy for the German authorities to track people down and arrest them. It also allows them to identify illegal refugees from other parts of the country or Jews who have moved out from the Jewish part of Warsaw, which is now being surrounded by barbed wire fences and will soon become a Jewish ghetto.

Wacek finds all his friends from before the war, when we lived in Warsaw and he attended the Warsaw Polytechnic. Many of them are active in the resistance, and Wacek has joined the secret Polish Union of Armed Struggle (Związek Walki Zbrojnej). His assignment will be railroad and bridge sabotage.

Two weeks after this, Wacek receives a registered letter requesting him to report immediately to the German administration office in Warsaw. I am terrified! What do they want? Have they discovered that he has joined the resistance? Or have they found out that he is Jewish, did not register as a Jew, and is not wearing the white armband with the blue Star of David that the Germans require all Jews to wear?[i] I know that because I am married to a Jew, I am also required to register as a Jew and wear the armband. It would be the end of both of us and the rest of our family, as hiding Jews is severely punished. Beating is the mildest punishment, but the Germans would more likely imprison and torture us and then kill or deport us to a concentration camp.

However, we have never considered registering as Jews, and we understand this so well that we have never even needed to talk about it. We will not allow Hitler to dictate who we are. But now, when the German authorities want to question us, should we flee again and go into hiding? But Wacek is trying to calm me down. He is always logical and rational. He says, "If they discovered I am Jewish or a resistance member, they would simply come and arrest me together with everybody else in the house. They don't send polite letters to arrest Jews or resistance members. They probably want something else, and I should comply and go." I am not fully convinced, but he goes the next day.

I sit on the edge of my seat waiting for him to come back; I am so worried that I am getting sick. Eventually, he returns and explains that the Germans

---

i Starting in September 1939, all Jews aged ten and above in the entire territory of German-occupied Poland were required to wear yellow badges in the shape of a Star of David on the back and front of their clothing. On October 8, 1939, the northern and western parts of Poland were annexed by the Third Reich and became a part of Germany. In that part of occupied Poland, Jews continued wearing yellow stars. On November 23, 1939, Hans Frank, the governor of the eastern part of German-occupied Poland (the General Government—Generalgouvernement), ordered all Jews aged ten and above to wear a 10 cm-wide white cloth armband bearing a blue Star of David on their right arms. These rules were still enforced after the Jews were confined to the ghettos.

have not discovered that he is Jewish. Quite the opposite. They have found German roots in his family—because his father, Józef Sterner, was of German origin. He was drafted into the army in World War I and killed in the first days of the war, but his body was never recovered. Mercifully, the Germans have not learned that Wacek's mother, Helena nee Neuding, was Jewish. She passed away in 1927 and now the authorities do not have accurate information on her ethnicity. They also have Wacek's religion listed as Lutheran Evangelical, after his father. Thus, thinking that Wacek is German, and not knowing his Jewish origins, the authorities have given him the opportunity to become *Reichsdeutsche* (a German citizen) or *Volksdeutsche* (a person of German origin, but without German citizenship)—both usually despised as German collaborators.

Of course, Wacek will absolutely not become *Reichsdeutsche* or *Volksdeutsche,* and therefore a German collaborator, although this would protect him from German persecution and could save his life. However, this is also an offer that one cannot refuse, as refusal would signal that he is an enemy of the German regime and make him a target. To avoid arousing suspicion, then, Wacek has politely said that he will definitely comply with their request. But he also knows that the German authorities are very persistent and will further investigate why he has not followed up on their request and punish him. We also worry that if they check other documents, the Gestapo could still find out that Wacek is Jewish, search for him, and arrest us.

So again, to avoid arrest and disaster, Wacek has to go underground and change his identity. He immediately goes to the city registration office and voids his residence in our apartment, leaving no forwarding address. As he is a member of the resistance, they give him fake Polish papers with the name Wacław Domański, my maiden name. Wacek thinks that another Domański living in this apartment will not be suspicious, because it is also the last name of my parents and brother, who are all living with us. Wacek also gets false documents that say he's a railway employee; he buys a railman's hat and always wears it outside. So, we still have a place to stay and manage to hold onto our situation, at least for now. Wacek, Tadeusz, and I get temporary jobs here and there, working in different stores and selling odds and ends, such as cigarettes that we make at home.

But we are constantly living on the edge, as all the time we hear about raids on apartment buildings and arrests. On one occasion, in the middle of the night, there was loud banging on the outside door of our building and German voices woke us. Have they come to get Wacek? The janitor opened the door to the building, and we heard Gestapo soldiers going up the stairs towards our apartment. But they passed it and rapped on the apartment door above us, where the wife of the former Warsaw mayor lives with her two sons. The Gestapo arrested and imprisoned her husband back in October 1939. This time, they arrested both her sons, but did not come to our apartment. We were so shaken that we couldn't go back to sleep.

Thus, frequent raids, arrests, and mass killings are now a part of our daily life under the German's. This is a well-planned campaign of terror and murder, called *Intelligenzaktion* (German for Intelligence action),[16] which has replaced the initial Operation Tannenberg. These are mass arrests and executions of the intelligentsia, on direct orders from Hitler, who said, "The Führer must point out that the Poles can only have one master, and that is the German; two masters cannot and must not exist side by side; therefore, all representatives of the Polish intelligentsia should be killed [*umbringen*]."[16]

Hitler's plans for our future are even grimmer. The first phase is to make us into uneducated slave laborers, according to the October 2, 1940, meeting of Hitler and Martin Borman (his secretary) with Hans Frank (the governor of occupied Poland). Borman recorded that the country would become a "reservation, a great Polish labor camp."[16] The second phase of Hitler's plan, known as the *Generalplan Ost* (The Master Plan for the East), is the total ethnic cleansing of Eastern Europe and its repopulation by Germans.[17]

Chapter 7

Birth

Back on March 24, 1940, Easter Sunday, just after coming back to Warsaw, we had a feast. Kazio, who is an excellent cook, prepared homemade ham from the pork he smuggled in. Everybody was enjoying it and saying it was the best ham they had ever eaten. But I started getting nauseated and couldn't even take a bite—to me, it smelled and tasted rotten. Since then, I have been getting more and more nauseated.

Now in May, I am sure that I am pregnant again. I cannot stop thinking about my previous lost pregnancy, which makes me even more determined to have the baby. Wacek and everyone else are very caring and encouraging. But I worry that all the hardship when we were fleeing from Krzemieniec to Lwów and then travelling to Warsaw affected my pregnancy. And I wonder why week by week my nausea is getting worse and worse instead of going away.

Finally, in June, I go to a doctor. His diagnosis is that, besides being pregnant, I have an ovarian cyst that is pressing on the fetus. I need surgery to remove it, otherwise it will continue to grow and could cause some fetal abnormalities or malformation. I come back home dizzy and distressed. The surgery is risky because of the constant shortages of all medications and hospital supplies. But Wacek, as usual, is very supportive and resourceful. He has a friend who is a surgeon in the Evangelical Hospital in Warsaw and can perform the operation. The surgery goes well, and after a week in the hospital I come back home.

Unexpectedely, in November the Germans confiscate our building and evict us from our apartment. I panic, as I am due any day and now we do not have a place to stay. But to our great relief Niusia promptly finds another apartment on 27 Szustra Street, also in the Mokotów district (fig. 21). Despite my advanced pregnancy, I go to the new apartment and wax and polish all the floors. The next day, we all move there—including Niusia's dental office—and I help with everything.

But our eviction is nothing compared with what our Jewish friends are facing. The Germans have ordered all Jews in all the cities and towns in Poland to live in designated areas, ghettos, typically surrounded by barbed wire fences or walls. The Germans have also ordered all Jews from the countryside to move into these ghettos, and if they do not the occupiers forcefully transport them there.[18, 19] Already on April 1, 1940, the Germans started constructing a ten-foot-tall brick wall around the Warsaw Ghetto with Jewish slave laborers. The Germans also deprived Jews of all legal protection, banned them from taking trains and other public transportation, confiscated Jewish-owned property, froze Jewish bank accounts, and allowed them only to have small amounts of money.[18, 19] However, several of our Jewish friends, like us, defied the German orders, did not move into the ghetto, and live outside it either in hiding or by passing as Poles using false papers.

We all try to keep our spirits high and not feel beaten down by all the difficulties. The more restrictions the German authorities put on us, the more ways we find to oppose or get around them. The cafes in Warsaw are still full of people who dress as fashionably as they can and carry on with their lives, as they do not know what tomorrow will bring.

A week after moving, I have an urge to go to a fancy hairdresser on Nowy Świat Street to have my hair done. I dress up and want to walk there, which is quite far, four kilometers—about an hour-long walk. I think some fresh air and exercise will be good for me. But everyone at home says I should not walk. They call for a *dorożka* (a horse-drawn carriage) and give me money for the fare. But I wave the *dorożka*, walk all the way there, get my hair done, which lifts my spirits, and walk back home.

Late at night, the contractions start and become intense. I have to go to the hospital, but because of the curfew, I must wait until the next morning. I want Wacek to be with me and take me to the hospital, and he obviously wants to come, but we know he cannot. To get to the hospital, we have to go first through the heavily patrolled German section and then through the ghetto. But now everything is in an upheaval, as Jews have been moving into the ghetto and everyone who isn't Jewish is moving out. If Wacek is caught with false Polish papers rather than living as a Jew in the ghetto, it will be the end of him (and us). In the morning, with no hesitation, Niusia summons a private ambulance, and we set out for the hospital.

When we get to the ghetto, we find that the gates are shut and heavily guarded; there is a long line of vehicles and people waiting to get in. We learn that four days ago, on November 16, 1940, the wall was finished. The ghetto has been completely closed and no one can get out anymore.[20] There is a big sign in Polish and German: "Typhus risk area. Only through-passage is allowed." Poles with proper documents can still enter through certain gates and drive through it, although this will soon end and to drive through the ghetto will require special permission from the German authorities. But now, after a long and thorough examination of our papers and inquiries about the purpose of our travel, the guards open the gate, and we can go through. "Thank God Wacek did not come with me," I think.

We arrive at the hospital in the afternoon. I am in labor for the rest of the day and night, and all I can think about is that, after all my hardships, the baby is born healthy. Niusia stays with me all the time and is very encouraging. Early in the morning, I deliver a beautiful, healthy baby girl. Niusia goes to the doctor's office and calls Wacek with the news. I am weak, but relieved and happy. We name her Barbara, but I affectionately call her Basia. It is November 21, 1940.

The next evening, Niusia takes us home; there is a shortage of beds in the hospital and I feel sufficiently well. We again go through all the checkpoints at the ghetto gates, this time with little Basia. Dark thoughts cloud my mind. What a somber world she is seeing on her first day! How can I shield her from all this cruelty? How can I make life better for her? I have no answers.

It has already gotten cold and in the apartment the temperature is 9°C [48°F]. The apartment has coal heating stoves, but there is a constant shortage of coal, and electricity is also rationed with frequent blackouts, usually in the evening and at night. When I change and bathe Basia, Niusia holds a heating lamp over her (if there is electricity); but despite this, Basia still shivers from the cold. Nevertheless, I think we are very fortunate to be able to use a heating lamp—because we have a higher electricity allowance on account of Niusia's dental office at home.

I choose my best childhood friend, Jania Marchwińska-Rabęcka, as Basia's godmother. Jania is now married to Henryk Rabęcki, a major in the Polish army. She does not know what has happened to her husband, as the Soviets took him prisoner when they invaded Eastern Poland. Jania is waiting for any news from him and hopes that he returns soon.

Basia is a very healthy and undemanding baby; she never gets sick, rarely cries, and never makes a fuss. I breastfeed her and I am surprised that I have enough milk on my poor diet. But breastfeeding makes me thin as a stick and all my clothes hang loose on me. As soon as I can get around, I leave her for a few hours at a time with my mother and Marysia, and do my odd jobs to make some extra money. This allows me to buy more food on the black market to supplement our inadequate rations.

One day, our childhood nanny, Teklusia, comes to our apartment. She raised us all until we finished high school and then retired to live in a convent in Warsaw on 6-go Lipca Street. But now, the living conditions in the convent have become very difficult. They were commandeered to move to Żelazna Street. She does not have a room and there is not enough food. We loved her very much and we ask her to live with us. She will sleep with Marysia in the kitchen.

All the stresses of daily life under the occupation are weighing us down, especially my father. He is seventy-eight years old, rarely goes out of the house, and is very weak and depressed. He cannot go for his usual treatments in the sanatorium in Krynica anymore and we are sad that there is not much that we can do to help him. On April 5, 1941, his heart gives up and he passes away. We bury him in the Bródno cemetery with heavy hearts.

In the fall of 1941, we get great news! Niusia receives a postcard from Kazio who's in Switzerland. Apparently, the mail from neutral countries still functions normally. He obviously does not say much, knowing that the mail is censored, but he is alive and well. One cannot imagine Niusia's joy and relief. She has been keeping his picture on her nightstand all that time, not saying much but hoping . . .

Chapter 8

Kazio's War Odyssey

It was only after the war that we found out what happened to Kazio. Back in March 1940, Kazio and his friend from the resistance, engineer Antoni Hergesel, got to Zakopane near the southern Polish border with Slovakia. Maybe they were already planning to leave Poland and join the Polish army that was regrouping in France, as he often talked about starting to fight the Germans as soon as possible. He probably wanted to see in Zakopane how feasible this was.

However, the Gestapo had already been looking for Hergesel and caught and arrested both of them. Kazio and Hergesel were armed with handguns tied to their belts. Carrying weapons was a crime punishable by death. The Gestapo soldiers confiscated these guns away. But they did not notice that Kazio and Hergesel also had small handguns tied to their ankles. When they were left with just two guards, they shot their captors and escaped. The Gestapo launched a big manhunt for them and pasted large posters with "Wanted" above Hergesel's picture all around town. Kazio and Hergesel had to flee Poland immediately.

They were joined by three other resistance members who also had to escape, and all five of them set out on foot through the Tatra mountains to the border. But they encountered a German border patrol and a gunfight ensued.

They got separated; Kazio and Hergesel hid in a stream and stayed there undetected for several hours, completely covered with ice and snow.

They avoided capture by the German patrol, but Kazio developed a severe cold and Hergesel badly twisted his ankle and could barely walk. They did not know what happened to their other three companions, and they never heard from them again; so it's likely they got captured and killed. Kazio and Hergesel managed to cross the border to Slovakia. However, Slovakia was occupied by the Germans, too, its government was allied with Hitler, and Slovak troops had participated in the invasion of Poland.

Kazio and Hergesel made it to Slovak peasant's hut and found temporary refuge there; Hergesel could not walk anymore and his leg was badly swollen. The peasant put them up in a barn with pigs. They stayed there until Hergesel's leg healed, but the peasant wanted a lot of money. Hergesel was well-off, though, and had a lot of gold dollar coins with him.

Then they walked across the border to Hungary, found a local train station, and traveled by train through Hungary, Yugoslavia, and Italy to France. I never found out how they managed to travel so far and cross so many borders. They must have somehow obtained false foreign passports, or maybe Polish passports were still recognized in these countries, which were not yet engulfed by the war.

In France, they joined General Bronisław Prugar-Ketling's Polish Second Infantry Fusiliers Division as noncommissioned officers. The Polish Second Division had about sixteen thousand soldiers and fought with the French and other international forces in the Battle of France in May and June 1940. The division's task was to defend the area around Belfort. They were poorly equipped, mostly with World War I rifles, but morale was high and they were eager to fight the advancing enemy. Kazio, a staff sergeant, was a squad leader.

On June 16, 1940, Marshal Pétain offered an armistice to the Germans, but the aggressors continued to make gains and the Polish Second Division continued to fight them. From June 17–19, in heavy fighting on the Clos-du-Doubs hills, near the Doubs and Saône rivers, they stopped the German attack, but lost a lot of men. Despite this success, the French army fled the area and the German forces surrounded the Polish Second Division. But the Polish forces refused to surrender, and during the night of June 20–21 they broke through and crossed the Swiss border. At 5:30 am, as the last soldiers were entering Switzerland, the German tanks closed in behind them. The soldiers had to leave their arms at the border and were interned in Switzerland.

The Polish Second Division remained interned for the rest of the war, and their new task was to defend the northwestern Swiss border in case the Germans ignored the country's neutral status. In the internment camp, conditions were hard, mostly because there was very little food; so they were constantly hungry.

Kazio continued his service as an officer in the division; and thanks to his dental degree, he could work in a hospital in Wiesendangen near Winterthur, about ten kilometers northeast of Zürich, which allowed him to leave the internment camp (fig. 11). He lived in Winterthur in a house owned by a widow, and even had a dog. He was doing prosthetic dental work and also started attending medical school there. The hospital soon discovered that Kazio was an excellent surgeon. He started performing abortions, and after a year, he was allowed to do other surgeries, such as appendectomies.

Several of his fellow soldiers enrolled at the Universities of Fribourg and Zürich. Kazio could easily support himself, live in the city, and pay for his medical studies, which were in German (he knew some German when he got there and learned quite a bit more). He could hike in the mountains, take biking and boat trips, and go skiing. He also sent care packages to us in Warsaw, which—amazingly—got through to us.

Everything was going well for Kazio until one day in 1943, when he ran into a group of German soldiers in a bar. One of them said to him, "You are a subhuman Polish swine [*Sie sind ein untermenschliches polnisches Schwein*]. You all are. We will wipe out your country and all of you from the map of Europe." Kazio could not hold himself back; as he used to box, he quickly knocked out the German soldier. But then he had to flee Switzerland to avoid retribution from the Gestapo. I am not sure what route he took and how he did this. Most likely, he went with Hergesel through Vichy France to Marseille, which was known for an active resistance network that was helping refugees to escape to British Gibraltar and then to Great Britain.

That is probably how Kazio and Hergesel got to Great Britain. There, they joined the Polish First Armored Division stationed in Scotland, Kazio as a dentist. Polish soldiers were not very welcome because they often seduced local girls. To make things worse for Kazio, he established a chicken farm and his birds constantly escaped onto neighboring fields, which was a great nuisance for local farmers. They tried to buy him out to get rid of his pesky birds. It's hard for me to imagine Kazio as a chicken farmer because I remember him as always dressed in a tailored suit with a white shirt and a tie.

Chapter 9

The Warsaw Ghetto

It is 1941 in Warsaw, and the Germans have completely closed the ghetto to everyone and deprived Jews of their livelihoods. The Jews cannot leave and sell their goods outside the ghetto and have no income. Polish Jews, who are all confined to ghettos in Poland now, including almost half a million in the Warsaw Ghetto, face starvation, extremely crowded conditions (with typically over nine persons per room), infectious diseases (including deadly typhus and tuberculosis outbreaks), and lack of medications.[20] The daily rations of nonnutritious food (mostly dry bread and lowest quality potatoes, groats, and turnips) in the Warsaw Ghetto are only one quarter of our already poor food rations in the rest of the city, which are about one third of what we used to eat before the war.[i]

Professor Ludwik Hirszfeld, who has been forced to live in the Warsaw Ghetto, compares the ghetto to a concentration camp: "We were put in a concentration camp [ghetto] created in order that people devour one another and die from starvation, epidemics, and disgust."[21]

---

i The daily ration of nonnutritious food in the Warsaw Ghetto was 177–253 calories per person per day, compared with 669–699 calories for Poles outside the ghetto; the Germans had 2,613 calories of nutritious food (see reference 20). The current recommended daily calorie intake of nutritious food in the US is 2,500 for men and two thousand for women.

For the Jews to survive, food must be smuggled in from the outside. According to pianist Władysław Szpilman, "The real, regular smuggling trade was run by such magnates as Kon [Kohn] and Heller.... Bribed police guards simply turned a blind eye at agreed times, and then whole columns of carts would drive through the ghetto gate."[22] But this is expensive food sold at high profits for the rich minority and the German collaborators, who frequent expensive restaurants and cabarets and pay little attention to the poverty and starvation of the poor majority. This poor majority depends on food smuggled by individuals, often children, daily risking their lives.[20, 23]

The miserable, unsanitary, and crowded conditions in the ghetto are best described by Szpilman: "Lice crawled over the pavements, up stairways, and dropped from the ceilings of the public offices.... Lice found their way into the folds of your newspaper, into your small change; there were even lice on the crust of the loaf you had just bought. And each of these verminous creatures could carry typhus.... [In] the center of the ghetto ... dense crowd ... was not walking but pushing and shoving its way forward.... At the slightest provocation the crowd would become panic-stricken, rushing from one side of the street to the other, choking, pressing close, shouting and cursing.... [P]rison cars drove ... prisoners ... after their interrogation: bloody scraps of humanity with broken bones and beaten kidneys, their fingernails torn out.... [T]he Gestapo men would lean out and beat the crowd indiscriminately with truncheons ... studded with nails and razor blades."[24]

It is too risky for me to enter the ghetto and see it myself, but Szpilman and Bernard Goldstein, who live there, write: "Dozens of beggars lay [on the streets] ... ragged apparitions ... with tubercular saliva, ... children covered with oozing sores ... [others with] blinded eyes, toothless, sinking open mouths, all begging for mercy at this, the last moment of their lives."[24] People in the ghetto are desperate for food: "Along ... Leszno Street ... sick children lay, half dead, almost naked, swollen from hunger, with open running sores, parchment-like skin, comatose eyes, breathing heavily with a rattle in their throats. The elders stood around them, yellow and gaunt, whimpering in their weakness, 'a piece of bread.'"[25] A "poor woman was carrying a can ... a ragged old man ... shivering with cold ... lunged forward, seized the can ... [which] fell on the pavement, and thick, steaming soup poured out into the dirty street ... he threw himself down full length in the slush, lapping the soup straight from the pavement ... ignoring the woman ... as she kicked at his head, howling, and tore at her hair in despair."[26]

We know that many people in the ghettos are dying from starvation, disease, and lack of medical help. The full extent of this tragedy is enormous—approximately ninety-two thousand Jews died in the Warsaw Ghetto from starvation and diseases (figs. 22 and 23).[20] How true and tragic is Szpilman's description: "In the ghetto, there was no way of burying those who died . . . [daily] the dead were stripped of their clothing—too valuable for the living to be left on them—and were put outside on the pavement wrapped in paper. . . . [The] wind blew . . . lifting it to expose naked, withered shins, sunken bellies, faces with teeth bared and eyes staring into nothing."[27] The dead were loaded on wagons and transported for burial in mass graves (fig. 23).

Chapter 10

Rescues

> If you are neutral in situations of injustice, you have chosen the side of the oppressor.
> —*Desmond Tutu*

Our family has many Jewish friends who, not knowing what their fate was going to be, stayed in the ghetto. We often hear from them about the horrific and worsening conditions in the ghetto, although no words can adequately describe this human misery and suffering. And now I am desperately looking for ways to help them. Some help comes from bribing the ghetto guards to allow me to get parcels containing food to our friends inside. In the same way, Jews can send me products made in the ghetto, primarily clothing, shoes, and accessories. I then sell the items in stores and send money or food back to the ghetto. I also often ferry letters and other documents between our Jewish friends in the ghetto and their friends and relatives on the Polish side. All of this is obviously not allowed and very dangerous, but it's something.

One day our good friend, architect Leszek Gryczyński, visits us. He is living in the countryside outside Warsaw with Polish papers, but his wife, her sister, and her mother are in the ghetto. He asks if we know anybody who can help to get them out. I have an old friend who is a chief financial officer in the court and finance building on 53/54 Leszno Street. This building is on the ghetto border and has two entrances—one on the ghetto side and the other on the Polish side. I say, "I'll ask him if he can help me get them out of the ghetto to the Polish side." I do, and he says that he will help us. We will all make an appointment with him and meet in his office. They will take off their white armbands with blue stars, and I will lead them out of the building through the exit on the Polish side. But to be inconspicuous, I can only take one person at a time.

All the ghetto gates have German, Jewish, and Polish police guards. But the doors to the court and finance building have just one Jewish and one Polish guard on the ghetto side, and only one Polish guard on the Polish side. This Polish guard will allow Polish customers to enter and leave the building, provided they show a pass for an appointment in the financial office. Thus, the Jews will need Polish passes to exit the building on the Polish side with me. My friend in the financial office will issue these passes for them. Once we are on the street on the Polish side, I will summon a *dorożka* and take the Gryczyńskis to our apartment. But what to do next?

To live outside the ghetto, they will need false Polish identification cards. Fortunately, Wacek has many contacts with the Polish underground and has already obtained his own papers through them. We also have other Jewish friends who are already passing as Poles and living on forged papers. I talk to one of them, Hala (Halina) Hermelinowa, and she tells me that her brother, Ziutek (Józef), is an especially skilled forger and that he can make the necessary documents.

I call Gryczyński's wife in the ghetto and tell her when and how to make an appointment with my friend in the finance building. Incredibly, the telephone lines between the ghetto and the rest of Warsaw still work and we are told that they are not bugged. Very apprehensively, I enter the finance building, meet Gryczyński's wife, and lead her to the exit on the Polish side. The Polish watchman checks our passes, and everything goes smoothly—he pays no particular attention to Gryczyński's wife's fake papers, which say that she also came for her appointment from the Polish side. He lets us out through the door and we both leave out of the building. But we are still very frightened because many guards and police are patrolling the building and the ghetto walls, scrutinizing everybody. We walk as casually as we can, pretending to laugh and chat, and get into a *dorożka*.

We arrive safely at Niusia's dental office in our apartment building (fig. 21). Gryczyński's wife goes into the building alone, pretending to be a patient, so she doesn't raise the janitor's or neighbors' suspicions. We are relieved as we get her into our apartment. Two days later, I make similar arrangements for Gryczyński's mother, and the following week for his sister-in-law. Each time, I lead them safely out of the ghetto through the finance building and bring them to our apartment. We take their photographs and give them to Ziutek, Hala's brother, and the Gryczyńskis stay with us for a few days while he makes their papers. They think it will be safer for them to live in the countryside rather than in Warsaw, and they leave.

So now we have a way to smuggle our friends out from the ghetto and rescue them. I know that the parents of my good friend, Lucek Kamiński, are in the ghetto. We stayed with Lucek in Lwów and he helped us a lot. But then he was arrested by the Soviet secret service and sent to Siberia, and we have not heard from him since. I have been in contact with his parents in the ghetto, and now I want to rescue them. We make the same arrangements for them as we did for Gryczyńskis and, again, everything goes smoothly. Through Wacek's friends in the resistance, we get them Polish documents and also help them find an apartment in Warsaw.

We continue rescuing our friends from the ghetto as fast as we can, and I lead them all out through the finance building. But as I can only accompany one person at a time, it takes us several days to rescue the entire family. Also, they have to be dressed in clean Polish-looking clothing and have Polish-looking haircuts, so that neither the watchman nor street patrols notice anything awry. Women with strong Semitic features wear hats with black veils, as if they are in mourning.

Eventually, word gets around and our Jewish friends give the phone number of Niusia's dental office to their families and trusted friends. The people smuggling becomes a regular activity, and it does not frighten me anymore. It does not look odd that so many people are passing through our apartment because many patients are constantly coming to the dental office. Also, our location in Mokotów is far from the crowded city center and immediately adjacent to the German residential area, so there are fewer patrols looking for Jewish escapees. The Germans probably think that Jews would not dare to hide in this part of Warsaw. We work undetected, then. We do not keep any records of the people we help in case we are denounced and raided by the Gestapo. We do not belong to any official organization, as this would make it easier to trace us and could endanger everyone involved.

We now also have several friends helping us with this operation. Ziutek, and other people who make the false documents, can somehow get the special paper and produce very authentic-looking identification cards.

The mayor of Warsaw, Stefan Starzyński, before his imprisonment by the Gestapo in October 1939, provided thousands of blank identification cards and birth registry forms to the resistance, but I am not sure whether these or other forms are used for the Jews we are helping. Other people help to find accommodations and other necessities, such as Polish-looking clothing.

We also have an apartment on nearby Odyńca Street, where our secret workshop to produce Polish documents is located. Our friends, the poet Seweryn Pollak and his wife and the writer Wanda Grodzieńska, made this apartment available to us. They moved out of Warsaw because they thought it was less dangerous to live in the countryside. We covered the windows in the apartment and installed a large padlock on the outside of the door so that it looks like the apartment is unoccupied. But the padlock can be locked and opened from both the outside and the inside. The families we help to escape from the ghetto either stay in our apartment on Szustra Street (fig. 21) and sleep on the floor in the dental office or stay in the boarded-up apartment on Odyńca Street.

My brother, Tadeusz, is helping us too. He moved into the apartment on Odyńca Street. One night when he was staying there, the Gestapo raided the building in the middle of the night. All the men were rounded up and taken away to the Majdanek concentration camp. But Tadeusz was in this locked apartment and stood by the door listening, afraid to move or to make any noise. But because of the padlock on the door, the Gestapo did not enter his apartment, as they thought it was empty.

Of course, we know that each stage of this activity is extremely dangerous if discovered. There are large signs prominently displayed on the ghetto walls and on the streets of Warsaw that say: "Any Jews trying to escape will be shot dead on sight" and "Anyone helping Jews in any way—by helping them to escape, taking them in for a night, giving them a lift in a vehicle of any sort, or feeding runaway Jews or selling them foodstuffs—will be punished by death." We know that the entire family could be executed. But we try not to think about it. There is no other way for us to live but to keep helping those in need. We are all the same people.

There are also setbacks. The Germans capture Ziutek, Hala Hermelinowa's brother, in a *łapanka* (fig. 24),[15] a random roundup of people on the street, and send him to a concentration camp, where he perishes. Ziutek is Jewish and was passing as a Pole, which was easy with his light blond hair and Polish facial features. He was very active in the Polish resistance; besides making false Polish identification documents, he kept an underground radio receiver and transmitter in his apartment and ran a clandestine cadet training school. Ironically, he was not arrested for these activities or as a Jew, but was caught completely randomly.

Nobody is safe these days. Roundups are more and more frequent and often in retaliation for anti-German resistance actions or for any form of civil disobedience. We read in the underground press that by now there are about four hundred daily victims of *łapankas* in Warsaw. Our family is not spared, either. Eugeniusz Dziarski, Kazio's brother, is caught in a *łapanka*, and we do not know where he is. Tadeusz Winiarski, Kazio's sister's husband, is arrested for his underground activities, tortured in the notoriously brutal Pawiak prison, and sent to Buchenwald concentration camp. We do not know if they are still alive.

We also find out that someone denounced the Gryczyńskis—the first family that we rescued from the ghetto, who then moved to the countryside. They were caught by the Gestapo, sent to a concentration camp, and did not survive. But Leszek Gryczyński was in Warsaw at the time of their arrest and was not captured.

Chapter 11

Passing and Hiding

One time in 1941, our phone rings and the caller is Dr. Edward (Edek) Kosman, our friend from before the war, who is now the head physician in the Jewish hospital in the ghetto. He does not want any help to escape from the ghetto, but asks for some medicines not available in the ghetto and for some nutritious food like butter and meat. "This is for the children in my hospital," he explains (fig. 25).

I know exactly what to do. Even though a tall brick wall topped with barbed wire or broken glass surrounds almost the entire Ghetto, on Elektoralna Street there is no wall—just a fence, with some openings cut in it. That's where I pass food packages in from the outside, collect goods from the ghetto to sell in Polish stores, and return the money from the sales. With help from the physicians we know, I get the medications and I buy some butter and meat on the black market. I go to the fence, bribe the guard with a few złotys so he looks the other way, and I hand over the items through the opening to a boy, as agreed. It is usual that Jewish children pick up the deliveries, as they are agile and can run fast and easily hide. Delighted, Edek asks for more of the same and each time I deliver them.

Late in the fall of 1941, in the evening, our doorbell rings. We think it may be a patient with a toothache emergency. Our housekeeper, Marysia, opens the door—and there is Zosia (Zofia) Kosman, Edek Kosman's wife. We quickly invite her in. The Germans picked her up for transport to a concentration camp, but she managed to slip out, hide, and then escape from the ghetto by joining a group of workers going to the Polish side.

We sit down in the kitchen, serve her supper, and start discussing how to help her. I've been in contact with Zosia but she never mentioned that she was planning to escape. And I'm under the impression that she's just got out, but she explains that she's been in hiding for two months with nowhere permanent to stay. She's been wandering around in Warsaw and then in Lwów, looking for place that Edek can also hide in. Now she is back in Warsaw, temporarily staying with her friends, also in Mokotów, but she cannot remain there long, and she certainly cannot take Edek there when he manages to escape. Well, we are obviously upset with her: Why didn't she come to us in the first place?

Zosia has nothing; she could not take any luggage with her out of the ghetto. But this is not a problem because she is petite, the same size as me and Niusia, and we can share our clothing with her. Most importantly, though, Zosia already has Polish documents and can easily pass as a Pole. She is a couple years younger than me, has dark-blond hair, and does not look Jewish at all, which, with proper documents, will allow her to live openly undetected.

Her family has known a Polish carpenter for some time, Mr. Żukowski, who has been helping them in the ghetto by supplying food. He has even visited them a few times, entering through underground passages or sewer tunnels. Mr. Żukowski's young daughter, Zofia Żukowska, was a seamstress and she recently passed away. He did not report her death and saved her documents, knowing that they would be useful for someone from the ghetto or for a Polish resistance member who must change identity. He generously agreed to give these documents to Zosia Kosman, and she has already picked them up from his other daughter, Eufemia. They are authentic documents and include birth and christening certificates—they are worth more than gold. Thus, Zosia Kosman has become a seamstress, although by education she is a biologist.

Now we need to find an apartment for her. Niusia's sister-in-law, Zofia Winiarska, has a nice three-room apartment on Wilcza Street in the center of Warsaw. This apartment is now empty because Zofia and her new-born daughter, Elżunia, are living elsewhere in Warsaw, in the Wola district, with Zofia's mother. Zofia did not want to live alone with her baby after the Gestapo arrested her husband, Tadeusz Winiarski, a member of the Polish resistance, and put him in the Pawiak prison. Niusia goes and talks to Zofia, and she agrees to rent her apartment to Zosia Kosman, although she knows how dangerous it is to provide an apartment for ghetto escapee. Zofia Winiarska is highly religious and believes that it is her duty as a Catholic to help people in need. She also hopes that her generosity will persuade God to spare her husband from death.

We are all delighted that we have found an apartment for Zosia Kosman, but now we need to prepare her for her new life. I buy her an old sewing machine from a secondhand store, and she learns how to use it. She speaks perfect Polish with no Yiddish accent. But she is highly educated and, to match her documents as a seamstress, has to learn how to speak as an uneducated Polish woman.

She must also pretend to be a Polish Catholic. I teach her how to pray in Polish, and take her to church with my mother; we show her how to pray in a church. This is very important, because the residents in her apartment building are Polish Catholics and they often gather in the courtyard and pray together and go to church on Sunday. If she does not pray with them or does not go to church, it will look very suspicious, and they could denounce her to the Gestapo.

I am not religious and do not go to church. And now I really doubt that God exists. Why does He permit such suffering and the slaughter of His people? Why doesn't He stop the hand of the executioner? I heard "Love thy neighbor" so many times when I was a child, but the words are so hollow now. All the prayers that we teach Zosia sound hollow, as nobody answers them. Yet, she must recite these meaningless prayers to protect herself from her neighbors, the Catholics who have forgotten how to "Love thy neighbor." I often talk with Niusia about it, and she has also lost her faith in God. Our mother supports our efforts to help Jews, but she clings on to her Catholic faith and it is very hard to talk to her about our doubts about God and religion. She thinks that, as good Catholics, we must help all those in need, but she cannot explain why God allows such suffering and the barbaric mass killings of innocent people.

To further protect Zosia and establish her image of a devout Catholic, we go to the market and buy several religious pictures for her apartment, as Catholics typically have them. These are critical survival lessons that we give to all the Jewish escapees that we host, but not all of them can easily adjust. It is especially difficult for those who do not speak fluent Polish and have Yiddish accents.

I help Zosia Kosman move into her apartment. We become close friends and I visit her often. She also often visits us at Niusia's. Life is very hard for her, both physically and mentally. She supports herself by buying horse meat on the black market, making it into pâté, and selling it to the stores. She does not have anybody. Her parents perished in a concentration camp. She has not heard from her husband, Edek, who stayed in the ghetto. She wants to save him when the appropriate time comes, but for now she's afraid that if she contacts him the Gestapo may discover her whereabouts. Edek has not tried to escape because he feels responsible for running the hospital and helping his patients. Zosia's sister is a physician, who was working for the Polish military when the war started; but nobody has heard from her since then.

One day in the winter of 1942, around noon, our apartment doorbell rings. It's Edek Kosman dressed just in a suit, with no winter coat and no hat. The Germans put him on a truck in the ghetto for transport to Wołomin. He knew Wołomin was a place where the Germans execute Jews. He was the last one sitting at the end of the truck, next to the German guard. When it left the ghetto and was on Bielańska Street heading towards Plac Teatralny, he shoved the guard, jumped off the truck, and ran away. The guards started shooting at him, but missed. Edek had nothing to lose because he knew he was facing certain death in Wołomin. He ran into a building's courtyard and escaped through the other side, as he happened to know that there were two entrances. This saved his life.

Edek had nothing with him—no money, no winter clothing—and he had to walk for over two hours from Plac Teatralny to our apartment on Szustra Street (fig. 21), going around the German district and taking side streets. This is the only address he had, as he did not know what had happened to his wife or where she lived. With his black hair and Semitic facial features, he looks like a typical Jew—obviously an escapee from the ghetto. But, luckily, he avoided police patrols and no one on the street did anything: nobody helped him, but, then, nobody reported him to the police, either.

I immediately go to Zosia's apartment to let her know. She is ecstatic and comes back with me right away. It is hard to describe their joy! They fall into each other's arms and kiss, laugh, and cry. Edek shaves and we give him a haircut, but he still looks completely Jewish, so we decide it would be risky for him to go out on the street during daylight. When it gets dark, Wacek gives him his winter coat, his hat, and glasses. We summon a *dorożka,* and Zosia and Edek go to their apartment.

Although Edek Kosman speaks perfect Polish, because of his obviously Jewish appearance they decide it is too dangerous for him to live openly and walk the streets. So he has to hide and secretly live in his wife's apartment on Wilcza Street. When she is not at home, he has to be absolutely silent—he can't walk, use the sink—even to drink water—and he cannot cook on the stove or go to the bathroom. If the neighbors hear that someone is in the apartment, they might get suspicious. He has to just sit still all the time when she is not in. When she is in, they can only whisper quietly because, again, the neighbors could hear that she has someone with her. They know they cannot take even the slightest chance of Edek being detected. We help them install a hiding place for him behind the bathtub in the bathroom that looks like a tiled wall. He immediately hides there every time someone knocks on the door or visits them, and must stay there motionless.

Zosia thinks it is beneficial if some neighbors visit her, because they know the apartment is not hers and she is only renting it. She wants to have witnesses in case the authorities question her about living alone there—especially because the apartment is large. She always has her sewing machine out with some clothing spread out, so it looks like she is working.

Also, the apartment building janitor has become an important person now. The German authorities have ordered building janitors to keep lists of tenants registered to live in every apartment and to make sure that nobody else lives there. Janitors also have the keys to the main door and can control who enters the building. When the police come, they always get this list of tenants. Thus, janitors can do a lot of good or a lot of harm. In our apartment building, the janitor, Mr. Saczkowski, is a very honorable man. When Wacek was living with us on false papers under the name of Wacław Domański, Saczkowski took a great risk and entered Wacek's false name on his list and stamped it with a forged stamp, although Wacek was not duly registered with the city authorities. Saczkowski did this to protect Wacek in the event that there was a police raid on our building. But janitors could also report illegal residents to the authorities; as in fact, they are required to.

Matters get worse for Zosia when Bronek, her apartment building janitor, takes a romantic interest in her and starts visiting her frequently. He will come in, get really close to her, and ask, "What is a pretty miss like you doing here all alone?," or "Why don't you come and visit me?," or "Why don't we go out together?" He often reaches out for her hand or tries to embrace her. She pushes him away and attempts to keep her distance, but he is persistent. He always goes around and inspects the entire apartment, probably looking for some sign of whether she has a boyfriend. He gives particular attention to the bedroom and bathroom, looking for men's clothing, shaving cream, or a razor. She follows Bronek there and tries to distract him and encourage him back out of the bathroom, where Edek is hiding. Zosia knows Edek can hear everything and how hard it is for him to restrain himself from jumping out to get rid of the irritating admirer. She can barely keep herself together. To get Bronek out of the apartment, she asks him, "My dear Bronek, can you help me carry out my carpet and mattress for cleaning? They're too heavy for me."

She knows she has to be nice to Bronek and be very careful not to anger, offend, or antagonize him. But, also, how can she get rid of him and stop these unpleasant, even frightening, visits? Apart from how hard it is for her to play this game, what if Bronek discovers some trace of Edek, such as an item of clothing? He would be jealous and who knows what he would do. And, as the janitor, Bronek has keys to all the apartments. What if he uses his key and enters her apartment in the middle of the night to make some amorous advances? These thoughts constantly torment her, even when he is not there.

There are other near misses, too. One day, Edek is in the kitchen when a neighbor unexpectedly comes in through the front door. Edek does not have time to hide in the bathroom, so he hides behind the kitchen door. The neighbor stays and talks with Zosia for a very long time; and finally, when it gets late, she gets up to leave. But the apartment has a second entrance through the kitchen and the neighbor wants to leave through there because she would come out closer to her apartment. Zosia cannot refuse and they both walk through the kitchen. If the neighbor looks back, she will see Edek behind the kitchen door. She doesn't—but Zosia's and Edek's hearts are in their throats.

Nowadays, we cannot trust anybody, and neighbors are especially dangerous, as they gossip and word spreads around. Someone may denounce another person to the Gestapo, which pays for information about people hiding Jews. These Polish collaborators are especially dangerous because they can easily identify Jews by their looks, speech, and behavior. The Germans can only identify Orthodox Jews—by their beards, sidelocks, praying shawls, and black hats and gabardines; but it is difficult for them to be sure about other kinds of Jews just by looking. So they rely on Polish denouncers. But the occupiers are very meticulous and can trace Jews using their documents—identification cards, birth certificates, and employment and bank records.

Edek Kosman lives with Zosia in hiding for over two years. To pass the time, he writes a Polish-English medical dictionary. I frequently visit them, and so does Niusia. They also become friends with Zofia Winiarska, from whom they are renting the apartment. These visits give Edek some company and he can relax a bit. Besides our family and Zosia, Edek has nobody else to talk to. And it is not suspicious for the neighbors and the janitor if women visit Zosia's apartment. Quite the opposite; people who live alone and do not have any Polish friends and family, are immediately suspected of being Jewish escapees from the ghetto.

Zosia and Edek realize they are fortunate to be alive and have a safe place to stay. But they are always afraid that any day Zosia's identity and Edek's hiding place could be discovered and communicated to the Gestapo. They fear that not only they would perish, but that this would bring harm onto our entire family for helping them. They are also tormented by the loss of their families and friends, that they could not save them and cannot help other Jews. But I admire Edek for staying so long in the ghetto until his arrest and risking his life every day to help as many people as he could.

Chapter 12

Working for the Enemy

Our entire household and efforts to help Jews depend on Niusia's steady income from her dental office, as our odd jobs are insufficient. With additional people from the ghetto staying with us, we must supplement our paltry rations with food bought on the black market at high prices. Marysia, Teklusia, and I are very careful to shop frequently and in different stores, as buying and bringing large amounts of food home all at once might look suspicious to the neighbors. In the spring of 1942, the situation becomes dire because Niusia gets sick and has to have surgery. We all worry about her health and how we are going to support ourselves and the recuperating patient.

At the same time, a letter arrives from the German Schmidt-Münstermann engineering firm in Warsaw addressed to Wacek, under his real name, Sterner. I am terrified simply at the sight of the letter. How do they know that Wacek, under his real name, is still living here? Wacek opens the envelope. The letter asks him to visit the company office to discuss an employment opportunity. Is it a trap? Do they want him to go so they can hand him over to the Gestapo as a Jew living outside the ghetto? But Wacek argues they could just notify the Gestapo that he is living here, which would simply come in the middle of the night and arrest him and the rest of us. He decides to go the next day.

Wacek is gone almost all day. I wait anxiously and worry more and more with every passing hour. Have they arrested him? At last, he comes back late in the afternoon. The company somehow found out about his prewar civil engineering experience and has offered him a job overseeing the construction of a labor camp and a German uniforms factory in Poniatowa, near Lublin, some 170 kilometers southeast of Warsaw. The German Walter C. Többens uniforms factory, now in the Warsaw Ghetto, will relocate there, together with the fifteen thousand Jews working there.

I am horrified and dumbfounded. Wacek, a Jew who helps Jews to escape from the ghetto, is now to collaborate with the Germans and build a forced labor camp—essentially no different from a concentration camp—to imprison Jews? My heart is pounding. I cannot hold back my tears. What is he to do? Flee and hide? Where?

But Wacek, as usual, is calm and rational. He says that they will build the camp and the factory regardless of whether he helps them. And he says, "If I take the job, I can actually save many people. I will have unlimited access to the Warsaw Ghetto and to the Poniatowa camp. I've already talked to my commanders in the underground and my assignment will be to recruit Jews from the Többens factory in the ghetto and from the Poniatowa camp for the resistance and help them escape. I can also provide the Polish resistance with information about the camp and the factory that could aid in sabotage and rescue actions. It is beneficial for us to infiltrate a German company; we will know what they are doing and what their plans are. If I don't take the job, someone else who takes it may not help the resistance and may not help the Jews." And then he adds, "Besides, working for a German company will be the safest work for me, because the Gestapo does not bother people working for the Germans and surely will not suspect that a Jew is working for a German company. I will not have to hide and live on false papers anymore."

Wacek's logic and sense of purpose calm me down and we decide he will take the job. He travels to Poniatowa a lot, spending more than half of his time there. They clear the forest and build roads, bridges, barracks, and the factory. He also finds a position for Tadeusz—supervising the workers in Poniatowa. Our living conditions improve, as he has a better income and larger food rations, as does Tadeusz. Also, Niusia recovers quickly after her surgery and is back to seeing patients.

We continue helping Jews to escape from the Warsaw Ghetto through the court and finance building on Leszno Street as much as we can. But Wacek now has a new way to help Jews in the ghetto. Working for Schmidt-Münstermann, Wacek often oversees Jewish workers in Warsaw, who leave the ghetto during the day to work on various construction projects on the

Polish side. These Jewish workers often smuggle out various items, such as clothing and shoes, which they want to sell or exchange for food. Wacek and I take these items from them; I sell them and then deliver money or food. We also help Jewish workers to pass letters and messages to their family and friends on the Polish side. This is especially important for those who want to find safe places to stay on the Polish side before they escape. And then, if some Jewish workers want to escape from the ghetto, Wacek also helps them slip away from the worksite.

In the summer of 1942, mass deportations from the Warsaw Ghetto start. The Jews are told they are being "relocated" to live somewhere else in the East, but soon we find out that they are being sent to the newly built death camp in Treblinka, just eighty kilometers from Warsaw. The situation in the ghetto is desperate. We read with utter horror the description of these deportations, printed and distributed by the Polish underground: "The daily quota of victims is 8,000–10,000. Jewish policemen have the responsibility of delivering them into the hands of German executioners. If they fail to do so, they will also perish . . . . Railway wagons wait at the ramp. The executioners stuff the condemned 150 to each wagon, on the floor of which is a thick layer of lime and chlorine covered in water. The doors to the wagons are sealed. Sometimes, the train leaves immediately after loading. Sometimes, it is moved into a siding where it stands for a whole day, two days . . . By now, this is of no significance to anyone. In the tightly packed wagon, those who die remain standing shoulder to shoulder with the living, who are slowly dying from the mists of lime and chlorine, a lack of air, a drop of water and food—no one remains alive anyway" (fig. 26).[28] There are no barracks for the Jews in Treblinka. They are herded directly from the train into the gas chambers. Just a few of the strongest men are allowed to live for a few more days, but only to be forced to burn the bodies of their families and friends killed in the gas chambers.[20]

But tragically, most people pay little attention to this slaughter unraveling behind the ghetto walls. And it is extremely depressing that we cannot really do anything more to stop this mass murder. We can only help one family at a time. Deliveries of food and money to the ghetto and arranging escapes have also become very difficult, practically impossible, because the ghetto is now especially heavily guarded.

The Warsaw Ghetto has been the largest ghetto in Europe, with 460,000 Jews imprisoned there. But in the fall, we learn that in less than two months the Germans have deported over three hundred thousand people from the

Warsaw Ghetto to the death camp in Treblinka, where they immediately killed them and burned their bodies. Through disease and starvation, and now this murder, its population has been reduced to only fifty-six thousand.[20] We hear that the Polish resistance is smuggling weapons inside, but we cannot help with that; we can only offer refuge to those who can escape.

On January 18, 1943, when the German troops enter the ghetto and round up people for a new wave of deportations to Treblinka, they are met with a barrage of fire from Jewish fighting organizations. All day, we hear intense fighting in the ghetto. However, in the end, the Germans kill several hundred Jews, suppress the resistance, and round up some five thousand Jews for deportation to the death camp.[20, 29]

Wacek is mostly in the Poniatowa labor camp, as the uniforms factory is being relocated there together with all the workers. This is a top priority project for the Wehrmacht, as it is very important for the morale of their soldiers to have excellent uniforms. Thus, the best tailors and seamstresses from the ghetto work there. To maintain the entire Jewish workforce for his company, Többens persuaded the authorities to appoint himself as a Jewish deportation commissioner for the Warsaw Ghetto and negotiated less stringent conditions for his workers in the Poniatowa camp. Although they are still prisoners and slave laborers, Többens lets them move with their children and their possessions. The security at the camp is not tight either. So it will be relatively easy for Wacek to arrange escapes for the prisoners to join the Polish resistance and provide them with false documents. There are many young men and women in the Poniatowa camp who could escape this way. However, only a few Jews decide to escape because Többens promises his workers that if they work in his factory they will survive the war. And, sadly, most of the Jews believe him, not knowing that eventually all of them will be killed.

On April 19, 1943, SS troops again enter Warsaw Ghetto to start new deportations, but they are once more met with armed resistance. Intense fighting breaks out. This is the beginning of the Warsaw Ghetto Uprising.[29] We lose all contact with the ghetto, and many SS and Wehrmacht troops surround it. But we learn about two unsuccessful attempts by the Polish resistance to blow up the ghetto wall. We hear machine gun fire and explosions. Everyone in Warsaw is talking about the uprising; some with admiration, but painfully, some with mockery (which makes me furious and ashamed).

We watch with horror as heavy dark smoke rises from the ghetto for over three weeks. The wind carries ash all over the city. At night, the sky is lit up with flames. The entire ghetto is burning while the resistance fighters and other residents hide in houses and underground bunkers. Eventually, they die or the fires and shelling force them to surrender (figs. 27 and 28). Niusia and I frequently visit Zosia and Edek Kosman, just to keep them company and help them cope with this terrible tragedy. The fighting ends on May 16, 1943, with a large explosion—the SS units have demolished the beautiful Great Synagogue of Warsaw. The Germans then raze the ghetto to the ground.[20, 29] Now we can only help those few who managed to escape.

But we also have another way to help the Jews in the Poniatowa camp. Many of them still have some valuables, especially gold and jewelry, because only rich Jews could afford the huge bribes that were required to get these jobs in the Többens factory. These jobs saved them from deportations to Treblinka death camp. Now they want to sell their remaining valuables to have some cash to bribe the guards or buy extra food and other necessities. So Wacek and Tadeusz bring their gold and jewelry to Warsaw, and I take it to pawn shops. After a few days, I collect the money and Wacek or Tadeusz take it back to the Jews in the Poniatowa camp. All of this is extremely dangerous, because if any of us get caught, we have no proof where the gold, jewelry, or money came from. The police will immediately assume it belongs to Jews or is connected to the resistance or some other illegal activity. Also, the pawn shops can easily cheat and not give me the money, which sometimes happens. Even worse, they could report me to the police.

What makes these trips even more perilous is that I look very Jewish—I have black hair, dark eyes, a dark complexion, and a Jewish-looking nose. In a trolley, I see people pointing at me several times and overhear them saying, "Look, a Jewess." I know that this is dangerous, and not just talk, because by now the German occupation has spawned a new underclass thugs, called *szmalcowniki*,[i] who roam the city in search of Jewish-looking people to extort money by threatening to denounce them to the Gestapo. Although I am Polish with Polish papers, I am married to a Jew; and under the Nazi law I am considered Jewish and obligated to wear an armband with the Jewish star and live in the ghetto. By rights, I should already be dead. Not only Wacek, Basia, and I are in danger—our entire household is, just for sheltering us.

---

i *Szmalcownik* (pl. *szmalcowniki*) is derived from *szmalec*, which in Polish means "lard"; but in a slang, *szmalec*, and more often *szmal*, means "money." A *szmalcownik*, then, is someone who obtains money in a despicable way, such as through threats and extortion. *Szmalcowniki* usually accosted their victims on the streets, whereas blackmailers would track down Jewish hiding places, demand large payments, would often come back for more, and threaten denouncing both the Jews and their Polish protectors to the Gestapo.

I do not think of people in terms of Jews and Aryans—we are all the same. But if arrested, how would I convince the Gestapo of that? Before the war, I could stand up to powerful bankers and the police when organizing workers' unions and strikes. I know I can stand up to *szmalcowniki,* but if they denounce me, the Gestapo in the Pawiak prison is so brutal . . . Would I be strong enough to withstand torture? I am not accosted by *szmalcowniki,* though. I do not know what would happen if I were. By giving them money, I would admit my guilt and they would never leave me alone . . . I try to keep these thoughts out of my mind and continue what I am doing.

Chapter 13

Blackmail

In the summer of 1943, Wacek comes back from Poniatowa distressed, which is quite unusual for him. My heart is already beating faster. He tells me that Obergruppenführer Odilo Globočnik inspected the Poniatowa camp. Finding that prisoner discipline is lax and their living conditions relatively comfortable, he ordered the camp commandant, Gottlieb Hering, to drastically tighten security and implement a harsher regime. It will be very difficult now to help the prisoners. In addition, Wacek thinks the Germans suspect his involvement with the Polish resistance. I immediately know that this is punishable by torture and death in the Pawiak prison. He needs to leave Poniatowa and disappear.

The next day, Wacek goes to the company headquarters in Warsaw and meets with the owner, Heinrich Münstermann—a fat, forty-year-old man in a civilian suit, who sits behind a desk in a richly furnished office. Wacek asks him to terminate his employment, but Münstermann becomes visibly upset and refuses because the company needs him at the camp. Wacek expected a negative answer, so he has prepared a story that he hopes will convince the owner to release him. There are many partisans in the forest in the Poniatowa area, and they target not only the Germans but also Polish collaborators.

Wacek has written himself a fake death threat from the partisans, and shows it to Münstermann. He says that he doesn't feel safe anymore and must find a position elsewhere.

However, Münstermann is not persuaded by this argument and tells Wacek that he has received several death threats from the Polish resistance, too, and that they mean nothing. He says that the Gestapo will protect Wacek, and that he has nothing to worry about. Wacek has to agree, takes all his work orders and new construction plans, and pretends to set out for Poniatowa. But instead, he goes into hiding and moves into his friend Leszek Gryczyński's apartment on Królewska Street in Warsaw. He stays there secretly, very much like Edek Kosman in his wife's apartment. In the meantime, Wacek's brother-in-law, Tadeusz, who is still working for Münstermann in Poniatowa, calls company headquarters in Warsaw. He tells them that Wacek left Warsaw two days ago, but did not make it to Poniatowa, and that the partisans have probably killed him.

The same day, I receive a phone call from Münstermann's office asking what has happened. I tell them that Wacek left two days ago and that I have not heard from him since. They order me to come for immediate interrogation. I am terrified. All I can think of are Wacek's stories about his employer's cruelty and ruthlessness.

Münstermann personally supervised the construction of the wall around the Warsaw Ghetto. He often beat his Jewish workers with a club or a whip. On one occasion, he threw bricks at a crowd of hungry Jews who gathered around his workers receiving their soup ration in order to disperse the crowd. Although he has not murdered any Jews himself, Münstermann has made a fortune extorting large sums of money from the Jews in the ghetto in exchange for employment in his company. This work gives them temporary protection from deportation to a death camp. For example, a wealthy Jew, Mr. Sztak, the prewar owner of an iron trading company, gave Münstermann one hundred gold dollars and three furs for employing his wife and child. And Jews working for Münstermann's company usually have to continue paying him to keep their jobs. If they cannot keep the money flowing, or if they are too weak to work, Münstermann himself escorts them to the *Umschlagplatz*, the collection point for transports to the death camps.[5, 6]

I have no choice. I take my two-year-old Basia with me and, trembling, enter the building at 5 Prusa Street. To my surprise, I am led not to the Münstermann's office, but to his partner Schmidt's office. I must act like a new widow—and it's actually very easy. I shake and cry so profusely that my face is swollen because I am truly frightened and worried about what will happen to us. I tell Schmidt, through an interpreter, that Wacek showed them the death threat and that Münstermann insisted on him continuing at the camp. I add that Wacek has probably been caught and killed by the partisans because he wasn't allowed to leave.

The next day, I get a phone call from Münstermann's office. He is furious that Wacek's death is likely not real; he is looking for Wacek everywhere. He has even been to two transit detention camps near Radom, where people rounded up in *łapankas* are held. They make threats: to force Wacek to show up, they will take me and Basia as hostages. I am completely terrified. I have heard stories of the Gestapo torturing children in front of their parents in the Pawiak prison. For the first time in my life, I do not know what to do and how to protect my little Basia. Everyone is advising me to go away somewhere with her and hide. But this would mean admitting they are right that we staged Wacek's death. Besides, I have no place to hide undetected with a small child. Even Wacek is having doubts about the wisdom of staging his own death, and we frantically look for a way out of the situation.

Finally, he finds a contact in one of the Polish resistance organizations, who works as a driver for Münstermann and Schmidt. The man goes and talks to Schmidt. I do not know what the driver told him, but Schmidt asks me to come to his apartment. With much trepidation and, again, crying desperately, I enter the apartment. But I am pleasantly surprised when he and his wife welcome me with an elegant dinner. They both speak good Polish, are very polite, and tell me I should not worry. Schmidt tells me he will make my problem go away, and then adds, "After the war, when all the dust settles, Wacek will surely come back."

I go back home puzzled, but relieved, and immediately call Wacek. Why is Schmidt sympathetic to me? Maybe he is just a decent man who understands what a terrible situation Poles have found themselves in through no fault of their own . . . Or maybe he is afraid of retaliation by the Polish resistance . . . Or maybe both . . . Weeks later, the driver tells me that he overheard Schmidt telling Münstermann: "If you don't leave Sterner's wife alone, I'll go to the Gestapo and tell them about all the illegal dealings that you have with the Jews and all the bribes you take from them. They can check all the money, gold, and diamonds that you are keeping in the safe at work, which you extracted from the Jews. Also, if Sterner is indeed dead, you will gain nothing. But if Sterner is alive and something happens to his wife and daughter, the resistance will surely find a way to put a bullet in both your head and mine."

But for now, Wacek continues to hide and, thanks to Schmidt, I do not receive any further threats. Eventually, Wacek returns home with new false papers, again under the name of Wacław Domański. But he still must keep a very low profile and steps outside only when absolutely necessary.

Soon we find out that the fate of the Jews in the Poniatowa camp has been the same as the Jews in the Warsaw Ghetto—brutal extermination. In Operation Harvest Festival (*Aktion Erntefest*), the Germans ordered the Poniatowa inmates to dig long anti-tank trenches. Then, on November 3 and 4, 1943, the SS guards ordered some forty-three thousand male and female prisoners to undress, get into the trenches, and then shot them. A few prisoners staged a revolt in one of the Poniatowa camp barracks, but the SS guards set the barrack on fire. One "Jew running from the flames was bludgeoned with rifle butts [by the SS] and thrown back into the burning building," and all the rebelling prisoners were burned alive.[30] Többens did not keep his promise that his Jewish workers survive the war.

Our dealings with Münstermann also confirm that he really is a ruthless war profiteer and has committed many crimes. Later, in the spring of 1944, the German authorities sued Münstermann for extorting large ransoms of cash, gold, jewelry, and furs during the liquidation of Warsaw Ghetto. The Third Reich considered all confiscated Jewish possessions the property of the state. They convicted Münstermann and expelled him from the capital. These crimes, however, saved his life, as he would probably have been killed during the subsequent Polish Warsaw Uprising. After the war, Münstermann was on the list of war criminals; but again, he was saved by two Jewish women who were both hiding their husbands at home. They gave Münstermann huge bribes, a veritable fortune, in exchange for hiring them and staying quiet about their husbands. Thus, ironically, Münstermann survived the war and was then spared from facing charges of war crimes because he saved the lives of these four Jews, whereas Schmidt was killed in 1944 in the first few days of the Polish Warsaw Uprising.

Chapter 14

The Underground

It is February 2, 1944, and, as usual, I am selling various items in Polish stores and, at the end of the day, I am coming back home in a trolley car on Aleje Ujazdowskie, going towards Piękna Street. Suddenly, I hear gunfire and see a German soldier running and carrying a bleeding child. The Gestapo and the German police are everywhere, stopping all the traffic and rounding everybody up on the street. A mass *łapanka*. All the passengers in the trolley car fall to the floor. I am wearing a brand-new light-blue coat, and I am reluctant to lie down flat on the floor and get my coat dirty, but someone yells at me and pushes me all the way down to the floor. The trolley driver accelerates as fast as the trolley can go, speeds through the Gestapo roadblock, and then stops at Piękna Street. Everyone on the trolley is relieved how lucky we got; the driver has saved us all. Only when I get to the market on Koszykowa Street do I find out what happened and can call home to tell Wacek and Niusia that I am safe.

Earlier that day, the Polish underground Home Army (Armia Krajowa, AK) assassinated Franz Kutschera, the chief of the SS and Reich's Police in Warsaw. Kutschera was especially brutal and ruthless, and he conducted frequent *łapanki* and executions of civilians. The news is hard to get, but we read in an underground publication that the AK operation squad comprised nine men and three women. When Kutschera's limousine was entering SS headquarters on Aleje Ujazdowskie, three AK fighters blocked the limousine with their car. They got out of the car and shot Kutschera dead at close range. A gun battle with SS guards ensued, and the Germans badly wounded three resistance fighters. All the partisans escaped in two getaway cars, but the two wounded fighters died later from their wounds. The Gestapo intercepted two other AK fighters on a bridge over Vistula River and wounded them in a gunfight. The injured fighters jumped off the bridge to their deaths.

In reprisal for Kutschera assassination, the Germans capture and execute three hundred Polish civilians and impose a fine of one hundred million złotys, which is collected as an additional tax from the residents of Warsaw. But this does not break the spirit of the resistance. Soon, graffiti on Warsaw streets appear: "100 million for Kutschera, 200 million for Himmlera" (Polish for Heinrich Himmler)[i]—meaning that next the underground will assassinate Himmler.

Such attacks, sabotage actions, and assassinations, especially of the most brutal SS officers, are now frequent. Poland has the largest resistance of all the occupied countries in Europe and it is a part of the Polish Underground State,[ii] a clandestine organization with all branches of government operating in secret.[31, 32] By the summer of 1944, the combined armed forces of the Polish resistance organizations number 650,000 people.[31] But because of all these anti-German attacks, everyday life is more and more difficult and dangerous for us due to the increased German repression, with frequent daily searches, raids, arrests, and random roundups.

However, we know that the Nazis are losing the war on the Eastern front and that the Allies are advancing in Italy. In May, we hear about the Allies' victory at the Battle of Monte Cassino, which involved many Polish soldiers. In June, we find out that the Allies have landed in Normandy and are gaining the upper hand, and that the Germans are retreating on all fronts. This fills us with a lot of hope that the war will end soon and Poland will be liberated.

---

i Heinrich Himmler was Reichsführer (chief) of the SS; he was one of the most powerful Nazi leaders and the primary architect of the Holocaust.

ii Unlike other Nazi-occupied countries in Europe in WWII, Poland never officially capitulated and never entered into any surrender agreements with the occupiers, but continued all its government operations underground and abroad. The Polish Underground State (Polskie Państwo Podziemne in Polish) was a single clandestine political and military entity formed by the union of resistance organizations in occupied Poland. It had all typical governmental institutions (political parties, judiciary, ministries, armed forces, treasury, and educational, cultural, and social services), all operating in secret. It was a legal continuation of the prewar Republic of Poland, loyal to the Polish government-in-exile in London.

We read that the Red Army is already in the Poland's eastern towns, and in July, that it is advancing towards Warsaw. We are happy, but also apprehensive, remembering the NKVD's hostility towards us in Lwów and Krzemieniec. Our anxiety is heightened by the news of a recent discovery in Katyń forest of mass graves of twenty-two thousand Polish military officers and civilians from the educated upper class, who were murdered by the NKVD in April or May 1940 (fig. 29).[33] The husband of my best childhood friend, Jania Marchwińska-Rabęcka, was one of the victims.

For the last several months, Wacek, Tadeusz, and their fellow resistance fighters have been training more and more intensely and preparing to fight. At the end of July, we can feel energy, hope, and anticipation in the city. There are many young people rushing around Warsaw carrying mysterious packages, probably weapons and explosives manufactured in clandestine factories by our resistance. Boldly, they now pay little attention to the Germans, who also ignore them, likely anxious and preoccupied with the approaching Soviets. We also see on the streets German soldiers and civilians fleeing the city, with their heads down, taking as many of their looted possessions as they can. They pay no attention to people openly swearing at them, which was unthinkable a few months ago and would have resulted in severe punishment, if not death. But we are also wary of the Wehrmacht moving their military equipment eastward and building fortified bunkers in and around the city.

Finally, in the last few days of July, we can hear the rumble of artillery fire far in the distance, getting closer and closer, coming from the east bank of the Vistula River. This is the Red Army approaching Warsaw, fighting the Germans. We all think that something big will happen soon—the liberation of Warsaw. But how and when?

Chapter 15

The Uprising

On July 31, 1944, Wacek and Tadeusz receive a secret message that an uprising to liberate Warsaw from the German occupation will start the next day, August 1, at 5:00 pm. It is delivered by a runner from General Bór (Tadeusz Komorowski), the commander of the Home Army, the largest resistance organization, which will lead the uprising. The Polish People's Army (PAL) and other resistance organizations will join the uprising under the Home Army's command. Altogether in Warsaw, they have some twenty thousand to forty-nine thousand fighters, but enough weapons for only a quarter of them.[34] They hope to capture more weapons from the Germans. The timing of the uprising was selected to coincide with the arrival of the Red Army and the First Polish Army—which is fighting alongside the Soviets—on the east bank of Vistula River, just outside of Warsaw. The uprising fighters hope to liberate Warsaw with the help of both the Soviet and Polish armies.

Wacek is overjoyed! Finally, he will get to openly fight the hated enemy. And most of all, he already feels free and will not have to worry about being denounced to the Gestapo or just caught on the street in a *łapanka*. This is the greatest burden he has been carrying with him the five years of the German occupation—constantly worrying about his triple jeopardy as a Jew, a Pole, and as a resistance member. Any encounter with the Gestapo or the SS would have led to the discovery that he is Jewish and death of our entire family. Thus, his greatest worry was never for himself, but that he was endangering me, Basia, and everyone else. He's never shown his fear and has always been optimistic, but I could feel how worried he was.

On August 1, Wacek and Tadeusz, wearing their makeshift uniforms and white-and-red armbands with the Polish flag, are already gone. Many of their friends join them, including Jan Mulak and Teofil Głowacki, whom I know very well. In the afternoon, from the balcony of our apartment on Szustra Street, I see a line of Polish resistance fighters armed with submachine guns running north on Kazimierzowska Street. My two good friends, Stefan Szmit and his cousin, Leon, are among them. The fighters are heading towards the school on Różana Street, a block away from our house, which the Germans converted into a bunker. I hear a lot of gunfire late into the night. But soon, sad news arrives—one of the first bullets killed Leon. The bunker was so strong that the uprising fighters could not take it—they were only lightly armed and did not have any heavy artillery.

The next day, the fighting intensifies. The uprising establishes its own radio station, and we hear that our fighters have captured the city's main power station, the German arsenal and supply depot, and a brewery with a large stockpile of grain. But I am terrified by all the shooting and fighting and spend all the time in the cellar of our building, together with Basia, my mother, and women from other apartments. All the firing and explosions bring frightening memories from my childhood of fighting in the streets of Warsaw during World War I.

I do not understand why I am so afraid, because I was never afraid to rescue and hide all the Jews from the ghetto, to sell their possessions for them, and to supply money, medicines, food, and other things to the ghetto—very dangerous activities. It is hard to understand what bravery is. I thought I was brave, but now I am not. Maybe it's because I am afraid of the worst, losing Basia, and I am not sure if I can protect her. Or maybe it's because I am also worried that Wacek, my mother, Tadeusz, and Niusia may be killed. Niusia is not with us, as she has joined the uprising as a nurse and is gone all day attending to the wounded. She tells us that great numbers of people are being wounded and killed, including many women and children. The streets are littered with bodies, which can only be collected at night. The Germans are also using Polish women and children as human shields. They walk them in front of their advancing troops and have them sit on their tanks.

The Mokotów division of the uprising has established its headquarters in our apartment on Szustra Street (fig. 21). After some time, we have to move into another building on Pilicka Street, and later we move again to avoid the heavy fighting with the strengthened German forces advancing on Mokotów (figs. 30 and 31). Wacek was first appointed as the head of B-3 company's engineer section; he's in charge of digging connecting trenches in the center of Mokotów and is also responsible for radio communication. Then he participates in the fighting for the cemetery in Czerniaków and the Mokotów Forts near Królikarnia. Later, with his company, he defends Puławska, Odyńca, Kazimierzowska, and Różana Streets.

Wacek and Tadeusz only occasionally stop at home to bring some food for us. A few times, they even manage to bring us fresh onions and tomatoes, which they picked from the adjacent fields at night.

Niusia continues as a nurse in nearby Elżbietanek Hospital, attending to the wounded. One day, the Germans bomb this hospital so heavily that it completely collapses and becomes a pile of rubble. All the patients and personnel are crushed by the collapsing building and killed. It is not even possible to identify the dead. The body of one physician, our family friend, is only identified by her shoes. Niusia did not go for her shift at the hospital that day because she was sick—this saved her life.

As I sit in the dark cellar of the apartment building, hiding from the fighting and holding little Basia tightly, I hear constant machine gun and artillery fire and bombs exploding. All day and night, I try to cover her with my body in case the walls or the ceiling collapse on us. Dark thoughts hang over me. I cannot help remembering the images from the battlefield that I saw when I was a child. I was around six years old during World War I. Soon after a bloody battle near Warsaw, I went with my parents to the battle site to see that all the dead were properly buried. Now, images of many huge, poorly dug and shallow graves, with people's hair or body parts partially sticking out of the ground, crowd my mind. When my parents tried to cover them with soil, they would start uncovering other dead or just body parts . . . I try to block these images out, but I cannot. I can only think about how to protect Basia from seeing such horrific things.

I know that, so far, we have been lucky. Many buildings have collapsed under the heavy bombing and artillery fire and killed the people hiding in the cellars. The German troops have also set many buildings on fire with flame throwers and are throwing grenades into the cellars. People are killed instantaneously, burned alive, or flee and are shot dead on the streets.

We keep waiting for the Red Army and the First Polish Army (*Berlingowcy*)[i] to come and aid the uprising. But help does not come. Finally, we hear on the Polish resistance radio station that several thousand Polish soldiers attempted to cross the Vistula River. However, neither the Polish uprising fighters nor the soldiers had been able to secure any of the bridges that the Germans destroyed by September 13.[34] Thus, the *Berlingowcy* tried to cross the river by boats under a barrage of machine guns and artillery fire from the heavily fortified riverbank. Although the Polish soldiers were very daring and brave, most of them were killed crossing the river or on the shore after the landing because they did not receive any support from the Red Army. Only a few hundred of them made it through the German defenses and joined the uprising. We are very proud of our soldiers, but deeply saddened by the great numbers of casualties. And we are highly disappointed by what we now see as the deliberate lack of support from the Soviet army.

The fighting has been going on now for over a month; not only is there no end in sight, but we are losing ground (figs. 30 and 31). We are exhausted and food is scarce. The German forces surround our Mokotów district and there is no communication with other parts of Warsaw controlled by the Polish fighters. Towards the end of September, we are separated from Wacek and Tadeusz, who are fighting somewhere else, but I don't know where, and they have stopped coming to see us. The Polish-held territory is shrinking because the single houses characteristic of Mokotów are very easy targets for tanks and heavy artillery—a couple of well-aimed shells can level one. The uprising fighters have no defense against tanks and artillery except for Molotov cocktails and grenades, but they cannot approach the tanks close enough to throw them because of the wide spaces between the houses.

At the beginning of the uprising, we were certain that the Red Army would continue the offensive and join us in the fight to liberate Warsaw, as we are all fighting a common enemy. But it is obvious now that the Soviets will not enter the city as long as we are fighting—and we understand why. The reason is that the Home Army is under the command of the Polish government-in-exile (in England), which wants to establish Poland as a Western democracy after the war. But the Soviets want Poland to become a communist country

---

i *Berlingowcy* was a popular Polish name for soldiers in the First Polish Army (Berling's Army), named after commander, General Zygmunt Berling. The army was under Soviet control and fought alongside the Red Army on the Eastern Front. After his attempt to support the Warsaw Uprising, the Soviets dismissed Berling from his post and sent him to Moscow.

under their control. For this reason, the Red Army is simply standing by and watching events in Warsaw. The Soviets will not make their airspace and air base—which is five-minutes flying time away from Warsaw—available either, from where the Allies could easily drop supplies and give air support. Only at the very end of the uprising, both the Allies and the Soviets drop some supplies. But by then the Polish-held territory is so small that the Germans intercept most of the supplies.[34] Thus, we are convinced that the Soviets want the uprising to fail and want the Germans to eliminate the Polish resistance forces, so they will have no say in the future of Poland.[34]

To add to all of this sorrow, in a radio broadcast, the Soviet-installed provisional Polish communist government in Lublin denounces the Warsaw Uprising fighters as traitors and Nazi collaborators. How can this be? They are fighting Hitler's army to liberate Poland from the German occupation. Will the long-awaited Soviet liberation of Poland turn into another occupation? But for now, our main worry is how to survive the German onslaught.

Eventually, we are squeezed into a small area of a few blocks of densely built tenement houses, tightly surrounded by the German forces. The uprising has reached a stalemate. The fighters are not only poorly equipped, but are now running out of food and ammunition. Without heavy weapons and outside help, they cannot displace the German forces from their strongly fortified bunkers and cannot stop the advance of the elite Wehrmacht reinforcements that are bringing in more tanks and artillery. We hear rumors that any day Mokotów will fall; civilian men who are not fighting start escaping through the sewer tunnels, as they are sure they will be executed on capture. Women and children do not dare to enter the sewers and are left behind.

On September 26, German airplanes drop leaflets urging all civilians to leave Mokotów during a two-hour ceasefire in the afternoon. Some people are so desperate for this ordeal to be over that they come out and turn themselves in. But we and most others do not, as we have heard about mass killings of civilians in other sections of the city that have fallen to the Germans. On September 27, I see German soldiers on the street, and I know the uprising is all over for us. There is no place to flee and all we can do is to hide and await our fate.

I do not know what has happened to Wacek and Tadeusz or if they are still alive. This not knowing is a strange state of mind. I am extremely worried that they could be dead, but I still have hope that they somehow managed to survive. These agonizing thoughts circle in my brain and I try to hold on to every ray of hope I have.

But the Nazis have accomplished their goal of crushing the uprising—they're proud of it, even though they are losing the war. The SS chief Heinrich Himmler has again evoked the First Battle of Tannenberg of 1410, as he wrote the following to Hitler when he learned about the Warsaw Uprising: "My *Führer*, . . . what the Poles are doing is a blessing. After five, six weeks . . . Warsaw, the capital, the head, the intelligence of this former 16–17 million Polish people will be extinguished, this *Volk* [people] that has blocked our way to the east for seven hundred years and has stood in our way ever since the First Battle of Tannenberg. After this the Polish problem will no longer be a great historical problem for the children who come after us, nor indeed will it be for us."[34]

Chapter 16

Wacek's Imprisonment

Wacek (Lieutenant "Boss") was a commander of a company of several dozen uprising fighters, of which only about a dozen survived by the end of September. On September 25, 1944, when the Mokotów district was about to fall, the uprising's command ordered fighters to evacuate through the sewer tunnels to the city center, which was still held by the resistance. There, the fighters would help to defend the city center. The news of this directive quickly spread among civilians and triggered panic and a desperate desire also to escape from Mokotów.

Early in the morning of September 26, a couple of dozen fighters entered the sewer through the hatch on Wiktorska Street. But soon the evacuation had to pause for several hours because of heavy artillery fire. Then the next group entered the sewer, but they quickly returned because it was blocked at Puławska Street. When it got dark and the fighting stopped, Wacek and the remainder of his company reported to another hatch that was opened on the corner of Bałuckiego and Szustra Streets. Wacek had not slept for four or five days, and his left arm was in a sling because of a recent gunshot wound to his hand. He had not eaten for two days.

Wacek and another fighter, Second Lieutenant "Henryk," were put in charge of guarding the hatch. There were several hundred fighters, including many wounded, waiting in line to enter the sewer. A large crowd of over one thousand civilians were also gathered around the hatch trying to enter the tunnel. The opening was just big enough for one man to enter at a time, and they could only do it under the cover of night. So immediately Wacek realized that there was not enough time before morning for everybody to enter the sewer. But there was nothing he could do about it, except keeping order and hurrying people along. They knew that the German offensive would resume in the morning, as usual.

When the morning came, there was still a large crowd of civilians and several dozen fighters left waiting to escape through the sewers. Wacek, having the highest rank, became commander of the remaining fighters. The desperate civilians felt abandoned by the fighters and could not think logically any longer, and didn't care that the fighters had orders to join the fighting in the center of the city. These civilians did not understand that this handful of lightly armed fighters were completely outnumbered and outgunned by the Wehrmacht and SS forces and could not defend Mokotów any longer. The crowd became hysterical, started chanting "Treason!" and demanded that the men stay and defend them.

Wacek could not disobey his orders and he could not persuade the civilians that defending Mokotów was not possible anymore. Staying and fighting with the remaining few fighters, no ammunition, and no other supplies, would be suicide. This was the most bitter day for Wacek. After years of dangerous work in the resistance, months of fighting, losing most of his men, and all his sacrifices, he was now called a "traitor" by the very people for whose liberation he was risking his life.

It was September 27, and soon the news came that Major "Burza" (Eugeniusz Landberger) and Lieutenant "Nerus" (Stanisław Poturęcki) had surrendered Mokotów. The crowd of civilians dispersed and went back into hiding, and around 150 remaining uprising fighters entered the sewer. Wacek and "Henryk" were the last ones to enter, and closed the hatch just before the Germans arrived.

The sewer tunnels under side streets were small, 120 cm tall, so everybody was moving slowly, as they had to crawl, which was especially difficult for Wacek because of his wounded hand. The main sewers were 180 cm tall, though, and they could walk. Soon after they entered the tunnel, they heard explosions. The German soldiers were throwing grenades into the sewer further down the street. Fortunately, it was far enough away that they were not hurt. Long, tightly packed lines of men silently crawled or walked for hours in total darkness, usually in ankle- or knee-deep sewage sludge, searching for the way to the city center. But all the known routes were useless because the Germans had either collapsed the tunnels or blocked them with heavy wood posts or barbed wire.

At some point, Wacek heard people ahead of him screaming, “Gas! Gas! Gas!” Panic ensued. The orderly column broke down, and everybody started running in the opposite direction, trampling each other. Wacek never found out whether the Germans really did drop poisonous gas into the sewers. But from then on, the column split into smaller groups, each searching for the best way out. Some fighters, out of total frustration and exhaustion, climbed out onto the streets. The men who remained in the tunnel heard them being shot.

Since the Germans had blocked all the sewers leading to the city center, Wacek’s group went south, in the opposite direction, planning to come out on the city outskirts and, under the cover of night, escape into the suburban woods. It was a long way, but it seemed to be the best and, in fact, only option. So the march in the darkness continued for several more hours. By now, they had completely lost any sense of time and did not know how long they had been trudging through the tunnels.

Everybody was getting weak and Wacek started to hallucinate. There were five of them now, all completely at the end of their rope . . . One fighter started screaming, “I cannot take it anymore! I am not gonna die in the tunnel like a sewer rat! I am coming out!” Silently, everyone agreed. They found the nearest hatch and lifted it with great difficulty. It was near dawn, which meant that they had been in the sewers for over twenty hours. They looked around. They were on the corner of Madalińskiego and Kielecka Streets—back in Mokotów!

The ruined houses around them were empty; the Germans must have already expelled all the residents. Wacek’s group decided to hide in an empty house during the day and at night make their way out of the city to the nearby Chojnowski forest. They selected the smallest and the least noticeable house that was relatively intact. They were all covered with stinking black sludge and completely exhausted. Once inside, the sight of beds and sofas was irresistible; they collapsed onto them, forgetting all safety precautions, and immediately fell asleep. Wacek had excellent new knee-high leather officer boots, and he only remembered to take them off moments before falling asleep.

Loud German voices and gunshots awakened Wacek. He hid under the bed. These were German soldiers looting the abandoned houses. They came to the room where he was hiding and took his boots, but did not notice him. When everything was quiet, he carefully came out from under the bed.

He was alone in the house. The Germans had arrested his four companions. He went through the house looking for some food, but did not find any.

Wacek realized that hiding in the house was not safe. So he left it, crossed the street, and hid in the cellar of another house. But soon he heard German voices and steps at the cellar door. There were bars over the small window and there was only one entrance—he was trapped. Wacek pulled out his pistol as he saw the soldiers entering the cellar. They jumped up, startled, when they saw him. There were about ten of them with submachine guns on their shoulders and grenades on their belts. They did not have their guns drawn as they expected the house to be empty. Wacek's one pistol was no match for them. He dropped it and raised his hands. But he was relieved to see that the soldiers were wearing Wehrmacht uniforms. The SS would have probably shot him dead on sight, as he had heard about their mass murders of uprising fighters and civilians in Wola and Ochota districts.

The soldiers took Wacek to a local Gestapo office on Rakowiecka Street. He was wearing a uniform with stars on his epaulets, so they knew he was a Polish officer in the resistance. They kept him standing facing a wall for about an hour while trying to decide what to do with him. Every so often, they kicked him on the butt and laughed when he fell forward against the wall. But Wacek was glad that they entertained themselves by just kicking him, rather than beating or shooting him. Finally, because he was still barefoot, they gave him a pair of old galoshes, and two soldiers escorted him to the German Sonderdienst (Special Services) headquarters on Willowa Street. On the way there, they passed many German soldiers from various services. Some of them threw stones at Wacek, shouting, "*Bandit! Blutiger Hund*!" (Bandit! Bloody dog!) For the first time, he was glad that he had his German escort. He was still covered with sewage and was extremely hungry, as he had not eaten for at least three days.

They brought Wacek to a richly appointed office with an elegant elderly lieutenant colonel sitting at the desk. The colonel came out to meet Wacek. Wacek saluted and introduced himself, *"Sterner, Oberleutnant der polnischen Wehrmacht!"* (Sterner, lieutenant of the Polish Armed Forces!). The colonel saluted, smiled, and shook his hand, saying, "Glad to meet you." To Wacek's astonishment, he then called all the other German officers into the room and asked them to introduce themselves.

The colonel then asked Wacek to sit down, called in an orderly and requested coffee, dinner, and cognac for Wacek. Soon a cup of coffee, a bowl of goulash, and a glass of vodka appeared. The colonel was very polite and patiently waited for Wacek to finish eating his dinner. Wacek spoke fluent German and they had a long conversation. The colonel asked him many questions about the uprising (its whys, whats, and hows), showing genuine interest in the fighters' motivations and actions. He praised the Polish fighters for their skill and bravery, and noted that the Germans won only because they deployed large numbers of elite Wehrmacht soldiers with heavy weapons, which the resistance lacked. He also told Wacek that the Germans recognized Polish resistance fighters as prisoners of war and that he was sending him to a detention camp near Skierniewice, where the other prisoners from the uprising were kept. From there, they were to be transported to a POW camp in Germany. Upon Wacek's departure, the colonel shook his hand again and gave him two packs of cigarettes. This gift was worth more than gold—later, in the camp, the prisoners used cigarettes as a form of internal currency and they carefully cut each cigarette into six pieces.

From the Sonderdienst headquarters, a German officer drove Wacek in a military jeep to the Wehrmacht headquarters near Okęcie. There, a surprisingly polite German captain conducted another lengthy interview with Wacek, asking him for his opinions about the war. At the end, to Wacek's surprise, the captain asked, "Who do you think will win the war?"

"The Allies, of course," he replied.

"Why?"

"Because the Red Army is at the Vistula and the Allies at Ren, and you cannot reverse their progress . . . "

"But Japan will decide in the Pacific who wins the war," said the captain.

"I wouldn't count on that. We counted on help from the Red Army, and you know the outcome."

The captain gave Wacek a friendly pat on the back and said, "You're right, lieutenant, one should only count on oneself."

Wacek was completely astonished by his gentle treatment, knowing all the atrocities and brutal, cold-blooded murders enacted during the occupation of Poland. Had he just come across some decent Germans trying to make the best out of the awful situation that they'd been put in? Was it Wacek's fluent German? Or did they now realize that they were losing the war and wanted to show their human face? He also wondered whether they would have treated him the same had they known that he was Jewish.

The Germans put Wacek in a barn, barely guarded, so he could go in and out as he pleased. They gave him soap so he could wash in a nearby water well, and soon a paramedic arrived to change the old and dirty dressing on

Wacek's wounded hand. Wacek could easily escape, but where would he go? The Germans controlled the entire area, and he thought that they had probably expelled all the Polish civilians.

After a few days, two Wehrmacht soldiers escorted him to the nearby suburban train station. It surprised him to see that the trains were running and that civilians were riding them. From there, Wacek and his guards took another train to Pruszków. His Polish uniform, which he had cleaned, was a sensation among the passersby and people on the train. Many women started handing Wacek bread, butter, eggs, fruit, and tomatoes. When his hands were full, someone gave him a nightgown to serve as a sack to carry the food. The soldiers escorting him did not interfere and did not pay any attention to people swearing at them and handing Wacek the food.

They arrived in Pruszków at the railway repair plant that had been converted into a prisoner detention camp. There were thousands of people chaotically moving about. A young Polish woman in a white doctor's coat, who introduced herself as a camp physician, greeted Wacek and his guards, and took them to an office in one of the auxiliary buildings. While Wacek's guards were completing the paperwork for his transfer, she brought coffee, bread, and scrambled eggs, which was a delicacy that he had not had in many months.

Wacek examined her thoughtfully—she was fluent in both Polish and German; she was seamlessly navigating the camp and the German guards appeared to respect her. She was obviously working for the Germans, but who was she loyal to—the imprisoned Poles or the Germans? And was she just pretending to be loyal to the Germans?

She asked him if he could recognize any fighters among the prisoners in the camp, so they could be transferred with him to the POW camp. He knew that many members of the resistance had avoided capture by blending into the civilian population—they did not trust the Germans. Wacek saw some familiar faces in the camp, but could he trust her or her German superiors? Years of underground work in the resistance had taught to trust no one. The rule in the underground was to never divulge any information. And who knew what fate lay in store for the prisoners and himself. His privileged treatment could easily end any time, and at the next destination he could face a firing squad. He decided not to expose anybody, although he wondered whether this was the right decision.

Wacek's guards received orders to transport him by train to a temporary detention camp in Skierniewice. Again, they took a passenger train, but this time they travelled in a separate compartment. Some fifteen hundred uprising fighters from Warsaw were already in Skierniewice; and those from Wacek's battalion enthusiastically welcomed him, as they had thought he was dead. The next day, there was a roll call of the prisoners. It surprised and overjoyed Wacek to see that the prisoner who was conducting the roll call was Tadeusz. So Wacek and Tadeusz were reunited and stayed together from then on.

In Skierniewice, Wacek found out that the fighters in the center of Warsaw had surrendered on October 2, 1944, after sixty-three days of battle (fig. 32). Altogether, about sixteen thousand resistance members and about nine thousand German soldiers were killed in the uprising, and the Germans took about fifteen thousand fighters prisoner. However, an additional five thousand to six thousand fighters escaped and disappeared into the civilian population. Under the terms of the surrender, the Germans agreed to treat the uprising fighters as POWs and send them to POW camps in various parts of Germany. Reportedly, this infuriated Stalin, who wanted all of them killed. The Germans also agreed "to treat the civilian population humanely."[34]

After a few days in long damp dugout barracks in Skierniewice, Wacek, Tadeusz, and all the other fighters were transported by train in cattle cars to a POW camp in Germany in Sandbostel, near Hamburg. There, they were thoroughly disinfected and treated for the lice which had infested them in Skierniewice. The Germans then issued each man an aluminum spoon, a small bar of soap, a thin cotton blanket, and a small box of shoe polish. They housed the men in Stalag XB, in wooden barracks with triple bunk beds, which were still infested with lice and rendered the disinfectant treatment useless. High watch towers mounted with machine guns loomed over the extensive camp, which was divided into sections. Each section contained prisoners of one nationality and was surrounded by barbed wire. Wacek was issued the prisoner number 224676 (fig. 33).

The camp authorities usually adhered to the Geneva convention, which meant that they did not force the officers to do any physical labor. The major problem was hunger. There was just ersatz coffee in the morning, a bowl of meagre beet soup and couple potatoes at mid-day, and in the evening more ersatz coffee, two hundred grams of dried-up bread, twenty grams of margarine, a small teaspoon of beet marmalade, and half a small teaspoon of sugar. But altogether, the Poles were glad that they hadn't ended up in a concentration camp or dead in Warsaw. Many fighters and civilians were killed in the uprising.

Chapter 17

Deportation

> You may not control all the events that happen to you, but you can decide not to be reduced by them.
> —*Maya Angelou*

It's the beginning of October 1944 and I am still in Mokotów, hiding from SS and Wehrmacht troops with Basia, Niusia, and my mother. We have eaten all our food and there is no way to get any more. There is no water in the pipes, but we can still get some from a nearby well. We take turns going there because it is very dangerous to walk the patrolled streets. For the same reason, we cannot go back to our apartment, and we do not even know if our building is still standing. But the worst is not knowing what will happen to us and what has happened to Wacek and Tadeusz.

We hear explosions and smell smoke from burning buildings. Wehrmacht soldiers herd us out of the cellar and set our building on fire with a flame-thrower. They order us to join a large column of marching people and guard us as we walk west towards Rakowiec. I am carrying little Basia because she cannot keep up with the group. Niusia, my mother, and my friend Krystyna

Żebrowska are with us. We only have the clothing that we are wearing and whatever fits into our handbags. From time to time, Niusia and Krystyna help me carry Basia. Almost all of us are women, many with children, and there are a few elderly.

There is total devastation everywhere. All the buildings we pass have been demolished or are still burning. There are armored vehicles and tanks on the streets. These sights are frightening and depressing. We do not know where we are going. We walk out of the city and keep going on a country road. There is nothing to eat or drink and the guards do not allow us to stop. I keep thinking about how to escape, but there is no way to slip out of the marching column; if caught, the guards would probably shoot us on the spot. Neither is there anywhere to go and hide—just empty ruins all around us. So we have no choice but to keep walking (fig. 34).

In the afternoon, after several hours of marching, we arrive in Pruszków at a railway repair plant, which seems to have been made into a large makeshift camp, called Dulag 121 (*Durchgangslager* 121) (fig. 35). There are nine big factory buildings, several smaller ones, and some old train cars without wheels. Because there are no obvious barracks or sleeping quarters for the prisoners, we think we will not be here long. But what will happen to us? Several hundred, or probably a few thousand, people, mostly women and children, are sitting on the ground or waiting in long lines. They all look dirty, exhausted, and forlorn. We stand in a long line and finally get some water and small portions of dark, dried-up bread. While trying to find out what is happening, we hear that the other lines are to enter one of the large buildings, Hall V, in which we will be sorted out. Able-bodied people will be sent to labor camps; no one knows the fate of people who are sick and unable to work. Polish physicians do the sorting, as the Germans are afraid of contracting diseases, such as typhus or tuberculosis, from the prisoners.

Finally, we enter Hall V. We scan the sorting stations, and luck has it that one of the examining doctors is our family friend, Dr. Łoza. We line up to be examined by him. After a long wait, we get to him. He speaks perfect German and commands a lot of respect from his German superiors, who trust his judgement. He pretends he does not know us and quickly rules that we cannot work because I have a small child and my mother is too old and frail. Then he says that Niusia has tuberculosis (which she obviously does not) and sends her to a temporary camp hospital for observation. When he starts examining Krystyna, she faints and slips to the floor. He reports that she has a heart disease and cannot work either, so she joins me, Basia, and my mother.

We embrace Niusia, and the guard directs us to join the group not fit for a labor camp; we are ordered to go to one of the other large factory buildings. Niusia goes to a different one.

We hope that the people unable to work will just be released, but we are put in Hall I with several hundred other people, all elderly or women with small children; and the guards order us to wait there. The hall has no sleeping facilities, so we sit on its dirty concrete floor. There are no showers or bathrooms; we cannot even wash our hands; and the lines for the latrines are so long that people often cannot wait and relieve themselves outside or in the hall. There is a strong odor of sweat, urine, feces, and rotting straw, which was thrown on the floor probably days or weeks ago. I spend the night holding Basia tight to my body under my coat to keep her warm, as it is getting cold and the hall is unheated, and we both doze off a little. In the morning we wait in a long line to get some warm, black ersatz coffee and black bread. Bread and a bowl of thin soup is again served in the evening.

But during the day we get a surprise. A woman working for the Polish Red Cross brings us two letters from Niusia, or, rather, two tightly folded little scraps of thin paper—one for my mother and one for me. She's written in tiny letters in pencil:

> I am staying in [camp hospital Hall] IIb . . . . The conditions here are good, very clean, the room not too large, heated by a stove, on which I heated some water yesterday and washed myself when everyone went to sleep. [Ersatz] coffee with milk in the morning, bread in any quantity, food [soup] without long lines, uncomfortable sleeping on multilevel bunks made of wood covered with corrugated cardboard. All patients want to stay here for as long as possible. The care is very good, all doctors and paramedics are Russians (not Ukrainians!),[i] very kindly disposed. Yesterday I talked to the colonel doctor

---

i While most of the guards in Dulag 121 in Pruszków were Wehrmacht soldiers, there were also some SS units, some Russian prisoners of war (who mostly cleaned and performed other auxiliary functions), and Polish medical and sanitary personnel and kitchen staff. The Polish medical personnel organized an auxiliary hospital in nearby Milanówek, to which they transferred some patients. The entire personnel in the tuberculosis unit was made up of Russian doctors and paramedics. Niusia stressed that they were not Ukrainians, because Ukrainian SS units that collaborated with the Nazis were often notoriously brutal concentration camp guards and frequently took part in deportations of Jews from the ghettos.

> [Aleksander Anikiejew, the head of the small infectious disease unit for patients diagnosed with tuberculosis], who said that he cannot send me to Hall I yet, for my own good, [because the conditions there are so much worse]. . . . I am with a nice patient who has a blanket [which she shares with me], she is very polite and gentle, only not very energetic . . . . [I will] either stay here or go to the hospital . . . [in] Milanówek or further away . . . maybe we can meet in Skarżysko or Milanówek . . . . Don't worry about me—I am no longer in any danger, and I'll be fine.

On the other side of the paper, Niusia has drawn a picture of Basia in a pretty dress with big bows both in her hair and on her dress, holding a leash with a small dachshund on the end of it. Basia is delighted. As soon as we find a pencil—a scarce commodity—next to the girl she draws a picture of Niusia, also with a dog (fig. 36). But we have no way to send the letter back.

The next morning, we are ordered to march to the train station. There is a train waiting with one passenger car at the front for the guards and several cattle cars at the rear. The guards tell us to get on the train. Once the cattle car is full, they close and lock the door. People are packed like sardines, and we stand because it is too crowded to sit on the floor. But we are lucky; as we were the last ones to board, we are standing right by the door and next to a narrow window with bars, through which we can get some fresh air.

The train leaves the station and moves slowly. From the stations we are passing, I can tell that we are heading south towards Kraków. Nobody knows where we are going, but everyone is terrified and people say that we are probably heading for Oświęcim (Auschwitz) concentration camp, which is near Kraków, as we are not fit to work in a labor camp. The doors are locked and every time the train stops, there are Wehrmacht soldiers guarding the train.

Chapter 18

Escape and Freedom

After we pass Radom, the train makes a somewhat longer stop in Skarżysko-Kamienna, perhaps to replenish coal and water for the steam locomotive. A Wehrmacht soldier stands outside the door guarding our train car. Krystyna starts talking to the soldier through the window. She speaks fluent German and somehow manages to sweet-talk him into opening the door for us and allowing us to down from the car. I carry Basia in my arms and we run across the tracks. We hear shots fired at us, probably by another guard, but an incoming cargo train blocks further shots. We run to a small cabin by the rail tracks with a rail worker inside, probably a signalman. He lets us in, and we all crouch on the floor in a tiny space of his cabin. After both trains leave and there is no one in sight, he lets us know we can come out and points the way to the city by side streets. He warns us to avoid the patrols around the nearby munitions factory.

It was very fortunate that the opportunity to escape presented itself in Skarżysko-Kamienna, a small town halfway between Warsaw and Kraków, because Henia, a friend of mine from Lublin, a schoolteacher, lives there with her husband. And, also, Niusia wants to meet us there when she is released from the Pruszków detention camp.

It is already evening when I find Henia's house. We are exhausted, dirty, covered with soot, and hungry, since we only ate a small piece of bread yesterday.

My mother, Basia, and Krystyna wait down the street and I knock on the door. Henia opens the door and looks at me, bewildered—she obviously does not recognize me. I must look terrible. Only when I start to speak does she recognize my voice: "Come in, come in, we have everything here for you—food, clothes, beds." We embrace, and I explain that I've escaped from a transport train with my mother, Basia, and Krystyna; and I go to fetch them.

We can finally wash in a warm and cozy house, and they treat us to a sumptuous supper and hot milk with honey. We discuss what to do next. Luck has it that next door there is a small unoccupied house with a kitchen and beautifully furnished rooms, fully equipped with clean linens, towels, and everything. It belongs to the school superintendent, whose wife is also a schoolteacher. He has been taken to a labor or a concentration camp and his wife has gone to her family in Kraków. She asked Henia to take care of the house in her absence and protect it from looting, especially by *Vlasovtsy*[i]—notoriously ruthless and greedy foreign SS units. The woman also asked Henia to use her house for someone in need and trustworthy. So we may move in. After all the hardship we have endured during the last two months, staying in cold and dirty cellars with shelling all around us, living in this house is like heaven!

The next day, I go to the town to get some necessities. Several people in Skarżysko-Kamienna know Wacek because they worked for him when he was supervising the construction of the road and bridges there before the war. I knock on their doors and they are extremely kind and helpful. Someone offers me a heap of coal in a horse-drawn wagon and takes me around town. People give me a chicken, a pot of butter, some sour cream, flour, and a large loaf of bread. They tell me to come back every week to get fresh bread. I am moved to tears by this generosity and return with all these gifts to our beautiful house.

Two men from the local county of Odrowąż come to our house. In Odrowąż, there are many carpenters and builders who also worked for Wacek

---

i *Vlasovtsy* (*własowcy* in Polish) were soldiers in the Russian Liberation Army (ROA, also known as the Vlasov Army), named after their commander, General Andrey Vlasov. They collaborated with Germany during WWII in fighting the Soviets, Poles, and Western Allies. They were mostly composed of Soviet POWs and "White" Russians opposed to Stalin and communist rule in the USSR. In colloquial language in Poland (as used here by the narrator), the term *Vlasovtsy* also often incorrectly referred to other Eastern European formations, mainly Russian, Ukrainian, Latvian, and Belarusian, that collaborated with the Germans. For example, the Kaminski Brigade (known in German as Waffen-Sturm-Brigade der SS RONA) participated in the German suppression of the Warsaw Uprising in 1944.

before the war, and they remember him fondly. As word got out that we are here, they all banded together and decided that they will support me and my family until the war ends and Wacek comes back. They hand me a letter pledging this support. They have also found another apartment for me, fully furnished and equipped. I am so moved by all this kindness that I begin to cry and have no words to thank them . . .

We live in this comfort and regain our strength, but we continue to worry about what has happened to Wacek and Tadeusz—and to Niusia. Have they realized that she isn't sick and sent her to a labor camp?

Two weeks later, we are overjoyed when Niusia shows up. She tells us that in the hospital in Pruszków, the conditions were much better than in the rest of the camp, but harsher than the description she gave in her note. She hadn't wanted to worry us. The most miserable aspect of her time there was that she had severe diarrhea constantly. But somehow, despite all the upheaval, she was carrying with her two pairs of very fancy women's silk stockings that Kazio had sent her from Switzerland and which she had never used. She used them to bribe the nurse to record persistent fever on her medical chart. Based on this fever, the camp physician ordered to release her from the camp so she would not infect the German guards and the other prisoners, and she was just allowed to go. This saved her from being sent to a labor or a concentration camp. She found out that our train left towards Kraków but did not know what happened next. With no telephones or other means of communication working, she first went to Milanówek looking for us, and then to Skarżysko-Kamienna.

I do not know what would have happened if we had not escaped from the transport train in Skarżysko-Kamienna, or to Niusia, if Dr. Loza had not sent her to the camp hospital. I think we were extremely lucky because the Polish civilian population faced severe retaliation from the SS, which did not keep its side of the uprising surrender agreement: "to treat the civilian population humanely."

We read in the underground press that in some parts of Warsaw captured by the Germans during the uprising, special SS, Gestapo, and Wehrmacht forces went from house to house, shooting the inhabitants regardless of age or gender and burning their bodies. During the uprising, the Germans killed some two hundred thousand residents of Warsaw,[34] including seventy thousand to one hundred thousand civilians in the Wola district alone, and ten thousand in the Ochota district (fig. 37).[34–36]

We also learn that after the defeat of the uprising, we were among the remaining 350,000–550,000 civilians, mostly women and children, whom the Germans expelled from the city. They all, like us, marched twenty kilometers to the camp in Pruszków (figs. 34 and 35). From there, the Germans sent about ninety thousand civilians to labor camps in Germany, about sixty thousand to death and concentration camps, and the rest to various rural locations, where they released them and ordered them to work on the farms.[34] Maybe the Germans ran out of space in the concentration camps, as they started to liquidate them ahead of the advancing Red Army, to destroy the evidence of the genocide. Were we heading for Auschwitz or another death camp or were we going to be set free?

Now back with us, Niusia immediately starts looking for work, but there are no dental offices here. So she goes to Kraków, and Krystyna, who is also looking for work and better opportunities, joins her. Krystyna has a good amount of money with her and has been helping us all along. She gives me two gold coins, ten and twenty dollars, now worth a fortune, and leaves with Niusia for Kraków. Niusia finds out that Sulina Hospital in Rabka, a small town seventy kilometers south of Kraków, needs a dentist. She goes there, is hired, and rents a room in the house of a local carpenter, Mr. Wójciak. She comes back to us with this news, and we all move to Rabka to live with her.

About a month later, a letter arrives from a long-forgotten friend, Mr. Klajn, from Milanówek, near Warsaw. In October 1944, he received two postcards signed by Wacek and Tadeusz, which said that they had survived, were healthy, and were in a POW detention camp in Germany. They asked him to notify us. I cannot contain my joy! I run to Niusia and my mother to show them the letter. They are also overjoyed; Niusia almost faints, starts crying hysterically, and cannot compose herself for a long time. Later that day, she tells me she had heard from one of the resistance fighters that Tadeusz perished in the Warsaw sewers during the uprising. She'd also received a message from the colonel of Wacek's unit, which said that upon news of the fall of the uprising, Wacek shot himself in the entrance to our house on Szustra Street, because he had been sure that as a Jew he would be killed by the Germans upon surrender. But she hadn't told any of this to anybody. Now she is crying and telling me how hard it had been for her to keep everything to herself and try to hope that it was not true.

I do not know how these postcards got to Mr. Klajn or how he found out where we were. Later, he received another postcard with the address of their camp. Now we can write to Wacek and Tadeusz, and even send them some parcels with black bread and cigarettes. We cannot send anything else because it is either not allowed or it gets stolen by the camp guards. A few weeks later, we receive a postcard thanking us for the parcels and signed "Wacek Tadeusz." We know they are alive and together.

We cannot wait for the war to be over and to return to at least some sort of normal life. In December 1944, we start getting ready to celebrate Christmas. For us, Christmas is a Polish tradition, not a religious holiday. Basia is four years old, and we want to get a present for her. At the market, we find a doll's head—the body is missing. Niusia very skillfully sews a body out of scraps of fabric, with hands, legs, and a dress, and attaches it to the head. When our host, carpenter Wójciak, finds out that she has made this doll for Basia, he carves a beautiful miniature rocking wooden cradle that's just the right size for the doll. He decorates it with engravings and paintings, varnishes it, and offers it as a present for Basia. I sew the bedding for the cradle. This present reminds us of our childhood, and we all are as happy with it—as is Basia.[ii]

At the end of January 1945, the Germans finally retreat from Rabka, without a fight, before advancing Red Army. But they set several buildings on fire, mainly the beautiful sanatoria and town offices, and blow up the bridge in Chabówka. We are apprehensive about the Soviets occupying the area, as we have heard stories of drunken soldiers looting houses and raping women. But the occupation of Rabka is nothing like that; it is very peaceful and orderly, and the soldiers are well behaved. We get to know one of the Russian commanding officers who is staying in the same house as us. We do not speak Russian, but we speak French (we had a French governess when we were growing up), and the officer also speaks good French and is very polite and cultured. We enjoy spending evenings with him and talking. After a brief stay, the Red Army leaves and continues westward, pursuing the retreating Germans. But for us, the war has finally ended!

Now that we are no longer under the German boot, Niusia looks for ways to set up her own dental office. But it is expensive, and we lost everything when we were expelled from Warsaw. Fortunately, it is easier for her to communicate with Kazio in Scotland now, and he sends her several parcels of everyday items with money hidden inside. To prevent the customs officers from stealing them, these items, such as soap or toothpaste, are inexpensive and unattractive. Sending money has to be done in this clandestine manner because the communists who now rule Poland arrest everyone receiving money from

---

ii The narrator's granddaughter still has this cradle and the doll.

abroad as an anti-communist foreign agent. Kazio's hard currency goes a long way in our war-ravaged, impoverished Poland. And as soon as Niusia has enough money, she goes to Kraków, buys dental supplies and an entire set of excellent dental equipment that was left behind by the Germans when they fled Kraków—dental chair, drilling machine, lights, cabinets with instruments, and everything else needed for the practice. She transports it all to Rabka and opens her own dental office.

One day, at the beginning of July 1945, someone knocks on our door in Rabka. I open it and there is Wacek! I cannot believe my eyes! He is wearing a fancy, unfamiliar uniform and looks fit and healthy. Laughing and crying, we fall into each other's arms. When Niusia has finished seeing her patients, Wacek tells us the story of how he managed to come back.

Chapter 19

Wacek's Return

On April 29, 1945, the Canadian army liberated Wacek's POW camp in Sandbostel. This was not a surprise to anybody. For some time, both the guards and the prisoners had known that the Allies were advancing and the days of the Third Reich were numbered. The guards stopped supervising the prisoners and allowed them to run the camp. When the Canadian army arrived, all the guards and commanding officers were waiting to turn themselves in, their bags packed and without weapons.

But the fate of the prisoners in the camp was completely unknown, and it appeared that they would have to stay there for a very long time. Therefore, to go back to Poland, Wacek, Tadeusz, and two other second lieutenants (Jerzy Duracz and Stanisław Piechocki) took matters into their own hands. They left the camp on foot with the intention of walking or hitchhiking their way to the Polish border through the British and Soviet zones of occupation. Out of military habit, Wacek, as the highest in rank, was the commander of the group. Unfortunately, on the way, Jerzy Duracz got sick, developed a high fever, and eventually passed out. Wacek went to the nearby British army command office and arranged for an ambulance to pick up Jerzy and take him to the military hospital.

Wacek, Tadeusz, and Stanisław were then taken to the commander of the British unit, Major Drayton, who was organizing a camp for displaced persons in Germany. Some of these people had been released from liberated concentration camps and labor camps, and some were former POWs. Major Drayton asked Wacek to stay in Germany and become the commander of a temporary displaced persons camp in a brick factory in Buchhorst. Wacek would be responsible for all the organizational and security aspects of the camp.

This offer surprised Wacek. As much as he and his companions wanted to go back to Poland, they could not refuse to help the 1.8 million Polish refugees in Germany. Wacek accepted the position and, as his first task, he organized moving the entire camp to a permanent location in Krümmel. With more and more refugees arriving, Wacek was then put in charge of organizing a new camp in Spackenberg, and Tadeusz became the commander of the one in Krümmel. Wacek oversaw the administration, security, food, education for children and adults, and even some entertainment, of both camps. They were often presented to the Red Cross and other organizations as model temporary accommodation for the displaced.

For Wacek, the main problem in running the camps was the lack of work for thousands of people in the camps and that this idleness was demoralizing. Even when there was some work available, most people did not want to do anything. Their attitude was either "Why bother? This is only temporary and food and shelter are provided free by the British" or "We've been imprisoned and tortured by the Germans for six years and now they should work for us." This and the growing loss of any work ethic was very frustrating to Wacek: he knew how much needed to be done in Poland to rebuild the ruined country. Would these men be able to work when they got back to Poland?

Unfortunately, negotiations about the repatriation of the Polish refugees had stalled because the Polish government-in-exile (London) did not trust the new Soviet-installed government currently in charge in Poland. The Soviets wanted control of Poland and the Western Allies wanted democracy—but the West had little leverage over the Soviets. It could be months, or more likely years, before over a million of Poles could return from the camps in Germany to Poland. For this reason, after fulfilling his duties, Wacek decided to go back to Poland on his own rather than wait for official repatriation.

Thus, on June 27, 1945, he set out from the Spackenberg camp. When he tried to cross the demarcation line into the Soviet-controlled zone, a Soviet border guard stopped him. The soldier asked Wacek who he was, where he was going, if he had a gun, and what he had with him. Once he saw cigarettes in Wacek's bag, he made an offer: "If you give me half of your cigarettes, I'll let you pass and take you to my commanding officer, who can help you.

Fair enough?" As they had to wait for the relief guard to come, they sat smoking and talking about the hardships of the war.

The commanding officer detained Wacek. But the Soviets did not really know what to do with him because nobody else was crossing the border going east—many people, mostly Germans, were fleeing west to the Allied-controlled zone. The Soviets put Wacek up in an abandoned house for the night with no guards; and in the morning, Wacek just walked away. The weather was warm and clear, the sun was shining, and the birds were chirping. He felt light and happy and whistled while he hurried through the mostly empty countryside.

But travelling was hard, because civilian trains were not running, and civilian traffic was not allowed. Infrequently on the roads there were only Soviet military vehicles and tracks, and they were not stopping for a hitchhiker in a British uniform. However, Wacek found a way to get a ride in the Soviet trucks. On all major intersections, there were energetic female Soviet soldiers directing the traffic. Wacek would strike up a conversation with them, and soon enough they would offer to stop a truck and get the driver to take him. They acted with a lot of authority for girls who were probably only in their teens or barely in their early twenties.

Food was hard to come by, as the stores were closed or empty, and Wacek had no money, anyway. But he still had American cigarettes that he could easily exchange for food with the Soviet drivers. They always commented that the cigarettes were not strong enough, however, compared with the Russian cigarettes that they were used to. Finding a room for the night was also not possible; everything was uninhabited. He saw no people in the villages. All the local houses were boarded up, abandoned, or locked up, and nobody would open the door. But he only had to sleep for one night on a bench in a deserted railroad station.

The next day, he got enough rides in Soviet trucks to reach the Polish border on the Odra River near Szczecin. Across the river was a military pontoon bridge that looked unguarded. But half-way across, a Soviet border guard emerged from a pontoon tied to the bridge and stopped Wacek. The guard told him that he had orders not to let anybody through. As Wacek did not want to turn back and could not go forward, he sat down next to the guard, gave him a cigarette, and they started talking. After a while, the guard made an offer: "If you give me some cigarettes and take out the water from my leaking pontoon, I'll let you through." That was easy enough, and soon Wacek was back on his way across the bridge.

On the other bank of the river, the Polish border guards enthusiastically welcomed him and told him he was the first Polish officer to come back from Germany. In the guardhouse, the commander of the border guard unit greeted Wacek, served him a superb dinner, and provided a room for him to spend the night. He told Wacek that the passenger trains were running and were free for all military personnel. The next day, Wacek was on a train heading for Warsaw. It was very crowded—there were twenty people crammed in an eight-people compartment—but this was one of the happiest days of his life.

Chapter 20

Back Home

Soon after Wacek's return, in the summer of 1945, we go back to Warsaw from Rabka to see whether we can move there. The destruction in Warsaw is unbelievable and depressing. The entire city is in ruins. Almost all the buildings are burned down or have collapsed. It is hard to find an undamaged structure. There are still charred corpses in partially collapsed vestibules and the stench of decaying bodies buried underneath the ruins is everywhere. The streets are dotted with bomb craters and filled with rubble. How did it happen? When we were expelled by the Germans from Warsaw after the defeat of the uprising, many of these buildings were still standing.

We soon learn that on October 17, 1944, the German SS chief Heinrich Himmler issued the following order: "[Warsaw] must completely disappear from the surface of the earth and serve only as a transport station for the Wehrmacht. No stone can remain standing. Every building must be razed to its foundation."[34] And, indeed, the order was thoroughly executed. The German demolition squads used flamethrowers and explosives to methodically destroy house after house. They especially targeted historical monuments, Polish national archives, and places of interest.[34] By the time the Red Army entered Warsaw on January 17, 1945, mostly abandoned by the Germans, over 85% of the buildings had been destroyed (fig. 38).[34]

We come back to Niusia's apartment on the second floor of a three-story brick stucco building at 27 Szustra Street (later called Dąbrowskiego, fig. 21). The house is still standing, but is partially destroyed. Much of the roof and a part of one wall are missing, but the rest of the building seems to be in good condition. There are no signs of fire damage; the wooden floors, doors, and window frames are covered with debris, but largely intact. Most of our possessions have been looted, except for a desk, an armchair, and a bookcase, which, surprisingly, are still there and only covered with dirt and shrapnel marks. Most of the other houses in the vicinity have been burned down.

We find out from our janitor, Mr. Saczkowski, why our building was spared from the fire. After the end of the Warsaw Uprising and expulsion of all civilians, the Germans set all the buildings on our street on fire with flamethrowers. But Mr. Saczkowski escaped from the column of civilians marching out of the city and, risking his life, returned to our building and put out the fire. Then, as soon as the Germans retreated from Warsaw, he moved back in and locked the doors to prevent further looting. In other buildings, wooden floors, doors, windows, and door and window frames that survived the fires have been looted and used as fuel for heating and cooking.

Wacek inspects our building and establishes that, despite the damage, it is safe and will not collapse. As we have no other place to go, we move into our apartment, or rather the ruins of it. There is no water, no gas, and no electricity, but we are still happy that we have a place to stay—and we are back home. Wacek, using his construction experience, draws plans for rebuilding the house. We hire some workers, and we all help with the work and with removing rubble from the street around our house. We do all this labor by hand, as heavy machinery is not available.

Niusia still has her dental office in Rabka; she goes back there to work and will return when the house is finished. In November, Tadeusz comes back from Germany, but soon he takes a position in Wrocław and moves there. Wacek's civil engineering skills and experience are in high demand now, as everything has to be rebuilt. He is appointed the deputy director of the Warsaw Reconstruction Directorate, works from dawn to dusk, and I see very little of him.

We also have unexpected guests. Kazio's sister, Zofia Winiarska, comes to our apartment with a young woman in a military uniform; we do not know her, but she looks very familiar. When they were passing each other on the street, Zofia Winiarska thought the woman with light blond hair, blue eyes, and light skin complexion resembled Zosia Kosman. She stopped her and quickly found out that the woman was Zosia Kosman's sister, Anielka. We are delighted to see her because nobody has heard from her since the beginning of the war and Zosia Kosman assumed she perished during the fighting. She is married now and seeking any news about Zosia Kosman, as well as trying to get papers to emigrate from Poland. Anielka and her husband, Ernest, stay with us for several days because they do not have any other place to stay. Finally, they get their papers and go to Germany first and then to Australia.

In the summer of 1946, Niusia moves her dental office from Rabka to her apartment in Warsaw. Besides her dental equipment, she also brings with her an entire set of furniture made for her by Mr. Wójciak, the carpenter in whose house we stayed in Rabka. These are her prized possessions and very scarce in devastated, burned-down Warsaw.

Kazio wants to return from Scotland, but he is not sure whether he will be safe in Poland. He knows that the Polish communist political police (UB, short for the Urząd Bezpieczeństwa), backed by the NKVD, arrest and prosecute many returning Polish soldiers, especially officers, who fought in the West and are associated with the former Polish government based in London. There is also a guerilla war going on in Poland. Although Armia Krajowa disbanded in January 1945, there are still many partisan units loyal to the government in London fighting the new Polish communist regime. These people, when captured, are often executed. Everyone associated with the Polish government in London is considered an enemy of the new Polish communist state. This includes members of Armia Krajowa who only fought the Germans during the war and are not fighting the communists. They are interrogated and imprisoned on various charges, such as fascism or foreign imperialism, and often executed or sent to the Soviet gulags, where they "disappear."[34]

However, Kazio's two best friends, Antoni Hergesel and Tadeusz Retmaniak, come back to Poland and let him know that it is safe to come back. Thus, at the beginning of 1947, Kazio decides to return to Poland and arrives by ship in Gdynia, where Niusia goes to greet him. But as soon as Kazio arrives in Warsaw, he is arrested by the communist secret service and put in the prison for political prisoners on Rakowiecka Street (fig. 39). What a welcome for someone who fought in the war for our freedom! We are all worried and distressed, and we fear for his life, as we know that some prisoners never come out. But fortunately, after two weeks of interrogation, Kazio is released.

Not all are that fortunate. On May 8, 1947, the Polish resistance fighter, Captain Witold Pilecki, is arrested and imprisoned in the same prison as

Kazio on Rakowiecka Street (fig. 39). During the war, Pilecki allowed himself to be captured by the Germans and was imprisoned in Auschwitz, where he organized a prisoner resistance movement and reported to the Polish underground and the government in London on the extermination of Poles and Jews. He then escaped from Auschwitz and fought in the Warsaw Uprising. On March 3, 1948, in a show trial, Pilecki is sentenced to death; he is executed on May 25.[37] For us, Pilecki is a hero.

One day, a large package arrives addressed to Teklusia, our childhood nanny, from her sister in America. Teklusia is no longer with us and we lost track of her. Just before the Warsaw Uprising, she moved back into the convent because she thought she would be safer staying with the nuns during the fighting. I go around Warsaw trying to find out what happened to Teklusia and her convent. Finally, to my horror, I find out that during the uprising, the SS took all the nuns from the convent, including Teklusia, and murdered them. The package for Teklusia with food and clothing arrived in vain and too late . . .

We hope our lives will slowly return to normal. Niusia and Kazio are both busy now working in their dental office. Wacek finds a house for us, a villa on 5 Płatowcowa Street in the Mokotów district, close to Niusia's apartment. He rebuilds it and we move in there. Basia is already seven years old, has started school, can already read very well, and is very precocious. I keep thinking that despite all our hardships, we are very fortunate that we all survived, as we were all involved in various underground activities in the resistance and helping Jews. But we lost many friends; almost one fifth of the population of Poland perished in World War II.

Epilogue—Zosia and Edek Kosman after the War

During the Warsaw Uprising and our subsequent exile to Pruszków, we got separated from Zosia and Edek Kosman, so we did not know what happened to them and if they survived. We lived in the Mokotów district and they lived in the center of Warsaw, both of which throughout the uprising were encircled by the Germans and separated from each other.

We also lost track of all the other Jews whom we had helped, and we did not know what happened to them and if they survived. Up to 240,000 Polish Jews survived the Holocaust in Poland or returned to Poland from the Soviet Union or other countries when WWII ended. But then most of these Jews emigrated from Poland to British Palestine (which in 1948 became Israel), America, Western Europe, or Australia. Between 1945 and 1948, some one hundred thousand to 120,000 Jews left Poland. In 1947, ninety thousand Jews remained in Poland and emigration continued.[18, 38, 39] By 2006, only several thousand or maybe tens of thousands of Jews remained in Poland, although probably substantially more, as many did not identify themselves as such.[38, 39]

A couple years after the war, we finally received a letter from Zosia and Edek Kosman that they were alive and well. We were overjoyed! It was a great relief that our most dear friends had survived!

When the Warsaw Uprising began, Edek Kosman came out of hiding and joined the Polish resistance fighters as an army physician, and Zosia was helping him. When the uprising was defeated, they were taken prisoner together with other fighters and sent to a prisoner of war camp in Germany. Somehow, at that point, the Germans had not discovered that they were Jewish. Then, the British forces liberated their camp. When the German camp commander went to negotiate the surrender, he took with him as an interpreter Edek Kosman, who was fluent in both German and English. After liberation, the Kosmans went to Belgium and applied to emigrate to Australia, where Edek Kosman's older brother had gone a few years before the war. They waited for the Australian visa for a long time, during which Zosia learned to weave and obtained a craft certificate; this allowed her to work as a weaver once they arrived in Australia.

But sadly, neither I nor Niusia and Wacek could stay in touch with Zosia and Edek Kosman. This was the time of repressive Stalinist rule in Poland and any contact with anyone in the Western countries was viewed with great suspicion by the government. They were accused of being Western spies and were, at minimum, repeatedly interrogated, or, worse, threatened with losing their jobs and imprisonment. For this reason, we could not correspond with them and Wacek had to ask them not to send any more letters to any of us. It was simply too dangerous, as Wacek would lose his job as the deputy director of the Warsaw Reconstruction Directorate. This was a very high-profile, politically sensitive position that required constant approval and interactions with high officials in the Polish Communist Party. There are photographs of Wacek with Bolesław Bierut, the Communist Party leader, touring the reconstruction of *Trasa W-Z* (East-West Thruway) in Warsaw (fig. 40). And Niusia and Kazio had been viewed with suspicion by the government since Kazio's return from Britain and his imprisonment in Warsaw. Like all other doctors, they were ordered to work in a state-run clinic, instead of their private practice. Such were the circumstances in those days. Although Poland was liberated from the German occupation, it was given away to the Soviets by the Western Allies at the Yalta conference.

After the death of Stalin in 1953, a partial, but incomplete, political thaw began. In 1956, the Polish Stalinist leader Bolesław Bierut was summoned to Moscow for the Soviet Communist Party Congress and mysteriously had a heart attack there and died. A new communist leadership in Poland was installed, which was somewhat more lenient and tolerant. Thus, in 1965, with less fear about political repercussions, Niusia gathered her courage and wrote a long and overdue letter to Zosia and Edek Kosman in Australia. Soon, she received from both Zosia and Edek a very emotional, warm, and long reply of December 4, 1965 (fig. 41).

Zosia wrote:

> Dear Niusia! I cannot describe to you what impression your letter made on us. I was crying for the first day and couldn't find a place for myself for the next few days and waited for it all to settle down, to write calmly and to the point. Your letter was really shocking. There are over twenty years of life on these two pieces of paper.

Zosia was reluctant to write about their difficult early years after they emigrated from Poland:

> I will not write about the old days at the beginning of my emigration. Those were hard years; Edek had to do a diploma (4 years), and I worked very hard. [Zosia worked as a weaver and did other odd jobs, as did Edek.] The price of emigration is very high, and we paid a lot for our present prosperity. I don't mean money, of course, which we didn't have, but the years of work and the difficulty of adapting. We were also at the age limit when this is possible at all, but never quite completely. In fact, all the war émigrés known to us, regardless of their nationality, religion, or origin, never feel at home, have not put down roots anywhere; they sigh and long for their country of origin until they go there to visit. Even Poles who went to visit their families shorten their stay and, if they are honest, are happy to come back and stop complaining about Australia. But nowhere do these émigrés feel at home. This is sad but true.

The reason for this disappointment of these emigrants visiting Poland was that they expected to find life in the country as they remembered it from before the war. But, instead, life in those days in still war-ravaged and poor Poland under communist rule was very hard and the repression was stifling. Most people in Poland were envious of Western prosperity and freedom and would have loved to escape to the West; but the borders were sealed and those who tried to cross over were shot dead.

In her letter, Zosia also wrote:

> The younger generation has it much easier. They feel at home, speak without an accent, and communicate with their parents either in English or barely understand what is being said to them. My niece is an exception: she speaks completely fluent Polish, has only a slightly strange accent, and sometimes uses words that do not exist. My sister Anielka, whom you probably remember from her visit to you after the war, is practicing medicine in Sydney. Her daughter (after her mother, of course) is studying medicine and is, as they say here, OK. The girl is already nineteen, finished at the conservatory (piano), and is in the third year of medicine; but the most important thing is that she has a good head on her shoulders, which is not often seen with young people here.

Zosia continued, writing about her friendship with Niusia:

> We have been bound by a cordial friendship over the years, and if we begin to count our debts of gratitude, I will be your eternal debtor for sure. I mean not only your material help, but the entire sea of warmth that allowed me to get through the hardest years of my life . . . . Your home was my refuge then, and even after the war when I was far away; I always thought of you as it used to be . . . in your home full of family and friends. Or maybe it's impractical sentimentality on my part . . . . Please write as much as you can about you, your sons, Zochna, and Basia. How you all look and how Basia is. I mean not only how you look outside, but also "inside."

In the same letter to Niusia, Edek wrote:

> Dear Niusia! With what joy we opened your letter, so longed for and so unexpected at the same time. With what mixed feelings we read this letter, rejoicing in its entirety, which allowed us to be closer to you and your sister for a moment, and at the same time regretting the parts of it, which for you were long tragic chapters in life. Scars remain and they

> hurt—sometimes less, sometimes more, but they always hurt. But one must live on.

Edek concluded:

> We are glad that you have two loving sons. Since they are studying English, maybe we could send them some books; please let us know what would be appropriate . . . . Except for one letter, I never wrote . . . never, because we concluded from Wacek's letter that it is better not to write to all of you. Still this paralyzing fear that we could harm someone . . . I hope that this time the correspondence will not stop and that in some way we will be of use to you. Honestly devoted, Edward.

And indeed, our correspondence started in earnest. Both Niusia and I wrote many letters to Zosia and Edek, and they always replied, often to both of us together or to one or the other, as they knew we were both reading all their letters.

We learned more details about their life in exile. After Edek obtained his medical license in Australia, he opened his private medical practice. In 1952, they bought a large house at 30 Old South Head Road in Vaucluse, near Sydney, in which they lived and set up their practice, which included an outpatient clinic, reception, waiting room, and a laboratory. They hired a housekeeper ("as in the good old days," they wrote), and Zosia, free of housework, worked in the office as one of the two receptionists and as a business manager. Edek's older brother moved in with them after his wife passed away. They did not have children, but they were happy that me and Niusia had such caring and supportive children, and they wanted to know everything about them. They mostly led peaceful and comfortable life and often wrote about their daily chores (fig. 13). They had some health issues—in 1976, Edek had heart surgery for blocked arteries, but he fully recovered.

We rarely wrote about the war years, as the memories were too painful for all of us, even though our friendship had developed during that difficult time. Occasionally, a mention of some event from those war years would bring all the memories back and evoke powerful feelings. For example, on September 3 and 9, 1992, Zosia wrote (fig. 42):

Dear Zochna! . . . Your letter touched me a lot, but it also "disturbed" me deeply. I can't explain it better. I do not understand how it could actually happen that people, in such a close relationship as both of us, remember the past in such different ways. After all, the fact that we are able to maintain this kind of closeness over so many years of not seeing each other shows a great understanding of our intimacy. Well, you mention that our meeting was accidental. But I remember that we were the two Zosias of our aunt Stefa Niedźwiedź; for both of us, she was an aunt through marriage—not an aunt related by blood. She was for me and Edek the dearest person from the previous generation—from a great family. She was the mother of Jasia and Staś. I came to you after two months of wandering between Lwów and Warsaw. I didn't want to be a burden or a risk for you because of Wacek. I had papers from Eufemia Żukowska and I survived on them until the end of the war. [The documents] of her deceased sister. I came to you for help in finding an apartment—or rather a corner—where I could bring Edek. I knew then for sure that I would either get him out of the labor camp or lose him. At that time, I was living in Mokotów with the Burkacki family, but I would be able to keep Edek there only temporarily, for a few days—not permanently. I came to you, not sure how I would be received, and I experienced a feeling of happiness—for the rest of my life . . . [*sic*] all of you were waiting for me . . . [*sic*]. You were worried about what happened to me, you were angry that I did not come right away. You told me then that in the papers which I handed you through the ghetto wall was the last letter from Stefa; she asked you to treat Edek and me as her children. The ways of human feelings . . . [*sic*] and events . . . [*sic*] are strange. Do you remember anything I am writing about? . . . I also want you and Basia to know (Niusia too, of course) that your house [fig. 21] was *the only one* where I did not feel that people would close the door behind me with a feeling of relief because I was a source of fear, tension, and risk. I spoke about it honestly with your mother—that my visits were a risk for the *entire* family. I said: "Your whole family and little Basia . . ." [*sic*]. She replied, "You are somebody's children too . . ." [*sic*]. These matters will affect us for the rest of our lives.

Zosia was not sure if we were getting any world news in Poland; but she usually avoided any political topics, fearful, as we also were, of the censorship of letters in Poland. However, some comments occasionally slipped through. On September 15, 1990, she wrote:

> We are getting involved more and more in the scary problem of the Middle East. Arabs are mostly fanatics—we've never seen such people and it's hard to imagine. I don't know what you see in the news from around the world. Here we watch masses of completely wild people who not only murder without hesitation, but also want to die in a "holy war" as soon as possible in order to get to heaven. Jewish fanatics are also terrible, but no one rushes to heaven, and if they murder it is in self-defense or defense of their own. Mostly they throw stones at cars if people drive on a Saturday. Four years ago, I was in Jerusalem for the Easter holidays; I could see the fanatics of the 3 religions up close, because they [their holidays] happened almost at the same time. It was difficult for me to decide who was the worst. . . . The longer I live, the more I am grateful to my parents that they did not force anything on us and brought us up without any religion. It probably wasn't easy or simple in practice, because the "pressures" were probably from all sides at the time.

In Australia, there were no such pressures, at least in Zosia's and Edek's circle of friends. Like us, they did not celebrate holidays because of religion, but as a tradition. In one of her letters, Zosia mentioned that they gathered for an Easter meal with five friends—three Orthodox Jews, two Catholics, and Zosia and Edek—two atheists. And they all got along just fine.

They rarely travelled, even after Edek closed his practice and retired in 1990. They never visited Poland, which was the graveyard of their parents and extended family; and because of their own experiences during the war in Warsaw even the thought of a trip was too traumatic. And such feelings of trauma were conveyed to them by their friends who visited Poland. They were also wary of the communist regime. In Australia, they had good neighbors and many acquaintances, but their interactions with them were superficial, and they often mentioned that the only true deep friendships they had were in Poland—with us and two other friends, with whom they were also corresponding, Zofia Winiarska (in Sopot) and Krysia (who moved to Canada).

They not only wanted to know everything that we did and how we lived, but intently watched the news about the situation in Poland. At the sight of any difficulties that we might be facing, they immediately offered help.

In the late 1980s, Zosia and Edek learned from the news about the dismal situation in Poland: the communist economy completely collapsed, the shelves in the stores were totally empty, and mass workers' strikes led to the birth of the Solidarity movement, then martial law, and finally the end of communism. In the early 1990s, the new Polish government implemented severe austerity policies during the change to a market economy. In those years, Zosia and Edek offered to help us. They sorted out all their unneeded clothes and sent them to us, and they also sent us several packages with essential food items. We were very moved and grateful to them.

On January 23, 1990, Edek wrote:

> Dear Zochna! We would so much like to relieve you in these difficult times. Help us and write honestly what would be useful for you or Basia and Małgosia [Basia's daughter, Małgorzta Kaczarowska]. I give you a heartfelt embrace, Edek.

Then, on September 15, 1990, Zosia wrote:

> Dear Zochna! I am responding to your letter of 8/11/90, the last one in which you acknowledged receipt of the last two parcels. If at least something came in handy, then good . . . . I often think about what difficulties you both live in—you whom I so warmly know, and [now I have] a feeling of helplessness in my heart. It is so difficult to live each day fighting for every daily need when, next to you, few have it better and many worse. It was like that during the war, and I remember it too well. But at least then there was a feeling that the war *must* end. Now somehow one doesn't see a solution for the better.

This letter was an exception, because only rarely we wrote about the war. In the same letter, Edek added an encouraging note:

> I write only a few words, but I would like you to be encouraged that this difficult period that you are going through will surely end. We would be very grateful for your photos—may I ask

> for them? May I also ask for a few words about Basia and Małgosia? I embrace you warmly, Edek.

At that time, Zosia's health was beginning to deteriorate—in 1989 she had a stroke and partially lost her eyesight. This made it very difficult for her to read and write, yet she continued writing letters, as much as she could, and sending us parcels. Moreover, in a letter of September 9, 1992, she insisted on including us in her will:

> Give me all your and Basia's personal information—the exact details. Is the bank account joint and is her divorce final? . . . My questions, you understand, are related to my last will and are actually from my attorney. Don't put off your answer. Z.

Zosia's health continued to deteriorate; but despite that, she continued writing to us (July 27, 1993):

> My Sweetheart Zochna! I only write a few words in a hurry so as not to postpone writing until tomorrow. Thank you very much for your letter—although a short one—but it's always a relief to find out what's going on with you. I also got a letter from Niusia with a beautiful photo of her with both sons. It is very noble of both of you to write to me—I will also try better. I have poor eyesight and aching hands, for which there is no treatment. I should be glad of what is because it could be worse . . . . I will write the next letter to Niusia. I kiss you and yours very warmly, Zosia.

In 1993, a short note containing devastating news came in a Christmas card from Edek: "Zosia's left side is paralyzed. Her speech remains, but the condition is severe." And then, in a letter of January 28, 1994, he wrote:

> My Darling [Zochna], Zosia died on January 11 [1994]. The paralysis of her left side, relatively mild at first, worsened steadily, and a cardiac complication ended everything. I cannot write about it calmly yet. I am looking at your last letter with wishes for Zosia's recovery. This was not to be. I send my best wishes to Basia and Małgosia. Thank you for a long and proven friendship. With a warm embrace, Edek.

After Zosia's death, Edek continued his correspondence with me and Niusia. But my health was also deteriorating, and my eyesight became so poor that it was difficult for me to read his letters and write. So Edek started corresponding with Basia, wrote letters to both of us, and she read them to me. Again, he always offered encouragement and help. On May 7, 1994, he wrote to me and Basia:

> Dear Zochna. Your last letter [with the diagnosis of Basia's breast cancer] made me very upset. One has to face adversities in the conviction that modern medicine has a large arsenal of new methods of treatment at its disposal. I know it is difficult for you to write and that is why I allow myself to attach a separate letter to Basia. I hope she will not blame me for my uninvited interference in her very personal matters. But I am asking you, if you can, for a few words not only about yourself, but also about Basia and Małgosia. I embrace you tightly, Edek.
>
> Dear Basia. The misfortune [diagnosis of breast cancer] came unexpectedly, but you will surely overcome it. If you can collect your thoughts, write me a few words about yourself, your treatment plans, and the consquences for your work. Please write honestly because I have the impression that drugs are still difficult to get in Poland. I would also like to know what your health insurance and state medical care status looks like. If you have photos of yourself and Małgosia, could you please send some to me? One feels very close, but photographs make the feeling even closer. Courage, *mon amie*! With a warm embrace, Edward.

And on June 29, 1994: "Thank you for the photos. They bring me even closer to you and make distance lose its meaning."

When Małgosia was about to finish high school, Edek came up with the idea that she might want to come to Australia; he invited her to stay with him and study at the University of Sydney. He sent her all the information and documents required for the application and offered to fully sponsor her studies. On May 18 and 29, 1995, he wrote (fig. 43):

> Dear Basia! I have received the initial information regarding [Małgosia's] admission to the University of Sydney and

> I enclose . . . the following papers: 1. A photocopy of the brochure . . . 2. Information about knowledge of the English language . . . 3. The application form. Please enter me as the "sponsor." I hope that when my letter reaches you, Małgosia will have graduated from high school with great results and will be able to calmly think and decide about her studies. You probably agree with me that you can advise and help in these matters, but you must not insist . . . . I send my best regards. Edek.

Although Małgosia decided to study at the University of Warsaw rather than go to Sydney, we were moved to tears by his generous offer.
On December 10, 1995, Edek wrote:

> Dear Basia! I apologize for the long silence, which does not mean that I am not interested in your life. On the contrary, I would like to ask first of all about Mom's [Zochna's] health, and if there is anything of use to her that I could send from Sydney . . . . What are Małgosia's studies like? Does her interest in biology promise to last? How are her studies progressing? What is the state of biology textbooks in Warsaw? Could I send her anything from here? Would she still like to study in Sydney for a while? . . . Australia is a happy side of the world compared to others. The country is well developed and, despite the frequently harsh political rhetoric, people are always ready to sit down and discuss disputed matters . . . My heart bothers me a bit, but at my age something has to bother one and one has to adapt to it . . . . I wish you and Małgosia the best and a lot of joy and good luck. Edward."

And on March 21, 1996, he wrote:

> Dear Zochna! I am so sad when I think about your problems with your vision. Unfortunately, neither here nor in the States . . . have there been any breakthroughs in this area . . . . Recently, in my conversations, I mention you more often and everything you did to rescue us . . . . With a tight embrace, Edek.

Even when Edek's health was progressively failing, he kept encouraging Basia and repeating his offer for Małgosia. On March 21, 1996, he wrote (fig. 44):

> Dear Basia! Your last letter is testimony, and not for the first time, to how positive your attitude towards life is . . . . I am sending words of encouragement to Małgosia . . . . If Małgosia wants to come to Sydney, I have told my lawyer that, regardless of my state, she can have my house, full board, and tuition for at least a year. I send my best holiday wishes. Edek.

Soon after, Edek's health took another turn for the worse. On November 15, 1996, he wrote:

> Dear Basia! I haven't written recently because I wasn't doing very well with my health. My heart ached, I had a few attacks, somehow pulled myself out, but with difficulty. I do not recognize myself. I have become slow, and everything is taking a lot more time than before, but I guess I shouldn't complain because I can still do the necessary shopping and cook a decent meal. Sharon, our longtime housekeeper, bravely helps me keep my house and garden in order. I will be grateful for news about you. I would like to know how you are doing and how Małgosia's studies are going. My heartiest greetings. Edward.

In the same letter, Edek wrote:

> Dear Zochna. I've had a few bad months, but I'm feeling better again. We have a full spring; it is pleasant to go out to the garden in the morning. My days pass quietly now, I listen to music a little, sometimes one of my friends comes by for a chat . . . . An ancient maxim that I remember from school constantly comes to mind: *Vivere non est necesse; navigare necesse est* [It is not necessary to live; it is necessary to sail]. . . . I hope you are well. With a tight embrace, Edek.

This was his last letter. On June 11, 1997, Edek's cousin, Judith Latham, informed Basia that Edek passed away on June 10, 1997, at 6:30 AM (fig. 45). I will never forget Zosia and Edek and they will always be my dearest friends.

Afterword

> The world is my country, all mankind are my brethren, and to do good is my religion.
> —*Thomas Paine*

The reader may ask: Why another book on WWII and the Holocaust? I had both general and personal reasons for writing this book. One of the general reasons was the reemergence of the Holocaust in the news—but, sadly, for pathetic and disappointing reasons. Neo-Nazis, neo-fascists, and antisemites have risen in Poland, Europe, and America. In the USA, there have been calls to teach Holocaust denial in schools and vaccinations and other public health measures have been compared to the Nazi policies. I wanted this book to be a somber reminder of the real Holocaust, a warning that the conditions that spawned it could reemerge, as well an uplifting story of rescues and survival during that dark period.

The many wars and genocides all over the world that occurred after WWII were another general reason for writing this book. Why have we not learned from history that war does not solve any problems and that, in the end, there are no clear winners—only misery and hatred? The perpetrators always have their reasons and justifications. For the Nazis, it was a desire for *Lebensraum* (living space) and a belief in the superiority of the Germanic peoples (*herrenvolk*—the master race) and inferiority of other races, especially Jews and Slavs, whom they regarded as *untermenschen* (subhumans). In the brutal war in Ukraine, the propaganda of authoritarian Russia is cynically exploiting the alliance between Ukrainian nationalists and Hitler during WWII. They have termed the democratic government in Ukraine and its people, who just want to live in peace, Nazis.

On a personal level, the narrator, Zofia Sterner, was my aunt. While it matters to me, of course, it should not concern the reader—they should see her and her family members as just some of many ordinary people who did extraordinary things during the war. Their courage and humanity give me hope and optimism that the good will prevail in the world.

By now, all the people in the story have passed away, but I want them to be remembered for what they did. I am truly grateful to my aunt for her willingness to talk and tell her story, as for many people the war years were too traumatic to talk about. This was the case with my parents, Janina Dziarska and Kazimierz Dziarski (Niusia and Kazio): they did not want to talk about WWII. My mother, when asked, would wave me away with her hand and only say, "The war was terrible, you would not be able to imagine it and you would never understand . . . eat your supper, you never know when bombs could start falling through the roof and there will be no more food left." She experienced hunger. She heard the cries of the children. She saw the rapes. She saw the wounded. She saw the killings. She smelled the stench of rotting and burning bodies. She narrowly escaped several times, most likely. She was probably brutally abused at some point. Maybe that is why she did not want to talk about her bad memories, just the good ones. Only Zosia Kosman, in one of her letters to my mother, Niusia, mentioned that my mother had been through a lot of pain. I imagine that it was easier for these two friends to share their experiences. Similarly, my mother did not want to talk about antisemitism. She wanted us to believe that people are good. I have written this memoir because I want everybody to understand what war was like for people who had to live through it.

Zofia Sterner and her family did not think of themselves as heroes and did not think they had done anything extraordinary. They just considered themselves people who helped people who needed it—just as they got help from others when they needed it—Poles, Jews, sometimes Russians, and even Germans. In an interview with Marek Halter for his book *La force du Bien*,[1]

Zofia Sterner said of the help she and my family gave Jews: "I thought it was something quite natural. We knew we must help . . . it's normal, that's all." I let the reader be the judge.

Most Holocaust rescuers thought the same.[40] They saw it as their moral duty to help and a natural human reaction to the enormous human suffering and genocide, or just to seeing one person whose life they could save. Thus, like Zofia Sterner, they did not think of themselves as heroes. Maybe this is why Holocaust rescuers have written so few memoirs—they thought their extraordinary stories were ordinary. But I strongly disagree: they did incredible things under incomprehensibly dangerous circumstances.

How many Jews did Zofia Sterner and her family help rescue? My aunt and my mother would only say, "Many—there were always people passing through our apartment." They would add, "Every life was precious." To protect their own safety, the safety of the rescued Jews, and that of all the other people involved in their activities, they did not keep any records. This was usual in those days—people in the resistance knew each other only by pseudonyms. One just needed to know what was necessary for the task at hand. The Gestapo was ruthless in torturing prisoners, and no one knew if someone could withstand the torture and keep names or addresses secret. But based on the duration and the extent of their rescue work, I estimate they saved between forty and one hundred people. I cannot stress enough how dangerous it was to help Jews during the German occupation of Poland; being caught offering a glass of water, a piece of bread, a ride, or shelter to a single Jew was a death sentence for an entire family.

History consists of microhistories—the stories of individual people that had a great impact on the events of the day or lives and fates of other people. The stories of Holocaust rescuers certainly belong to this genre; and this is why I wanted to chronicle the activities of Zofia Sterner and her family. They were both Poles and Jews, although they did not make this distinction and thought of themselves simply as people. This is a story of how Poles and Jews worked together to survive the war and the Holocaust. Jews were not only passing as Poles: they also rescued other Jews and fought the Germans.

Postface

> History, despite its wrenching pain, cannot be unlived, however, if faced with courage, need not be lived again.
> —*Maya Angelou*

The descriptions and statistics of WWII and the Holocaust are horrific and hard to grasp, yet they are true. Here, I provide some additional historical background to the events described in this memoir. I also offer a glimpse of Polish-Jewish relations before and during the Nazi occupation of Poland. The complexity of this period defies the usual stereotypes and generalizations.

The Jewish Situation in Poland before WWII

> The human race tends to remember the abuses to which it has been subjected rather than the endearments. What's left of kisses? Wounds, however, leave scars.
> —*Bertolt Brecht*

In the tenth century, when Poland emerged as a country, Jewish traders were already settled and active in the country's towns. They were also likely in charge of the Polish financial system, as Polish coins with inscriptions in Hebrew were used.[38, 39] In 1264, the duke of Greater Poland, Bolesław the Pious, gave Jews special (and unprecedented for the time) legal rights in the Statute of Kalisz.[41] This statute guaranteed freedom of worship, full protection of life, property, synagogues, and cemeteries, and the right to trade and travel. It prohibited the Catholic Church from accusing Jews of *blood libel* (false notion that Jews murder Christian children and use their blood in religious rituals).[42] It also granted exclusive jurisdiction over Jewish matters to Jewish courts and established separate tribunals for criminal matters involving Christians and Jews. Furthermore, it set punishments for Christians engaged in antisemitic acts.[41] The Statute of Kalisz was later ratified and extended to the entire Kingdom of Poland by the subsequent Polish kings: Casimir III the Great in 1334, Casimir IV Jagiellon in 1453, Sigismund I the Old in 1539, Stephen Báthory in 1581, and others.[38, 39, 41, 43] In 1573, the Polish national assembly signed the Warsaw Confederation, which granted religious freedom to people from different ethnic backgrounds and religious denominations, including Jews, thus establishing Poland as the most religiously tolerant country in Europe.[44]

Facing mass expulsions from Western European countries, Jews found refuge in Poland, which guaranteed their rights, safety, and freedom of religion.[39] In 1606, Poland (that is, the Polish-Lithuanian Commonwealth) was named a "*Paradisus Judaeorum*" (Paradise for Jews) in a text celebrating the wedding of Polish king Sigismund III Vasa to Constance of Austria.[45] The expression was meant to praise the favorable conditions for Jews in the kingdom. Indeed, by 1750, 70% of the world's Jewish population lived in Poland.[38] But the words "*Paradisus Judaeorum*" were turned into a cynical proverb with antisemitic overtones: "heaven for the nobility, purgatory for townspeople, hell for peasants, paradise for Jews." People believed that Jews were over-privileged in Poland.[45]

Jews in Poland, in contrast to most other countries in Europe, were not confined to certain areas and were usually allowed to live anywhere, although they still faced some restrictions. They were not required to wear clothing identifying them as Jews, such as yellow hats. They usually formed tightly knit communities in towns and villages, spoke mostly Yiddish, practiced Judaism, and strictly followed Jewish laws and customs. Most were traders, shop owners, tailors, small-scale manufacturers, innkeepers, and millers, and except for business contacts had little or no social interactions with ethnic Poles and other Christians. Jews frequently worked for the Polish nobility, managing their estates and finances, and serving as medics and translators, as they often spoke many languages.[39, 46]

Poland, like the rest of Europe, had a feudal system, in which only the nobility (*szlachta*, 10–20% of the population) had the exclusive right to own land and hold office. *Szlachta* had almost unlimited power over the peasants, who were bound to the land. Jews had a similar social position as Polish townspeople (burghers), as they were not "owned" by the nobility and could freely move; and, like burghers, they could not own land or hold national offices.[39]

Jewish communities were self-governed. Each community had a body of elders (kahal) led by a rabbi, which oversaw all aspects of life of the community and selected representatives for regional and national councils (vaad) and rabbinical courts (beth din). In the sixteenth century, a central body of Jewish authority in Poland was established, the Council of Four Lands (Va'ad Arba' Aratzot), which represented Jewish interests in the Polish parliament (Sejm).[38, 46, 47]

Jews enjoyed five centuries of prosperity in Poland, from the fourteenth to the middle of the seventeenth century, and had the support and respect of Polish kings and the nobility. There were Jewish academies in Lublin, Kraków, Brześć, Lwów, Ostróg, Zamość, and other towns, and the country became the world center of Jewish scholarship and culture.[39] Many Jews acquired substantial wealth, equal to the Polish nobility, but there were unavoidable tensions between Jews and Polish townspeople, as they competed for the same markets in trade and manufacturing. There was a constantly simmering undercurrent of antisemitism, fueled by the Church which, despite the official ban, kept bringing up the accusation of *blood libel* and in its teachings often labelled Jews as Christ killers. But anti-Jewish riots and overt antisemitism were the exception, rather than the norm, and were usually punished under the laws against antisemitism, which were supported by most Polish kings. Overall, then, Jews were satisfied with their lives in Poland and foreign visitors often commented on their freedom and prosperity.[39, 46]

The country's prosperity ended in the middle of the seventeenth century due to a series of wars (referred to as the Deluge) that devastated villages and towns and resulted in the slaughter of one-third of the Polish population, including one hundred thousand Jews (out of a total of 450,000).[38, 39, 48] The economic situation and living conditions for most people in Poland, including Jews, became very difficult; and the country never completely regained its former prominence and prosperity because of this devastation, an increasingly dysfunctional parliamentary system, a weak monarchy, competition between magnate families, and the interference of foreign powers.

An attempt to modernize Poland politically, economically, and socially culminated in the Polish-Lithuanian Commonwealth parliament adopting the May 3 Constitution in 1791. The constitution was a product of the Enlightenment and "the first constitution of its kind in Europe."[49] Besides guaranteeing the tolerance and freedom to all religions, it granted townspeople (including Jews) "popular sovereignty"—the right to purchase land, serve as military officers, and hold public offices, including seats in the Sejm, treasury, police, and judiciary.[49] Until then, these rights were strictly reserved only for the nobility.

The progressiveness of the May 3 Constitution threatened the privileges of Polish nobility and was also opposed by neighboring feudal monarchies. Russia, with the support of Prussia and Austria, attacked Poland, quickly won the war, nullified the constitution, and partitioned Poland.[49] Thus, in 1795 the Polish-Lithuanian Commonwealth ceased to exist for 123 years as an independent entity (until the end of World War I in 1918)[50] and its inhabitants, including Jews, came under the rule of the occupying powers, which were less tolerant of the minorities.[38, 39]

The occupation of Poland by Russia, Prussia, and Austria stressed Polish-Jewish relations because most Jews accepted the rule of the occupiers, in contrast to ethnic Poles who never accepted it.[51] However, a small Jewish minority joined ethnic Poles in fighting the occupiers in the Kościuszko Uprising of 1794, the November Uprising of 1831, the January Uprising of 1863, and the Polish Legions in WWI in 1914–1918.[38, 51, 52]

In partitioned Poland, Jews faced increased discrimination, forced conscription into the military service, increased taxes, restrictions on where they could live, and pogroms—which were frequent at the end of the nineteenth and the beginning of the twentieth centuries in the eastern regions occupied by Russia. The pogroms prompted large numbers of Jews from the Russian-controlled territories to move further west to the Austrian-controlled territories or to emigrate to the United States.[52, 53] Despite these difficulties, Jews maintained their traditional, tightly knit communities. With increased trade during the Napoleonic wars, and then with the emergence of industrialization, many Jews improved their living conditions and gained new economic power. Some Jews became very wealthy (which caused considerable resentment among the Polish population and a rise in antisemitism), although most Jews were still poor, like the rest of Polish society. Younger Jews were becoming more open to interactions with the rest of society and politically active outside their Jewish communities. In 1897, they formed a socialist party, the

General Jewish Labor Bund, which sought to unite with Russian socialists and achieve a democratic and socialist Russia.[52, 54] Several other Jewish political parties were also formed.[39, 52]

In the Second Polish Republic—Poland regained its independence in 1918 after WWI—the legal situation of Jews improved.[39, 50, 52] In independent Poland, all minorities, including Jews, were granted full Polish citizenship, equal rights, and freedom of religion, language, and ethnic culture. The constitution abolished hereditary and class privileges and titles and protected women and children from abuse. Moreover, compulsory education for all children aged seven to fourteen was introduced. Indeed, Poland was one of the first countries in the world to recognize women's suffrage and in 1918 granted women the right to vote, although in Jewish local government elections only men could vote.[39, 50, 52]

The Polish government, headed by Józef Piłsudski, was sympathetic to Jews and protected their rights. Nevertheless, during the first two years of Polish independence, some two hundred to three hundred Jews were killed in several antisemitic attacks during the border wars with Ukraine and the Soviet Union, mainly because the killed Jews were accused of collaboration with Russian communists.[39, 52, 55] In 1921, hundreds of thousands of Jews moved from the Soviet Union to Poland, which met with resentment and the reemergence of antisemitism, as it stressed an economy weakened by years of exploitation by the occupying powers. Many Russian Jews were shopkeepers and professionals, and they moved to Poland because they were forbidden to work and own their businesses under the Soviet system.[38, 39, 52]

During the interwar period, the Jewish population in Poland grew by half a million and Jews comprised about 10% of the population.[50, 52] Most Jews still lived in relatively closed communities, separate from ethnic Poles, who comprised 65–70% of the population, and from Ukrainians, Byelorussians, Lithuanians, and other Christian minorities, which comprised 20–25% of the population. Most Jews (77%) lived in cities, spoke primarily Yiddish, and attended Yiddish or Hebrew schools.[52]

Jews in Poland at that time were highly diverse. Maria Ciesielska writes:

> There were Polonized Jews who considered themselves an integral part of the Polish nation. There were Bundists, secular Jews who pursued the Jewish values of social justice and were treated with disdain by the Orthodox. There were Zionists . . . [with] a passion for the Land of Israel, preparing to physically

> return to Zion . . . . The *Hasidim* were deeply religious, dreaming of the Land of Israel in the time of the Messiah . . . . The *Mitnagadim*, those who opposed the *Hasidim*, were also deeply religious and preferred little or no interaction with Polish people . . . . City Jews, suburban Jews, and country Jews covered every degree on the circle—from total poverty in the *dorfs* (small villages) . . . to rich bankers in urban centers.[56]

In everyday life, as described by Eva Hoffman,

> the streets of Poland's cities and the paths of its shtetls did not seethe with hatred. In some spheres, there was interaction between Jews and Poles, and moments of genuine fraternity . . . . [P]eople [mostly] left each other alone in their customs and beliefs, but they also worked and joked together, negotiated with each other, got used to each other.[57]

For the first time, many Jews broke with Jewish Orthodox traditions, became educated in Polish schools and universities, and entered mainstream life in Poland. In 1923–1924, Jews made up 26% of all students at Polish universities—63% of dental, 34% of medical, 29% of philosophy, 25% of chemistry, and 22% of law students were Jewish.[38, 39] In 1931, more than half of the doctors in private practice and half of the lawyers in Poland were Jewish.[58] Jews were also successful business owners and industrialists and controlled many major industries that employed over 40% of the Polish labor force.[58]

The Jewish cultural scene was especially vibrant. Over 150 Yiddish-language newspapers and journals were in circulation. Numerous books were published by Jewish writers—for example, the Nobel Prize-winner Isaac Bashevis Singer, who wrote in Yiddish, and Janusz Korczak, Bruno Schulz, Julian Tuwim, Jan Brzechwa and Bolesław Leśmian, who wrote in Polish. There were also many famous Jewish musicians, such as Artur Rubinstein; singers, composers, painters, theater directors, and filmmakers, and prominent scholars (mathematicians, economists, scientists), politicians, and chess-players.[52, 59] The first Polish encyclopedia was mainly sponsored by the Jewish Olgerbrand family.[59] Furthermore, mixed marriages between Jews and ethnic Poles became socially acceptable for the first time, although the practice was still strictly forbidden by the Orthodox Jews. For example, the famous singer, Jan Kiepura, had a Jewish mother and a Polish father.[39, 52]

However, this was also the time of the rise of nationalism and fascism in Europe; and in Poland, right-wing nationalist parties gained popularity. During the Great Depression, after the death of Józef Piłsudski in 1935, Jewish prominence and success, and the increasing numbers of Jews in Poland, began to cause resentment and led to the emergence of widespread antisemitism. The right-wing nationalist parties—Endecja and its fascist, far-right, ultra-nationalist splinter group the National Radical Camp (Obóz Narodowo-Radykalny, ONR)[60]—energetically promoted antisemitism and called for Jews to emigrate to Palestine. Indeed, the Polish government supported this proposal. Endecja even lobbied the League of Nations to create a Jewish state in Palestine, which also had a support of the Jewish Zionist party.[39, 52] The ONR formed a paramilitary wing which attacked Jews and leftist politicians, destroyed Jewish stores, businesses, and property, and promoted boycotts of Jewish businesses.[60] The ONR was outlawed in July 1934, after three months of existence, but continued its activities illegally.[60]

This rise of antisemitism led to the introduction of quotas and the assignment of separate seats for Jewish students at several universities, which effectively rejected the guarantee of equal rights under the Polish constitution but was justified by claims of "academic freedom."[52, 61] These antisemitic actions in turn resulted in protests by professors and students opposed to such practices. The people in this memoir took part in these protests and sat together with Jews on the benches designated for Jews to show solidarity with Jewish students.

The antisemitic atmosphere intensified before WWII and resulted in many anti-Jewish attacks: seventy-nine Jews were killed and five hundred injured between 1935 and 1937.[39] By then, antisemitism was widespread and was promoted not only by right-wing nationalists but also by the Catholic Church. Cardinal August Hlond, the primate of Poland, wrote in 1936:[62]

> So long as Jews remain Jews, a Jewish problem exists and will continue to exist . . . . It is a fact that Jews are waging war against the Catholic church, that they are steeped in free-thinking, and constitute the vanguard of atheism, the Bolshevik movement, and revolutionary activity. It is a fact that Jews have a corruptive influence on morals and that their publishing houses are spreading pornography. It is true that Jews are perpetrating fraud, practicing usury, and dealing in prostitution. It is true that, from a religious and ethical point of view, Jewish youth are having a negative influence on the Catholic youth in our schools.

However, Hlond did also admit that

> There are very many Jews who are believers, honest, just, kind, and philanthropic. There is a healthy, edifying sense of family in very many Jewish homes. We know Jews who are ethically outstanding, noble, and upright.[62]

He agreed with boycotts of Jewish businesses, but forbade attacking Jews or their property:

> One may love one's own nation more, but one may not hate anyone . . . it is forbidden to demolish a Jewish store, damage their merchandise, break windows, or throw things at their homes . . . it is forbidden to assault, beat up, maim, or slander Jews. One should honor and love Jews as human beings and neighbors.[62]

Hlond's point of view was typical and shared by many Catholics in Poland. Endecja and the government also opposed attacks on Jews and did not pass any major antisemitic legislations in the Sejm. However, the government still supported economic boycotts and implemented several restrictions on Jewish businesses and employment.[39, 50, 52, 59]

But what did Jews think about their situation in Poland at that time? Rafael Scharf asks, "if it was so bad, why was it so good?" He then answers:

> The inter-war years, despite the growing impoverishment and the rising tide of antisemitism, could be seen as a sort of golden age of Polish Jewry. Jews were born, grew up, had families, studied, earned their livelihood through craft and trade and the practice of professions, maintained "cheders" and "yeshivas", secular schools and institutions of higher learning, built synagogues and theaters, played and danced and enjoyed themselves, wrote books . . . pursued their manifold and diverse interests . . . . They lived, on the whole peaceably, among their Polish neighbors, separately yet together, and made an enormous contribution to industry and commerce, to Polish literature and culture . . . . There was total freedom of worship . . . political parties . . . Jewish members of the Sejm and Senate . . . . [Yet, there were] pressures of growing up and

> living as a Jew in a country where Catholicism dominated . . . [and] antisemitism permeated the space.[63]

According to Emmanuel Ringelblum, only "shortly before the war [WWII] broke out, the Polish community . . . understood that anti-Semitism in Poland was a weapon in Hitler's hand."[64] And then WWII dramatically changed the situation for both Poles and Jews.

Polish-Jewish Relations, Polish Help, and Polish Antisemitic Atrocities in WWII

> Many of the greatest crimes in history were caused not by hatred, but rather by indifference. They were caused by people who could have done something but did not even bother lifting a finger.
> —*Yuval Noah Harari*

Margaret Thatcher once said, "Europe is a product of history." The animosities between peoples in Europe are deeply rooted in history and not easily forgotten—they have persisted for millennia. Adolf Hitler drew from this history to fuel his regime's nationalist propaganda, justify invading Poland, and launch his campaign of ethnic cleansing. Hitler's Operation Tannenberg[10] and then *Intelligenzaktion*[16] aimed to destroy the Polish intelligentsia; his *Generalplan Ost*[17] aimed to eliminate ethnic Poles.

Hitler's plan for all Jews was total extermination. On January 30, 1939, he said in the Reichstag, "the annihilation of the Jewish race in Europe" would ensue if another world war were to occur;[65] and it was with the invasion of Poland on September 1, 1939 that Hitler started WWII. Initially, Poles and Jews heroically fought together to defend the country; but the terror of the German occupation strained Polish-Jewish relations to breaking point.

The situation of Poles and Jews during WWII in Poland is aptly summarized by Hoffman:

> The Nazi occupation of the country was, even by the brutal standards of the time, exceptionally ruthless. Poles, in the Nazi hierarchy, were next only to Jews and Gypsies in the order of inferior races—slated for complete subjugation and, in the more visionary Nazi plans, for eventual extermination.

> The Poles, then, were fighting against just about hopeless odds, while the Jews in their midst were being exterminated with no odds on their side at all.[66, 67]

At the beginning of the war, the Nazis focused on exterminating the Polish intelligentsia to eliminate all potential resistance leaders: they were either killed immediately (figs. 16–19) or sent to perish in Auschwitz.[16] To prepare for the extermination of Jews, the Nazis herded them into closed ghettos, where they died from disease and starvation. And in January 1942, the Nazi leadership, at the Wannsee Conference just outside Berlin, approved the plan for the complete extermination of European Jews known as the Final Solution (*Endlösung*).[68] The plan was highly secret and initially most Germans were not aware of it. Death squads, the Einsatzgruppen, carried out the first phase of the Final Solution.[14] These death squads, which had been operating in Poland since the beginning of WWII, systematically killed Jewish and Polish civilians, including women and children (figs. 16–19, 46, and 47)[14]— 618,000 to 800,000 Polish Jews.[68]

The second phase of the Final Solution was the extermination of Jews in death camps.[68] In occupied Poland, it was known under the codename Operation Reinhard (*Aktion Reinhardt*).[69] The Germans converted existing concentration camps (the most well known being Auschwitz—Oświęcim) into death camps and built new ones—Auschwitz II–Birkenau (Brzezinka), Bełżec, Chełmno, Majdanek, Sobibór, Treblinka, and others.[69, 70] The mass extermination of Jews was first carried out in eastern Poland and then in Warsaw and other major cities. By mid-1943, the Nazis had murdered most of Poland's 3.5 million Jews. They were killed in gas chambers and burned in crematoria or open-air pits, or shot and buried in mass graves (figs. 47–49).[18, 68–70]

How could this happen? Could Jews have been saved? And how could Polish people have helped to save them? Jewish and Polish analyses differ. As Hoffman put it: Jewish "survivors . . . think that anti-Semitic hatred was the Polish norm, and that during the war, the anti-Semitism lurking in every Pole came out and showed its true virulence"; whereas Poles think that helping Jews "represent[ed] the Polish norm, and also the normal human instincts . . . [and] the murderers and informers were the aberration."[71] The truth is that only a small minority of Poles helped Jews and not all Poles were antisemitic. In reality, Polish-Jewish relations in WWII were complex and defy generalization.

The major criticism by most Jewish writers is that Poles did nothing or did not do enough to save Jews because of their antisemitism. Emmanuel Ringelblum wrote:

> The blind folly of Poland's anti-Semites, who have learned nothing, has been responsible for the death of hundreds of thousands of Jews who could have been saved despite the Germans. The guilt is theirs for not having saved tens of thousands of Jewish children who could have been taken in by Polish families or institutions. The fault is entirely theirs that Poland has given asylum at the most to one percent of the Jewish victims of Hitler's persecutions.[72]

Mordekhai Tenenbaum had a similar view:

> If it had not been for the Poles, their aid—passive and active—in the "solution" of the Jewish problem in Poland, the Germans would never have dared to do what they did. It was they, the Poles, who called out "Yid" at every Jew who escaped from the train transporting him, it was they who caught the unfortunate wretches, who rejoiced at every Jewish misfortune—they were vile and contemptible.[73]

But many Polish writers argue that Poles provided as much help to Jews as possible and give many examples, with extensive documentation, of Polish help and the German oppression that prevented even more.[74, 75]

Jewish survivors were grateful to the Poles who helped them. However, they often lost their entire families and recounted many Polish betrayals—denunciations, extorsion, blackmail, robbery, murder, or simple hate, indifference, and an unwillingness to help—that they attributed to antisemitism.[23, 76–82] There certainly was widespread antisemitism; it was even acknowledged and bemoaned by Polish writers, such as Aurelia Wyleżyńska (who was hiding Jews herself): "A wave of anti-Semitism has engulfed the Polish people . . . . We are surrounded by a nest of wipers [vipers], characters from the underworld of crime . . . . For every hundred evil men it is hard to find even one noble soul."[83]

Jewish authors and survivors often mention attacks by Poles on Jews, pogroms, and examples of Poles who were glad that the Nazis murdered

Jews.[77, 83–87] Ringelblum wrote: "the younger generation of Endecja openly approved of Hitler's programme regarding Poland's Jews."[86] Joseph Kermish cited Adam Polewka: "Poles will bring flowers to his [Hitler's] grave as a token of gratitude for his freeing Poland from the Jews";[83] and S. Zemiński stated that "Many people condemn the German crimes and are revolted by them . . . but not a few think that . . . the Germans are in fact doing us a great service—solving the Jewish problem."[87]

Widespread antisemitism in Poland made Jewish survival very difficult. Hirszfeld pointed out that while in Warsaw and other large cities most of the people in his circles—scientists, artists, doctors, and other intellectuals—supported and sympathized with Jews, in the country most people were antisemitic: "I discussed these matters [the plight of Jews] with many people: landed gentry, peasants, and policemen. Almost all were anti-Semites, but no one approved of these methods of liquidating the problem [exterminating Jews]."[88] Nechama Tec notes that although Poles were habitually antisemitic and "felt that the presence of Jews in Poland was an economic and social problem, . . . they never dreamed of solving it by murdering Jews."[89] Indeed, many Poles with antisemitic views helped to rescue Jews.[74, 90] Gunnar Paulsson notes the distinction between the Polish and Nazi antisemitism: "the Nazis consciously and deliberately rejected all ethical restraints, whereas the Catholic Church and the great majority of Poles did not."[91]

Yet there are many despicable and tragic examples of Polish atrocities. Before Jews moved into the ghettos, Polish mobs—usually composed of youths—attacked Jews and their properties. For example, the February and April 1940 attacks in Warsaw left many Jews injured.[84, 85] But most horrific were the pogroms in June 1941 in Szczuczyn[92] and in July 1941 in Wąsosz,[93] Radziłów,[94] Jedwabne,[95] and other surrounding towns and villages. Polish mobs (or rather organized groups of murderers), some with German assistance, brutally murdered three hundred, seventy, six hundred to two thousand, and 340 to 450 Jews, respectively, often burning them alive and looting their houses. The Germans took the remaining Jews to labor camps and later exterminated them. Only very few Jews survived with help from a few local Poles.[92–95]

The motives for these pogroms were more complex than those for the attacks on Jews in other parts of Poland. Certainly, the antisemitism in these eastern regions of Poland dominated by Endecja and other right-wing nationalists was very strong. However, it increased after September 1939, when the Soviet Union invaded Poland and occupied the east. The Red Army only left

Poland when the Germans began their invasion of the Soviet Union in June 1941. For Poles, the Soviet and German invasions and occupations were equally bad, as the Soviets murdered tens of thousands and sent many more to labor camps in Siberia.[13, 33] But most Jews believed the Soviets would protect them from the Nazis' antisemitism; many greeted the Red Army with flowers and red banners, and some joined the Soviet apparatus of terror.[96–98] Educated and wealthy Jews remained loyal to the Polish state and became, like Poles, victims of the USSR.[96, 97] But antisemitism grew because many Jews supported the Soviets; prewar stereotypes of Jews as communist sympathizers revived and Poles turned against Jews.

Once the Germans took over the Soviet-held Polish territories, the antisemitic Poles used this as a pretext to take revenge on all Jews—Soviet collaborators, as well as everyone else, including women and children—in the abovementioned pogroms. In Jedwabne, an organized group of Polish murderers, in full view of the town's Polish population and with the Germans taking pictures, forced forty to fifty Jewish men to demolish the statue of Lenin and, after murdering them, buried their bodies together with the head of the statue. Then the murderers burned alive most of the remaining several hundred Jews in a barn.[95] Sadly, even Polish clergy refused to intervene to prevent or halt these atrocities and murders.[92–95]

Many antisemitic right-wing Polish AK partisans and civilians also killed Jews hiding in the forests or villages.[99, 100] Especially ruthless were the National Armed Forces (Narodowe Siły Zbrojne, NSZ) partisans, who "killed Jews regularly without any moral qualms."[101] Polish partisans or civilians killed or betrayed to the Germans about twenty out of the three hundred Jews who escaped from the Sobibór extermination camp in October 1943.[102] A cold-blooded murder of thirty to fifty-eight Jewish escapees from the labor camp in Skarżysko-Kamienna was committed by the Barwy Białe AK unit in August 1944.[103] The same unit, on other occasions, also murdered at least eleven Jews and some Russian and Polish communist partisans in Armia Ludowa (AL, the People's Army).[103] The motives for all these killings were antisemitism and the perception that Jews were communist sympathizers. Murders of Jews suspected of collaboration with the Soviets increased starting in 1943, when the AK was not only fighting the Germans, but also Soviet partisans, and then the advancing Red Army and their supporters.[99]

Antisemitism manifested itself even during the Warsaw Uprising. When Jews came out of hiding and joined in the fight, they were usually welcome. But sometimes the Polish population did not trust them and turned them away from bomb shelters. In one incident, a right-wing renegade AK unit murdered twenty-three Jews on Prosta Street, suspecting that they were German spies and collaborators, or maybe just because of antisemitism.[104] Tragically, then, there were many horrific pogroms and murders, and although they were not ubiquitous, they were often supported or tolerated by the general population. Many of the killers were prosecuted after the war,[18, 103–105] but often leniently.[106]

There are also many reports of other forms of Polish hostility against Jews. Polish peasants often attacked and robbed Jews who had escaped from Nazi transportation trains of their money, jewelry, and other possessions. (There are, though, accounts of railway men helping Jews.) Those who escaped from the ghettos and trains heading to death camps frequently went from house to house asking for help, which was usually denied. Many peasants in the countryside turned Jews over to the Germans or reported their hiding places (as ordered by the occupiers) or simply killed and robbed them.[107] Jews who did eventually find places to hide were constantly under the threat of exposure by antisemitic neighbors or *szmalcowniki* and blackmailers; this on top of frequent German raids. Thus, Jews lived in an atmosphere of constant fear and terror.[23, 76–82, 105, 108]

Kermish reiterated Ringelblum's conclusion: "at a time when the Jews were condemned to merciless extinction without exception and only a small handful succeeded in fleeing, [Polish] Government circles did nothing to save the remnant of Polish Jewry."[109] He attributed this lack of help to the antisemitic views of most of the members of the Polish government-in exile.[109]

Polish writers and historians acknowledge the barbarism and the tragedy of the Holocaust,[75, 110] and in recent years they have made significant progress in uncovering Polish antisemitic atrocities.[99, 103, 107, 111] However, they usually stress that there were many Polish efforts to help Jews[74, 75] and the difficulties that had to be overcome.[75, 110] Poland was the only German-occupied country in which helping Jews, or even making the smallest gesture of sympathy, was punished by the death of an entire extended family or household.[18, 112, 113] Sometimes, the Germans even murdered entire communities or villages, often by burning all the inhabitants alive.[112, 113] The Germans amplified the terror by torturing captured Jews and Poles until they revealed the names of everyone who helped Jews; public executions of all those involved would follow and the victims' bodies would be kept on display and their names posted.[18, 112, 113] Because secrecy was vital in the resistance, the general impression was frequent denunciations and executions and very little help. The story in this book is an example of such secret help only known to the people involved.

Before the Jewish ghettos were established, when the Germans banned "non-Aryan" lawyers from practicing law, all members of the Warsaw Bar Council (with only one exception) voted to retain the right of Jewish lawyers to practice. Immediately, however, the German authorities called in all members of the Warsaw bar for personal interviews and arrested and sent to Auschwitz all eighty Polish lawyers who opposed the ban on Jewish lawyers. Most were murdered. Among them was Jerzy Czarkowski, who was a leader of the ONR and a known antisemite, but who not only supported Jewish lawyers but was also helping Jewish prisoners in Auschwitz.[114, 115]

As soon as Jews were forbidden from leaving the ghettos, Poles were essential in providing food. Ringelblum wrote: "Smuggling of food into the Ghetto, as well as the smuggling of goods out of the Ghetto, was a very important part of Polish-Jewish cooperation . . . . The mildest punishment for smuggling is death, carried out on the spot."[116]

When industrial-scale extermination of Jews started in 1942, the Polish resistance repeatedly sent reports to the Polish government-in-exile in London, which transmitted the information to the Allied governments and the media; initially BBC did not believe in this information and refused to broadcast it.[18, 37, 117–122] Witold Pilecki of the Polish Home Army (AK) allowed himself to be captured and imprisoned in Auschwitz, from where he reported on the treatment of prisoners in July and September 1942 and on the gassing of Jewish prisoners.[18, 37, 120] In 1942, Jan Karski twice entered Warsaw Ghetto, observed living conditions there and met with Jewish leaders to discuss how the Allies could help Jews in Poland. Then, disguised as a Ukrainian camp guard, he visited Izbica Lubelska camp (a transit camp for Bełżec death camp) and sent a microfilm with his findings to the Polish foreign minister in London, who provided the Allies with this eyewitness account of the Nazi Holocaust.[117, 118, 121, 122] Polish prime minister in exile Władysław Sikorski in 1941 and 1942, Polish ambassador to the USA Jan Ciechanowski in 1942, and Karski in 1943 met with President Roosevelt at the White House; each time, they delivered reports on the Holocaust in Poland to the president and to other leaders and the media in the US.[117, 121–123]

In 1942, Szmul Zygielbojm (a Jewish representative in the Polish government-in-exile) wrote: "The Polish population gives all possible help and sympathy to the Jews . . . . The Polish and Jewish population keep in constant touch, exchanging newspapers, views and instructions. The walls of the ghetto have not really separated the Jewish population from the Poles."[124]

Polish Jews, through Karski and Zygielbojm, requested that the Allies take decisive action against the Third Reich, such as carpet bombing German cities, and call upon them to stop the exterminations. However, the Allies refused to take any such action. In protest and an appeal to the "conscience of the world," Zygielbojm committed suicide on May 12, 1943,[124, 125] but help from the Allies for the Jews still did not come.

Biuletyn Informacyjny (*Bulletin*) was the official weekly underground paper of the AK (the largest Polish resistance organization), with a circulation of some twenty thousand to over forty thousand.[126] Joshua Zimmerman wrote that throughout the entire German occupation of Poland, the *Bulletin* devoted "a full 43% of the paper" to the coverage of Jewish persecution and extermination and presented "the most sympathetic treatment of the Jews."[126] The weekly repeatedly printed "the statement of the Polish government-in-exile banning Poles from . . . participation in anti-Jewish actions organized by the Germans."[126] In August 1942, the Polish underground, despite the antisemitic views of many of its members, distributed, in Warsaw, five thousand copies of a leaflet protesting the barbaric treatment of Jews during the Warsaw Ghetto deportations.[28] However, the *Bulletin* initially "stopped short of calling on Polish society to physically intervene."[126] Only later did the underground press appeal to the Polish population to aid escapees from the ghetto.

In September 1942, the Polish underground established the Council to Aid Jews (Żegota), whose purpose was to help Polish Jews to survive the Holocaust. Poland was the only country in German-occupied Europe with such a government-sponsored underground organization. Żegota helped Jews (mostly children) get out of the ghettos, found safe places for them to live, and provided identification documents and relief payments to thousands of Jewish families.[127, 128]

The organization was financially supported by the Polish government-in-exile. Funds were delivered from London by airplanes containing parachutists carrying between fifty thousand and one hundred thousand dollars. These missions were very dangerous and only about half of the flights were successful.[129] Unfortunately, this work was not always as swift and wholehearted as necessary because it was not supported by Endecja and the other nationalist parties.[105] Yet, the Polish government-in-exile managed to deliver about five million dollars in Jewish aid,[18, 128–130] although critics argue[131] that actually less than 1% of the total aid of thirty-five million dollars that the government-in-exile sent to the country[128, 129] was designated for Żegota. But commentators have pointed out that this amount was larger than one million dollars of aid for Polish Jews sent from all the other Western countries combined. This Western money was also delivered very late in the occupation—in 1943—and after most of the ghettos had been liquidated. Moreover, the money was initially wasted because American Jewish organizations naively channeled it through a German organization and it never reached its intended recipients.[129]

The Polish underground provided small amounts of weaponry, ammunition, explosives, and training to the Jewish Fighting Organization (ŻOB, Żydowska Organizacja Bojowa) and the Jewish Military Organization (ŻZW, Żydowski Związek Wojskowy).[132, 133] Calls for mass breakouts and escapes from the ghettos in order to form large partisan units in the forests were also made by the Polish underground,[134] but most Jews were unwilling to take the risk. The Polish underground also offered aid, albeit very limited, during the Warsaw Ghetto Uprising. Two unsuccessful attempts to blow up the ghetto wall were made with heavy losses; Henryk Iwański's AK unit entered the ghetto and fought alongside Jewish fighters, sustaining many casualties, and the AK carried out some other operations supporting the ghetto uprising from the outside.[135–137] The AK also helped Jews to escape from the ghetto through the sewers.[135–137] The Polish underground press praised the Jewish fighters and urged Poles to aid people who escaped from the ghetto (although ultra-right papers continued their antisemitic attacks),[138, 139] and a good number of AK members provided such service.[74, 75, 81, 99]

The Polish underground made several efforts to curb denunciations and extortion. In 1943, the Council to Aid Jews issued a decree that blackmailing and denouncing Jews and Poles hiding them would be punished by death by ruling of a special court—and several executions were carried out,[140–142] which was extensively publicized in the *Bulletin*.[126] And finally, when the Warsaw Ghetto Uprising started, the *Bulletin* issued "a call for Poles to aid the ghetto population. For it was their 'duty to aid those Jews who are fleeing from the burning ghetto . . . [and] that our duty is to provide assistance in sheltering and protecting [the Jews] from the Germans!'"[126] Sadly, only some Poles answered the call and fulfilled this "duty."

In summary, regarding the activities of the AK, Zimmerman concluded that "the wartime record of the Home Army was varied, ranging from atrocious acts of murder to extraordinary acts of aid."[143, 144] About 70% of the testimonies of Jewish survivors reported AK abuses and atrocities; 30% rescues and protection.[143]

The Catholic Church, at best, had a mixed record in helping Jews. Pope Pius XII did not condemn Nazi atrocities against Jews and "the Pope's official silence . . . suggested tacit approval of these policies [although the Pope himself personally helped Jews]."[145] With no official guidance from the Church leadership, it was left up to the individual priests and nuns to decide whether to aid Jews. Some Polish priests helped Jews in various ways, mostly by providing Christian birth certificates and encouraging others to get involved. But many others preached in their sermons that Polish Christians should not help and shelter Jews. However, many Polish nuns distinguished themselves by sheltering Jewish children in convents and orphanages.[142, 146, 147] Forty-nine out of seventy-four religious orders took part in sheltering at least twelve hundred Jewish children,[148] and in the Warsaw area virtually every convent hid Jewish children.[149] During the mass deportations from Warsaw Ghetto in 1942, Polish clergy offered to take and save several hundred Jewish children, but the Orthodox Jewish leaders rejected this offer for religious reasons, despite assurances that the children would not be baptized and converted to Christianity.[150–152] This position was not universal, as many Jewish parents were desperate to save their children at all costs, and, for example, rabbis in Lwów advised parents that the children should be sent to nuns and saved.[153]

But most of the help for Jews was provided by hundreds of thousands of usually anonymous Poles.[142, 154–166] One of the most celebrated was Irena Sendler, who, with the help of her friends and Żegota, rescued between several hundred and 2,500 Jewish children from the Warsaw Ghetto.[142, 157–159] Dr. Eugeniusz Łazowski saved eight thousand Polish Jews in Rozwadów from deportation to death camps by simulating a typhus epidemic;[142] Zofia Kossak-Szczucka helped to save several thousand Jews, mostly children;[160] Antonina Żabińska and Jan Żabiński helped save hundreds of Jews;[161–164] Matylda Getter hid 550 Jewish children in Polish orphanages;[142, 160] Marek Dunski helped to save five hundred Jewish children by placing them in convents and orphanages.[165] And there were many others who helped (including Zofia Sterner and her family), and many who paid with their lives for their acts.[40, 142, 147, 154–156, 158, 160, 166]

As of January 2021, 7,177 Poles have been recognized as Righteous Among the Nations,[160] a distinction awarded by Yad Vashem to those who altruistically risked their lives to save Jews from extermination during the Holocaust.[167] Poles have the highest number of Yad Vashem awards in the world (over a quarter of the 27,921).[160, 167] Some have argued that there should be more Polish recipients, considering that the country had the largest number of Jews and that the largest number of Jews were murdered by the Nazis on Polish soil.[168]

But there are several counterarguments. Poles could not have saved Jews brought to the extermination camps in Poland from other countries. Regarding saving Polish Jews, several historians believe that the number of Polish Yad Vashem recipients represents only a small portion of Poles who saved Jews—and for many reasons.[142, 160] The repressive communist government in Poland after WWII strictly censored all contacts with the West, and especially with Israel, and regarded such contacts as anti-communist activity and spying. All publications were also strictly censored, and most people did not even know that Yad Vashem existed. Moreover, rescuing Jews was automatically linked to the underground activities of the AK (which typically provided forged documents and often financial assistance), and belonging to that organization (considered by the communist regime as a hostile organization) was often punished by imprisonment or even death.

The actual number of Poles who helped to rescue Jews is impossible to determine: records were not kept for fear of discovery by the Gestapo; rescuers who were discovered were executed by the Nazis together with the Jews they were helping; and, by now, most of the rescued and the rescuers have passed away. The estimates of the numbers of Polish rescuers vary from 160,000 to 1.2 million, which is 1% to 8% of those adults in a position to do good.[142, 160]

Out of 3.5 million Polish Jews,[70, 169] about 350,000 survived the Holocaust.[18] Of these, some 230,000 survived in the Soviet Union, thirty thousand to seventy thousand survived in labor and concentration camps, and thirty thousand to sixty thousand[18]—perhaps even as many as between one hundred thousand[18, 170] and 120,000[171]—survived by hiding among the general population. Thus, about 10% of all Polish Jews survived the Holocaust. But if we exclude the Jews who survived in the Soviet Union, about 3.4% of Polish Jews survived in German-occupied Poland, and, if we also exclude those who survived in the labor and concentration camps, only 1% to 2% lived.

Why did so few Polish Jews survive?

Peter Hayes noted that the survival of Jews mostly depended on the extent of control the Germans had in each occupied country and on the timing of exterminations.[172] The Nazis first eliminated Jews in Poland because they were in complete control of the country and most European Jews lived there.

They combined brutal terror, such as shooting on the spot anyone who even slightly disobeyed orders, with skillful deception, such as giving two-day rations of bread with marmalade to starving Jews for a two-hour trip to a death camp or by forcing Jews at gun point on arrival at the death camp to write letters to their families saying they were comfortable and working in some far-off location. Only later, in 1943–1944, after murdering most Polish Jews, did the Nazis start to exterminate Jews in other occupied countries, which had collaborationist governments and fewer Jews. But by then, Germany was already losing the war and the support of puppet governments, and eventually the Nazis ran out of time to finish the killings.[172]

Paulsson examines the question of Jewish survival using the Warsaw Ghetto as an example.[173] This was the largest ghetto in Europe with a population of 460,000 Jews at its height,[20] of which 2.5% (11,500) survived by escaping and hiding among Poles in Warsaw.[173] Even though this number is shockingly low, Paulsson calculates that it was about the same as in other German-occupied European countries, such as the Netherlands and Denmark, despite the more severe terror and punishments in Poland than in Western European countries.[174]

The major factors that enabled the extermination of enormous numbers of Jews were surprise, speed, and efficiency[175]—310,322 Jews were deported from Warsaw Ghetto and exterminated in less than two months from July 22 to September 12, 1942.[176] Bernard Goldstein wrote that already in April 1942 the Bund knew of the exterminations in Chełmno and Brześć and called for resistance: "We of the Bund were sure that this [deportations] was a disguise for extermination." But "People tried to convince themselves that all that was intended was a deportation of sixty thousand and then set about to avoid being among the sixty thousand . . . . Great sums of money, diamonds, gold jewelry . . . were used to buy a working card [which would temporarily protect an individual from deportation]."[177]

Even during these deportations, the Jewish leadership and most Jews in the ghetto believed or hoped that they were just "relocations," despite eyewitness reports from survivors from other ghettos in the east or from Treblinka.[178] The prevailing view was: "The Germans will not dare to exterminate the largest Jewish community in Europe. They will still have to reckon with world public opinion. And finally, there is the assurance of [German] Governor General Frank, that Warsaw, Radom, and Kraków [ghettos] will remain."[179] It was unimaginable that millions would be murdered.

Zysie Frydman said: "I believe that a miracle will take place. God will not allow that His people should suffer annihilation. We ought to wait, to wait for a miracle."[180] Marek Edelman wrote:

> people were convinced that if the Jews quietly supplied the requested quota, the rest of the ghetto would remain where it was. The instinct of self-preservation slowly changed people's psychology in the direction of saving themselves even at the expense of others. None of them as yet believed that the expulsion meant death. But the Germans were still able to divide the Jews into two parts—one condemned to death, the second still hoping to remain alive. And slowly, with time, the Germans were able to set one of these parts against the other so that the Jews would lead one another to death in order to protect their own lives.[181]

It was only when this wave of deportations ended that most remaining Jews realized that all the deported had been murdered and asked how the tragedy could have been prevented. On October 15, 1942, Ringelblum wrote:

> Why didn't we resist when they began to resettle 300,000 Jews from Warsaw? Why did we allow ourselves to be led like sheep to the slaughter? Why did everything come so easy to the enemy? Why didn't the hangmen suffer a single casualty? Why could 50 S. S. men (some people say even fewer), with the help of a division of some 200 Ukrainian guards and an equal number of Letts[i] [Lithuanian guards], carry the operation out so smoothly? . . . How could Jews have dragged women and children, the old and the sick, to the wagons—knowing they were being driven to the slaughter? . . . Very often, the cruelty of the Jewish police exceeded that of the Germans, Ukrainians, and Letts . . . . The resettlement should never have been permitted. We should have run out into the

---

i *Letts* was a colloquial term that usually meant Latvians (see Wikipedia, s.v. "Latvians," https://en.wikipedia.org/wiki/Latvians), but in his *Notes from the Warsaw Ghetto*, Ringelblum uses this term most likely to describe Lithuanian guards that were trained by and collaborated with the SS.

> street, have set fire to everything in sight, have torn down the walls, and escaped to the Other Side.[182]

But, realistically, as Wolf Biermann wrote, "how could these people, all civilians, how could women and children and old folk abandoned by God and the world, how could starved, sick men in fact have defended themselves against such a perfect extermination machine?"[183]

Thus, only after these mass deportations and exterminations, fifty-six thousand Jews that remained in the Warsaw Ghetto desperately started to search for ways to save themselves. The ŻOB and ŻZW started arming themselves and training in preparation for defending the ghetto.[132, 133] But they managed to recruit fewer than one thousand fighters and they knew they could not win against the vastly superior German military. They would defend their honor by dying on the battlefield rather than in the gas chambers.[29]

There were two survival tactics. The method of choice was to build extensive underground bunkers, equipped with beds, water, and food, in which large numbers of Jews hoped to outlast the next wave of deportations. Significant effort and expense went into smuggling cement and building these bunkers.[184–186] The second tactic was to escape from the ghetto and try to survive among Poles with their help.[187] But the freedom of being able to live for centuries in large and mostly closed and highly traditional communities now had tragic consequences for Polish Jews. It was difficult for many to seek help from outside—over three-quarters knew little Polish or did not speak the language at all, and did not know any Polish people they could turn to for help. Thus, in Polish communities, they could be easily identified by dress, physical features, language, and behavior.[50, 52, 188] Many Jews had large families and were reluctant to abandon or separate them. They also expected a hostile reception on the Polish side—they were hunted by the German police and Gestapo, the Polish Blue Police, an army of *szmalcowniki* and blackmailers, and hostile antisemitic Poles. "[T]hese negative expectations were not wrong, but exaggerated."[189] Jews also had to acquire Polish documents, find food and places to live, and find Poles who would provide them with these necessities and protection.

After the liquidation of the ghettos, the Germans turned their terror apparatus against Poles—"the terror throughout all of Poland entered a more severe and terrible phase . . . . Day in and day out, hundreds of Poles were dragged away"[190] and many Jews were discovered and apprehended in these daily searches, raids, and roundups.[191] Jews faced double jeopardy and extraordinary difficulties, then. Their hiding places were often compromised by antisemitic neighbors and they had to move frequently.[23, 82, 158, 192, 193] Yet, some twenty-three thousand Jews escaped from the Warsaw Ghetto and found some kind of safety among Poles, in addition to some five thousand Jews who were already living outside the ghetto before the 1942 deportations started.[187] All those who stayed in the ghetto died. The bunkers could not protect them; the Germans shot Jews, blew them up with shells or grenades, poisoned them with gas, or burned them alive.[20, 29]

As the Germans knew that some Jews had escaped from the ghetto and were hiding among Poles, in addition to raids and searches, they set up another trap: *Hotel Polski* (Polish Hotel). Jewish Gestapo collaborators sold, at exorbitant prices, forged foreign passports from neutral countries with the promise that buyers could "officially" emigrate to those countries. Despite warnings from the Polish underground that it was a trap, about 3,500 Jews, desperate for a "normal" life, came out of hiding, bought the passports and train tickets, and were then deported by the Germans to death camps.[194, 195]

How do we reconcile many reports of help with many reports of murder, hostility, or indifference? Describing the survival of Jews in Warsaw, Paulsson introduces the term "secret city":

> The flight of twenty-odd thousand Jews from the Warsaw ghetto . . . was probably the greatest mass escape from confinement in history, and the life of these fugitives in hiding for anything from one-and-a-half to more than four years is a dramatic story that has few parallels . . . . [T]hat . . . secret city consisted of some 28,000 Jews in hiding, in addition to 70,000—90,000 Poles who helped them and a few thousand criminals and policemen who preyed on them.[196]

Other estimates indicate twenty thousand Jews in hiding[197–199] (but range from ten thousand to thirty thousand)[72, 200, ii] and forty thousand to sixty

---

ii There are no definitive data on the number of Jews who lived outside the ghettos and the number of Poles who were helping them because hiding or passing as Poles had to be done in secret. While hiding in Warsaw, Ringelblum wrote: "It is difficult to estimate the number of Jews in hiding in Poland. In Warsaw there are said to be about ten to fifteen thousand Jews hidden; some people even estimate twenty-five to thirty thousand, but to my mind this is greatly exaggerated. Probably no more than fifteen thousand" (see reference 72). Havi Dreifuss writes that "accepted estimates . . . of Jews who hid in Warsaw . . . [according to] Israel

thousand Poles helping them;[72] still substantial, given the ferocity of the German terror and the frequency of denunciations. The great majority of Poles (90%) were indifferent, and neither helped nor exploited or denounced the Jews in hiding.

But the "secret city" altogether amounted up to 10% of the total population of Warsaw outside the ghetto and was, Paulsson continues, a "remarkable achievement, made possible by the initiative, courage and perseverance of the Jews, the heroic altruism of some Poles and the common decency of many others, and some of the Germans as well."[202] The characters in this book, Zofia Sterner, her family, and the Jews they helped were some of the heroes of this "secret city."

Of twenty-eight thousand Jews in hiding in Warsaw, seventeen thousand (61%) survived until the 1944 Warsaw Uprising, and the rate was 69% among those who avoided the *Hotel Polski* trap. Many Jews (5,400) were killed by the Germans in the last months of the war in the Warsaw Uprising (together with two hundred thousand Poles)[34]; so 11,500 (41%) Jews survived the entire war by hiding among Poles in Warsaw.[173, 199, iii] Paulsson concludes that the percentage of Jews who survived in hiding among the Poles in Warsaw was high and comparable to the figures for other Western European countries. For example, 40%–60% of Jews in hiding survived in the Netherlands—but it must be remembered that the German occupation there was much less repressive and there were no bloody uprisings.[173, 174]

However, the survival of Jews who escaped from the ghettos was much lower in the countryside (15% according to one estimate)[203] because of

---

Gutman . . . [were] 15,000 to 20,000" (see reference 200). Ringelblum's figure for helpers was based on his estimate of fifteen thousand Jews in hiding (see reference 72). A larger number of Jews in hiding would have likely required a larger number of Poles helping them.

iii Historians who cite lower numbers of Jews hiding in Warsaw (fifteen thousand to twenty thousand) also suggest there were lower numbers of Jewish survivors, "few" to "several" thousand (see reference 200)—i.e., an approximately 30% final survival rate. Regarding the frequently acrimonious debate about the exact numbers of the perished, rescued, rescuers, bystanders, and murderers, Joseph Lichten, a Holocaust survivor who lost his entire family, wrote: "I do not intend to get involved in statistical games. The value of Jewish lives and the heroism of the many who saved them cannot be evaluated by figures alone; . . . that [the rescuers] form a small minority . . . makes their efforts more significant, more courageous, more humanitarian . . . . But it is hard not to remember the millions who were indifferent . . . . We know that they could have been executed for giving help; we know that it is difficult to transform ordinary men into heroes. We are willing to be rational . . . but our hearts object" (see reference 201). The exact numbers are important for accurate historical records, but the enormous moral tragedy of WWII and the Holocaust is more important.

stronger antisemitism, greed for Jewish possessions, and the coercion system implemented by the Germans. This system was a milder version of the tactic in which the Germans forced the *Judenräte* (Jewish Councils) and Jewish police to deliver Jews for deportations to the extermination camps. The Village elders, held as hostages under penalty of arrest or death, were responsible not only for the delivery of the prescribed quotas of food, but also Polish workers for labor camps and all Jews and other unauthorized people hiding in the village (such as runaway prisoners).[204] Moreover, all villagers, also under penalty of death, were required to report all sightings of unauthorized people. To enforce this rule, Gestapo agents or their collaborators sometimes walked through villages dressed as partisans, runaway prisoners, or Jews, and took note of villagers who saw them. If a villager did not report a sighting, the Gestapo would come back the next day and kill them.[204] The Germans also recruited Jewish collaborators, who went to the villages, sought help, and then denounced those who helped them.[204] This system was very effective because everyone in a village knew each other and the Germans pitted villagers, who were often antisemitic, against the Jews and other hunted people.

Distinctions between helpers, bystanders, and perpetrators were not absolute, either. There are many examples of helpers becoming murderers, exploiters becoming rescuers, and antisemites becoming helpers.[74, 90, 205, 206]

Who, then, is correct? Ringelblum, who bitterly wrote, "The fault is entirely theirs [the Poles']"[72] and Tenenbaum, who had a similar view,[73] or Bartoszewski and Iranek-Osmecki, who argue that Poles provided all the help they could and that the Nazis bear entire responsibility for the Holocaust in Poland?[74, 75]

Sadness, disappointment, and the negative attitudes of Jewish survivors towards Poles are justified and understandable, as Jews faced rejection or discrimination and often lost their whole families. Hoffman suggests an explanation: "during the time of hiding, as they [Jews] struggled to survive amidst such deadly danger, it was impossible for them to think of those who were hiding them as equally threatened or vulnerable . . . [as they] were . . . in a position of power."[207] She continues:

> it took several people to save a Jewish life; it took only one person to cause the deaths of many . . . and paralyze many others . . . . Polish betrayals . . . were unforgivable, and . . . in survivors' memories one can often discern . . . a kind of elision of hatred, a transference of it from the first-order cause of their

> suffering [Nazis] to the one nearer at hand [Poles]. After all, it is hard to direct true, living hatred at an impersonal death machine, at monolithic Nazis.... It is possible that Nazis were beyond hate.[208]

Jan Grabowski's explanation, based on more recent discoveries of many Polish atrocities on Jews,[107] is: "Betrayal, denunciation, or outright murder of... former neighbors, compatriots, or friends left deep scars and a sense of bitter and profound disappointment."[209]

Antisemitic attacks and frequent reluctance to return the Jewish property after the war further amplified the bitterness and resentment of Jewish survivors toward the Polish population. From 1944 to 1947, some three hundred to two thousand Jews were killed in Poland, many because of the still widespread antisemitism.[210] The worst was the Kielce pogrom in 1946, in which a Polish communist militia and an antisemitic mob murdered forty-two Jews, followed by the killings of additional thirty Jews in other incidents triggered by this pogrom.[210, 211] Most other attacks were due to the ongoing civil war, lawlessness, "general postwar disorder, political violence and banditry"[210] or by pro-Western nationalistic partisans, historically often antisemitic, fighting communists and killing Jews who supported the communist government.[210] Tens of thousands of people were killed in Poland during that tumultuous time.

Doris Bergen analyzes Polish-Jewish relations in the Holocaust and compares three prevailing positions: "Poles as arch-antisemites" participating in the Holocaust; "Poles as equal victims" (as similar numbers of Polish Jews and ethnic Poles perished in WWII); and "unequal victims" (as about 10% of ethnic Poles compared with 90% of Polish Jews perished in WWII).[18, 212] Bergan concludes that such a "competition in suffering" is not morally valid in face of this unprecedented genocide and human suffering.[212] Hayes also calls "for understanding and for suspending mutual blaming and competing claims to having suffered worst."[213] Hopefully undertakings like The Neshoma Project, Bridge to Poland,[214] and the POLIN-Virtual Shtetl[215] will increase understanding.

In summary, several authors conclude: "The guilt rests not with Polish anti-Semitism but with the German Government" (Hirszfeld);[216] "The Nazi intention to eliminate Jews was the first and last cause of the Final Solution.... But some lives would have been saved instead of being wantonly eliminated" (Hoffman);[217] and "while Polish anti-Semitism facilitated and contributed to Jewish annihilation, it was not responsible for it. The ultimate responsibility for the creation and implementation of the Final Solution lies with the Nazis. Moreover, their policies and actions [terror, death sentences, public executions, and collective responsibility] functioned as the most powerful obstacles and barriers to Jewish protection" (Tec).[218]

Large-scale help by Poles to save the country's three million Jews was out of the question, short of a general uprising, which would have been suicide for all. The Germans were at their greatest power and the Poles themselves were defeated on the battlefield, terrorized, hunted, and subjugated, and could not prevent the Nazis from murdering nearly three million ethnic Poles. Moreover, there was no help from the Western Allies, and Hayes concludes that even they could not "have done much more to impede the killing [of Jews]."[219]

Could Polish atrocities have been prevented and the doors of all Polish homes (or at least more) opened up for Jews? Yes! And it is a great tragedy and disgrace that they did not. "More courage to help on the part of non-Jews would have produced more survivors"[219]—probably at least forty thousand to one hundred-sixty thousand, or more.[203, 220–226] This is a horrifying number of lost lives, and Polish society must come to terms with this tragic aspect of its history.

A national debate started in earnest after the publication of Jan T. Gross's groundbreaking and incendiary book *Neighbors: The Destruction of Jewish Community in Jedwabne, Poland*[227] about the Jedwabne pogrom,[95] and it is still ongoing.[227–229] Anna Bikont calls Polish atrocities against Jews a "moral tragedy" for Poland.[230] However, one hundred thousand wantonly lost Jewish lives is still less than 3% of the over three million murdered by the Nazis. But whether the numbers are larger or smaller does not change the tragedy and the burden of moral responsibility. In those days, the brutality of war numbed people to all the atrocities, suffering, and death. As noted by Szpilman, "the war has turned his heart to stone"—he refers to Jews,[231] but it applies to all, including Poles and Germans.

As Jerzy Jedlicki notes,

> If there had been only the Gestapo, how much easier it would have been to survive in hiding and count on a network of human solidarity . . . . What [was the] nationwide balance sheet? Heroism or baseness? . . . There is no way to subtract one from the other or offset one with the other . . . . We do not have to do penance for murderers and collaborators who,

> incited by invaders, volunteered sixty years ago to perform a task that would horrify any normal human being. . . . We will bear responsibility for what we make of our past, for how we reconcile its glory and its shame.[232]

Those Poles who denounced or murdered Jews are beneath contempt. It is also disappointing, shameful, and tragic that only a few Poles helped the Jews. We cannot even imagine the disappointment, helplessness, and terror of those who knocked at one door after another only to find rejection or even death. However, we cannot fully condemn those Poles who did not offer help, as we cannot demand the ultimate sacrifice of their lives and the lives of their loved ones. From our present comfortable life, it is easy to blame "neutral bystanders" for not defending the persecuted. We cannot even imagine what a mother thought when faced with a choice to protect her children or help a stranger. Was she paralyzed by fear and terror of the German occupants and all the denouncers and blackmailers? Could she not bring herself to risk the lives of her entire family, or was she indifferent or hostile?

We admire the few selfless and courageous Poles who helped Jews and wonder what motivated them to risk everything to help strangers. Ringelblum called them "idealists,"[233] and we should never forget them. In this memoir, Zofia Sterner modestly says, "it was something quite natural."[1]

The Human Cost of WWII

> Peace cannot be kept by force. It can only be achieved by understanding.
> —*Albert Einstein*

Paulsson describes the human cost of WWII in Warsaw, a city of 1.3 million people at the beginning of WWII, as follows:[234]

> Ninety-eight per cent of the Jewish population of Warsaw perished in the Second World War, together with one-quarter of the Polish population: in all, some 720,000 souls [400,000[20] to 480,000[234] Jews and 240,000[234] to 320,000[169] Poles], a number that dwarfs the destruction of life in Hiroshima and Nagasaki combined [129,000 to 226,000 people][235] and is undoubtedly the greatest slaughter perpetrated within a single city in human history.

The Nazi-orchestrated Holocaust in WWII aimed at the complete extermination European Jewry, and resulted in the systematic slaughter of over six million Jews, about two-thirds of all Jews on the continent.[70] Poland was the main site of this massacre, mainly in death camps, as it had by far the largest Jewish population in Europe and Jews from other countries were also shipped to camps there. Out of 3.5 million Polish Jews, which was 10% of the entire Polish population, over three million were killed, along with almost three million other Polish citizens—almost one fifth of the entire pre-war population.[70, 169] Thus, out of all the countries in Europe, Poland was the country that lost the highest percentage of its population in WWII.[236] Most were civilian victims of war crimes and crimes against humanity during the occupation by Nazi Germany and the Soviet Union.[70, 169, 236]

Altogether, some seventy to eighty-five million people perished worldwide in WWII, including about twenty to twenty-five million military personnel and fifty to fifty-five million civilians.[236] These grotesque numbers are impossible to comprehend and should not be forgotten; and it is hard to imagine the sum of human misery. But each victim was a person with a human face—and their killers were not faceless, either.

Imagine a Jewish child, who asked: "'Mummy, when they kill us, will it hurt?' 'No, my dearest, it will not hurt. It will only take a minute.' It only took a minute—but it is enough to keep us awake till the end of time."[237] Millions of children among the fifty-five million civilians murdered in WWII probably asked this question. We should never forget that.

Growing up after WWII, I drew strength and optimism from the courage of people who defied Nazi oppression, defeated the Axis powers, and prosecuted the perpetrators of WWII war crimes at the trials in Nuremburg and elsewhere.[238–241] I was encouraged by the relatively long period of peace in Europe, mostly peaceful dissolution of Soviet regimes, and the creation of the European Union. Former adversaries, such as Germany, France, Italy, Britain, and other countries, led the peace efforts in Europe and advocated for tolerance and democracy. However, sadly, peace in Europe has been shattered again.

Napoleon Bonaparte famously said: "There are only two powers in the world: the saber and the spirit. In the long run, the saber is always defeated by the spirit." A century and a half later, in a similar vein, Mahatma Gandhi said: "When I despair, I remember that all through history the way of truth and love has always won. There have been tyrants and murderers and for a time they seem invincible, but in the end, they always fall—think of it, always."

I agree. But tragically, in many conflicts, justice comes too late, and we cannot bring back the dead.

Thus, we need to remember those dark days of WWII and guard against the conditions that spawned both the war and the Holocaust.[241] As Hayes writes, "The veneer of civilization is thin, the rule of law is fragile, and the precondition of both is economic and political calm."[242] "The countermeasures put in place then [after WWII] are now under attack"[243]—they are threatened by widening economic disparity, by the resurgence of nationalism, and by the growth of neo-Nazi, neo-fascist, and white supremacist groups. With sadness, shame, pain, and disgust, I watched pictures of the reborn antisemitic and fascist ONR marching in Poland,[60] despite its small numbers, and of antisemites converging on Kalisz and burning a copy of the Statute of Kalisz.[244]

Also, tragically, there are still many wars and conflicts around the world. We have all seen footage of the horrifying genocides, bombings, and artillery, rocket, and tank attacks in Rwanda, Congo, Iraq, Syria, Afghanistan, Yemen, and now Ukraine—and thousands or millions of civilians fleeing for safety. My children commented, "This is just like the first chapter in this book, Dad." But I still hope history stops repeating itself. If we could only learn from it . . .

A Note on Terminology

The terminology that I have used is a faithful translation from Polish accounts of the characters in this story. At the time, the parts of Warsaw outside the ghetto were usually called Polish, rather than "Aryan," which in Nazi ideology designated "non-Jewish Caucasian". The term "Aryan" was not commonly used at that time by the people in this story, maybe because they abhorred the racial classifications imposed by the Hitler's regime.

The English-language descriptions of events in WWII, especially in the US, use the term "Nazis" instead of "Germans," implying that WWII and all its atrocities were carried out by the Nazis but not by all Germans. This is fair, but not strictly correct, as the term "Nazi" implies a member of the Nazi Party and could, perhaps, also be extended to Nazi sympathizers. The members of the Nazi party, including the SS and the Gestapo, were especially ruthless and brutal, but the Nazi Party membership constituted only about 7% of the population of Germany in 1939 and 10% in 1945.[245] However, the entire German war effort had the support of most of the Third Reich's population[246] and required the willing (or unwilling)[246] participation of most of the country's population.[246, 247] The term "Nazi" was not commonly used in Poland during WWII. Instead, the Polish word *Hitlerowcy* was often used, which translates as "Hitlerites" (supporters or followers of Hitler). But this term is rarely used in English-language texts and not all members of the Wehrmacht were supporters of Hitler; many were drafted into the military.

Polish accounts from WWII usually use the phrase "the Germans" to designate those who invaded and occupied Poland—and this is the terminology that I have used. Thus, here, "the Germans" refers to the specific German occupiers described in this story. It does not mean "all Germans" and is not equivalent to "Germans" (or "a German"), the term that refers to all members of the German nation.

There were many types of German forces that occupied Poland during WWII, such as the Wehrmacht—the uniformed armed forces that consisted of the Heer (the army), the Kriegsmarine (the navy), and the Luftwaffe (the air force)—and various uniformed and nonuniformed security forces, such as SS (Schutzstaffel—the Protection Squadron), SD (Sicherheitsdienst—the Security Service), SA (Sturmabteilung—the Storm Detachment), the Order Police (Ordnungspolizei), the Special Services (Sonderdienst), and the Gestapo (Geheime Staatspolizei—the Secret State Police). But the term "Gestapo" was also often used for all the security forces. I have used the specific terms only when the distinction is made by the people in this story.

Acknowledgements

I am most grateful to my aunt, Zofia Sterner, for jotting down her diary notes, for many conversations that I had with her, and for her willingness to talk and tell her story. I am also grateful to my parents, Janina Dziarska and Kazimierz Dziarski, who rarely talked about their experiences in WWII, but still shared some memories on several occasions, and to my uncle, Wacław Sterner, who also shared some memories and wrote an enlightening book about his experiences as a prisoner of war.[7] I am grateful to my cousin, Barbara (Basia) Kaczarowska (Zofia's and Wacław's daughter) for providing her mother's diary notes (with explanations and additional information) and for answering many questions. I am also grateful to my cousin, Andrzej Domański (Tadeusz's son) for interviewing Zofia and taping and transcribing the interviews. I am grateful to Małgorzata (Małgosia) Kaczarowska (Zofia's and Wacław's granddaughter) for her comments and providing Zofia and Edward Kosman's letters, family photographs, and documents. All the information that they provided and their help made it possible for me to write my aunt's memoir.

I am also grateful to my wife, Dipika Gupta, my children, Matthew, Alisha, and Anjali, my brother, Michał, and my friend, Katarzyna (Kate) Dzięgielewska. They encouraged me to write this book and read and provided many comments and suggestions on various versions of the manuscript. I am also grateful to Eva Fogelman for writing the foreword and to Stuart Allen for his thorough editing of my manuscript.

FIGURE 14. The First Battle of Tannenberg of 1410, also known as the Battle of Grunwald, painted by Jan Matejko, after which Hitler's Operation Tannenberg was named.

FIGURE 15. Twelve-year-old Kazimiera Mika cries over the body of her fourteen-year-old sister Anna killed by machine gun fire from a low-flying Luftwaffe plane in a field near Warsaw on September 13, 1939; no military targets were there, just a few women working in the field.

FIGURE 16. Public execution of twenty-five prominent Polish citizens in front of the Municipal Museum in the Market Square of Bydgoszcz on September 9, 1939; to terrorize the remaining population, the Nazis displayed the bodies for six hours (top). Execution of civilians by Einsatzgruppen in Kórnik on October 20, 1939 (bottom).

FIGURE 17. Polish civilians wearing blindfolds photographed just before their execution by Einsatzgruppen soldiers in Palmiry forest near Warsaw in 1940. In Palmiry, about seventeen hundred Poles were murdered in secret executions between December 7, 1939 and July 17, 1941.

FIGURE 18. Mass execution of fifty-six Polish civilians in Bochnia near Kraków on December 18, 1939 (top) and public execution of Polish civilians in Kraków on June 26, 1942 (bottom).

FIGURE 19. Magirus-Deutz gas van near Chełmno used by the Nazis for suffocation of civilians (top). A teenage boy stands beside his murdered family shortly before his own murder by the Einsatzgruppen in Zborów near Lwów (Polish part of Ukraine before WWII) on July 5, 1941 (bottom).

FIGURE 20. Polish girls in the Nazi labor camp in Dzierżązna near Zgierz (1942–1943).

FIGURE 21. Current view of the house on 27 Szustra Street (currently Dąbrowskiego Street) in the Mokotów district in Warsaw, where Niusia's apartment #3 containing her dental office was located and where Jews led out from the ghetto by Zofia found refuge.

FIGURE 22. Destitute and dying Jewish children on the streets in the Warsaw Ghetto (January–August 1941).

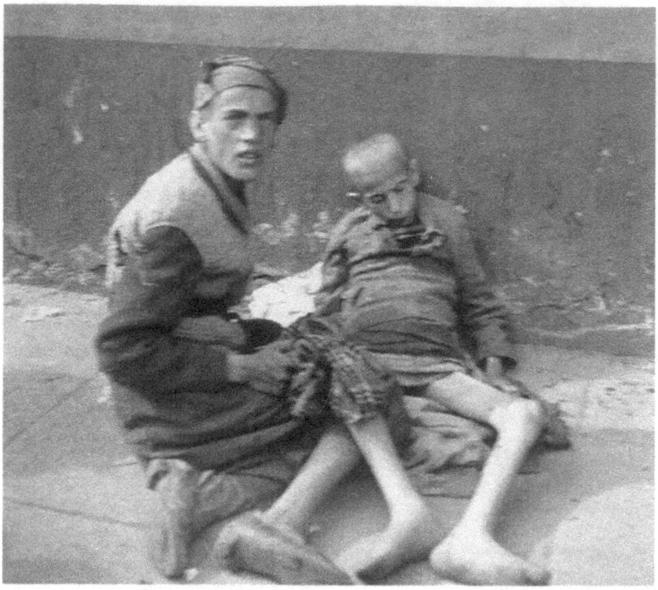

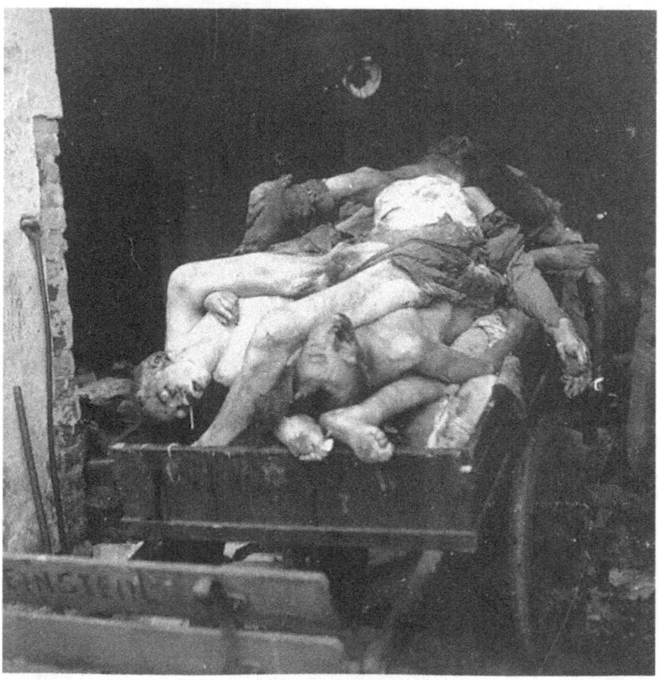

FIGURE 23. A young unconscious woman dying on the street in the Warsaw Ghetto (top); and dead bodies collected daily from the streets in the Warsaw Ghetto on a wagon for transport to a mass grave (bottom), September 19, 1941.

FIGURE 24. *Łapanka* in Warsaw in 1939.

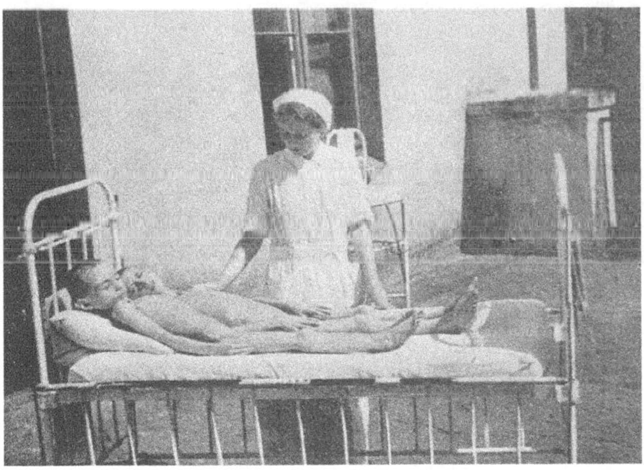

FIGURE 25. Two starving children with a nurse in a hospital in the Warsaw Ghetto (1942).

Figure 26. Jews awaiting deportation at the *Umschlagplatz* in the Warsaw Ghetto (top); and Jews from the Warsaw Ghetto being loaded onto cattle train cars for transport to Treblinka death camp (bottom), 1942–43.

FIGURE 27. Jewish mothers and children surrendering after the defeat of the Warsaw Ghetto Uprising in 1943 (top) and being escorted to the *Umschlagplatz* (bottom).

FIGURE 28. Jewish resistance members captured by the SS during the Warsaw Ghetto Uprising in 1943 (top). Jews pulled from a bunker by the German troops in the Warsaw Ghetto Uprising in 1943 (bottom).

FIGURE 29. Katyń massacre—a mass grave of Polish military officers and upper-class civilians murdered by the Soviet NKVD in April and May 1940.

FIGURE 30. Polish Resistance fighters from the Warsaw Uprising in August to October 1944, including young teenage fighters (bottom).

FIGURE 31. German anti-tank gun (top) and Luftwaffe Stuka bombing the city (bottom) during the Warsaw Uprising (1944).

FIGURE 32. End of the Warsaw Uprising: Polish resistance fighter coming out of a sewer tunnel is taken prisoner (top); Polish resistance prisoners marching out of Warsaw on October 5, 1944 (bottom).

FIGURE 33. Wacek Sterner's tag from the prisoner-of-war camp in Sandbostel, Germany, with his prisoner's number 224676 (1944–1945).

FIGURE 34. People of Wola leaving the city after the Warsaw Uprising in 1944.

FIGURE 35. Prisoner refugees from Warsaw in Dulag 121 in Pruszków after the Warsaw Uprising in 1944.

FIGURE 36. Picture of Basia sent to her in a letter from Niusia with a picture of Niusia then drawn by three-year-old Basia during their imprisonment in the Dulag 121 detention camp in Pruszków in October 1944.

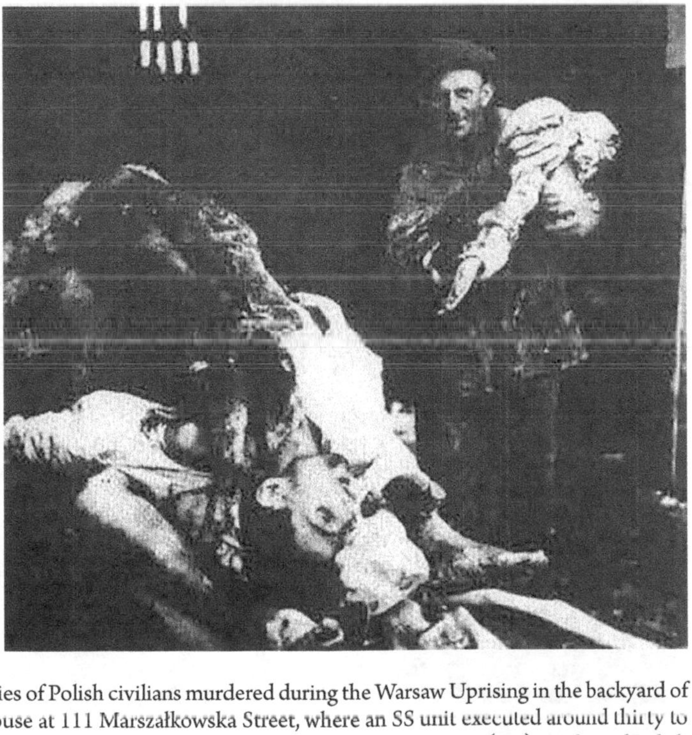

FIGURE 37. Bodies of Polish civilians murdered during the Warsaw Uprising in the backyard of the tenement house at 111 Marszałkowska Street, where an SS unit executed around thirty to forty-four Polish men, women, and children on August 2 and 3, 1944 (top). Bodies of Polish civilians after the Wola massacre before they were burned by the *Verbrennungskommando Warschau* (Warsaw Burning Detachment), a slave labor unit formed by the SS (bottom).

FIGURE 38. Destroyed Warsaw: ruins of the Royal Castle (top), city center and area of the Warsaw Ghetto in January 1945 (middle), and panorama of the city still mostly in ruins five years later in 1950 (bottom).

FIGURE 39. Current view of the watchtower and the wall of the prison on Rakowiecka Street where the postwar Polish communist government housed political prisoners. Kazio and Witold Pilecki were imprisoned and interrogated there and Pilecki was killed. There is now a museum devoted to the memory of the political prisoners it held.

FIGURE 40. Bolesław Bierut, Polish Communist Party leader and president, viewing the model of reconstruction of the *Trasa W-Z* (East-West Thruway) and touring its construction site in Warsaw in 1947. Top: Bierut is the third from the left and Wacek, wearing glasses, is the fifth from the left. Bottom, in the foreground, from the left: Wacek, Bierut, and minister of reconstruction, Michał Kaczorowski.

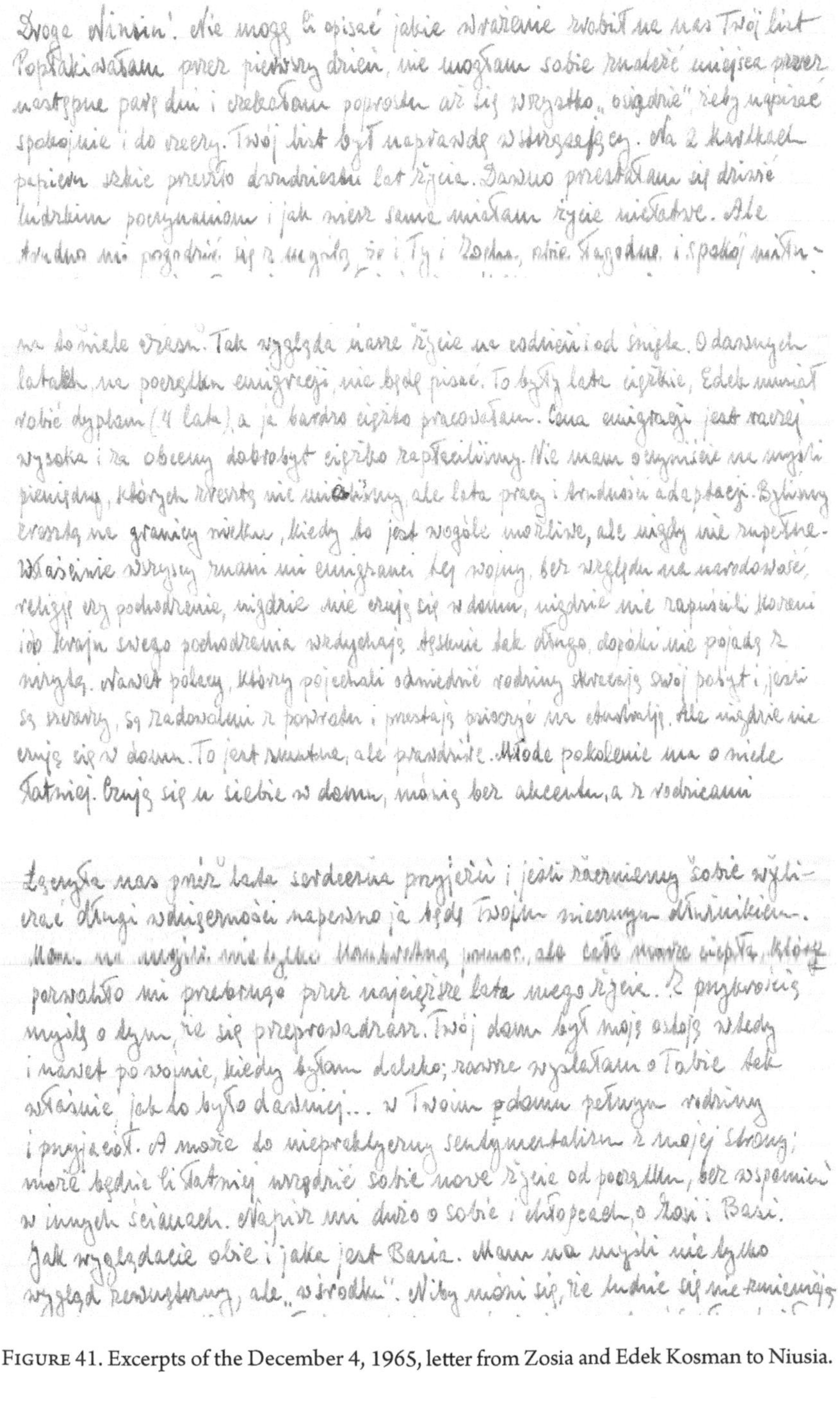

Droga Niusiu! Nie mogę Ci opisać jakie wrażenie zrobił na nas Twój list. Popłakiwałam przez pierwszy dzień, nie mogłam sobie znaleźć miejsca przez następne parę dni i czekałam po prostu aż się wszystko „osiądzie" żeby napisać spokojnie i do rzeczy. Twój list był naprawdę wstrząsający. Na 2 kartkach papieru takie przeszło dwudziestu lat życia. Dawno przestałam się dziwić ludzkim poczynaniom i jak wiesz same miałam życie niełatwe. Ale trudno mi pogodzić się z myślą że i Ty i Zosia, które łagodne i spokój miałyś-

[illegible] czasu. Tak wygląda nasze życie na codzień i od święta. O dawnych latach, na początku emigracji, nie będę pisać. To były lata ciężkie, Edek musiał robić dyplom (4 lata), a ja bardzo ciężko pracowałam. Cena emigracji jest raczej wysoka i za obcemy dobrobyt ciężko zapłaciliśmy. Nie mam oczywiście na myśli pieniędzy, których zresztą nie mieliśmy, ale lata pracy i trudności adaptacji. Byliśmy zresztą na granicy nędzy, kiedy to jest wogóle możliwe, ale nigdy nie zupełne. Właściwie wszyscy znani mi emigranci tej wojny, bez względu na narodowość, religię czy pochodzenie, nigdzie nie czują się w domu, nigdzie nie zapuścili korzeni i do kraju swego pochodzenia wzdychają tęsknie tak długo, dopóki nie pojadą z wizytą. Nawet polacy, którzy pojechali odwiedzić rodziny skracają swój pobyt i jeśli są szczerzy, są zadowoleni z powrotu i przestają [illegible] na obczyźnie. Ale nigdzie nie czują się w domu. To jest smutne, ale prawdziwe. Młode pokolenie ma o wiele łatwiej. Czują się u siebie w domu, mówią bez akcentu, a z rodzicami

Łączyła nas przez lata serdeczna przyjaźń i jeśli zaczniemy sobie wyliczać długi wdzięczności napewno ja będę Twoim wiecznym dłużnikiem. Mam na myśli nie tylko [illegible] pomoc, ale całą masę ciepła, które pozwoliło mi przetrwać przez najcięższe lata mego życia. Z przykrością myślę o tym, że się przeprowadzasz. Twój dom był moją ostoją zawsze i nawet po wojnie, kiedy byłam daleko; zawsze myślałam o Tobie tak właśnie, jak to było dawniej... w Twoim domu pełnym rodziny i przyjaciół. A może to niepraktyczny sentymentalizm z mojej strony; może będzie Ci łatwiej urządzić sobie nowe życie od początku, bez wspomnień w innych ścianach. Napisz mi dużo o sobie i chłopcach, o Zosi i Basi. Jak wyglądacie obie i jaka jest Basia. Mam na myśli nie tylko wygląd zewnętrzny, ale „wśrodku". Niby mówi się, że ludzie się nie zmieniają

FIGURE 41. Excerpts of the December 4, 1965, letter from Zosia and Edek Kosman to Niusia.

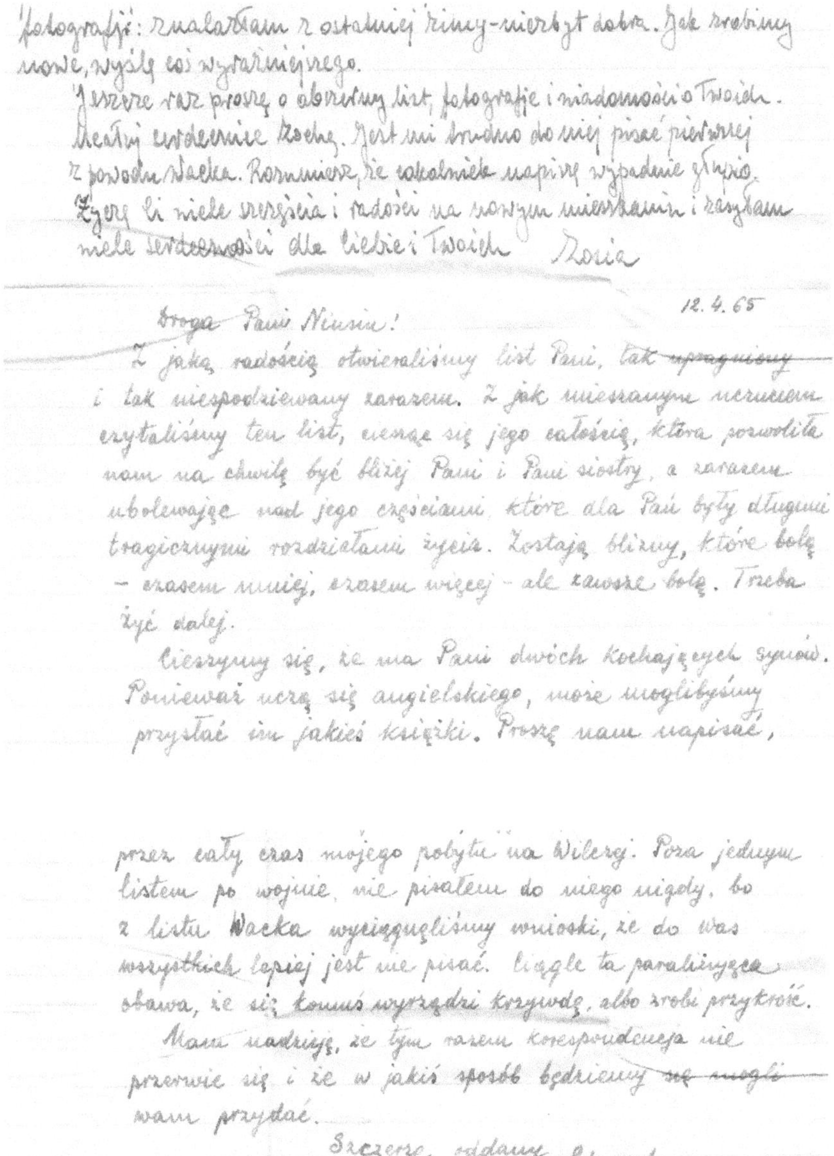
fotografii: znalazłam z ostatniej zimy — nie był dobry. Jak zrobimy nowe, wyślę coś wyraźniejszego.
Jeszcze raz proszę o obszerny list, fotografie i wiadomości o Twoich. Ucałuj serdecznie Roche. Jest mi trudno do niej pisać pierwszej z powodu Wacka. Rozumiesz, że cokolwiek napiszę wypadnie głupio. Życzę Ci wiele szczęścia i radości na nowym mieszkaniu i przesyłam wiele serdeczności dla Ciebie i Twoich Zosia

12. 4. 65

~~Droga~~ Pani Niusiu!
Z jaką radością otwieraliśmy list Pani, tak ~~upragniony~~ i tak niespodziewany zarazem. Z jak mieszanym uczuciem czytaliśmy ten list, cieszące się jego całością, która pozwoliła nam na chwilę być bliżej Pani i Pani siostry, a zarazem ubolewające nad jego częściami, które dla Pani były długimi tragicznymi rozdziałami życia. Zostają blizny, które bolą — czasem mniej, czasem więcej — ale zawsze bolą. Trzeba żyć dalej.
Cieszymy się, że ma Pani dwóch kochających synów. Ponieważ uczą się angielskiego, może moglibyśmy przysłać im jakieś książki. Proszę nam napisać,

przez cały czas mojego pobytu na Wileręj. Poza jednym listem po wojnie, nie pisałem do niego nigdy, bo z listu Wacka wyciągnęliśmy wnioski, że do Was wszystkich lepiej jest nie pisać. Ciągle ta paraliżująca obawa, że się komuś wyrządzi krzywdę, albo zrobi przykrość.
Mam nadzieję, że tym razem korespondencja nie przerwie się i że w jakiś sposób będziemy ~~się mogli~~ wam przydać.
Szczerze oddany Edward

Figure 41 continued. Excerpts of the December 4, 1965, letter from Zosia and Edek Kosman to Niusia.

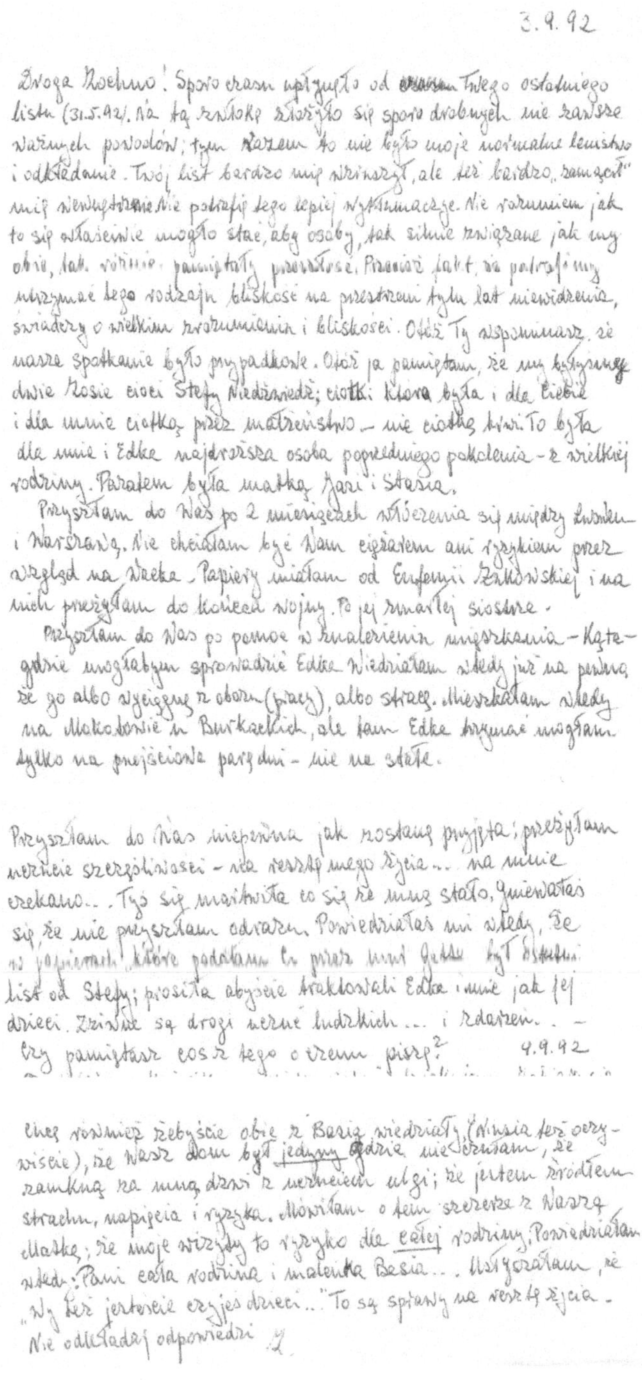

3.9.92

Droga Zochno! Sporo czasu upłynęło od ~~czasu~~ Twego ostatniego listu (31.5.92). Na tą zwłokę złożyło się sporo drobnych nie zawsze ważnych powodów; tym razem to nie było moje normalne lenistwo i odkładanie. Twój list bardzo mię wzruszył, ale też bardzo „zamącił" mię wewnętrznie. Nie potrafię tego lepiej wytłumaczyć. Nie rozumiem jak to się właściwie mogło stać, aby osoby, tak silnie związane jak my obie, tak różnie pamiętały przeszłość. Przecież fakt, że potrafimy utrzymać tego rodzaju bliskość na przestrzeni tylu lat niewidzenia, świadczy o wielkim zrozumieniu i bliskości. Otóż Ty wspominasz, że nasze spotkanie było przypadkowe. Otóż ja pamiętam, że my byłyśmy dwie Zosie cioci Stefy Niedźwiedź; ciotki która była i dla Ciebie i dla mnie ciotką przez małżeństwo – nie ciotką krwi. To była dla mnie i Edka najdroższa osoba poprzedniego pokolenia – z wielkiej rodziny. Zarazem była matką Jasi i Stasia.

Przyszłam do Was po 2 miesiącach włóczenia się między Lwowem i Warszawą. Nie chciałam być Wam ciężarem ani ryzykiem przez wzgląd na Wacka. Papiery miałam od Eufemii Szakowskiej i na nich przeżyłam do końca wojny. Po jej zmarłej siostrze.

Przyszłam do Was po pomoc w znalezieniu mieszkania – gdzie mogłabym sprowadzić Edka. Wiedziałam wtedy już na pewno że go albo wyciągnę z obozu (pracy), albo stracę. Mieszkałam wtedy na Mokotowie u Burkackich, ale tam Edka trzymać mogłam tylko na przejściowe parę dni – nie na stałe.

Przyszłam do Was niepewna jak zostanę przyjęta; przeżyłam wówczas szczęśliwości – na resztę mego życia... na mnie czekano... Tyś się martwiła co się ze mną stało, gniewałaś się, że nie przyszłam od razu. Powiedziałaś mi wtedy, że w papierach które podałam ci przez mur getta był ostatni list od Stefy; prosiła abyście traktowali Edka i mnie jak jej dzieci. Dziwne są drogi wśród ludzkich... i zdarzeń... – Czy pamiętasz coś z tego o czem piszę?

4.9.92

Chcę również żebyście obie z Basią wiedziały (Ninsia też oczywiście), że Wasz dom był <u>jedyny</u> gdzie nie czułam, że zamkną za mną drzwi z westchnieniem ulgi; że jestem źródłem strachu, napięcia i ryzyka. Mówiłam o tem szczerze z Waszą Matką; że moje wizyty to ryzyko dla <u>całej</u> rodziny. Powiedziała wtedy: „Pani cała rodzina i malutka Basia.... Usłyszałam, że „Wy też jesteście czyjeś dzieci..." To są sprawy na resztę życia. –

Nie odkładaj odpowiedzi Z

FIGURE 42. Excerpts of the September 3 and 9, 1992, letter from Zosia to Zofia (Zochna).

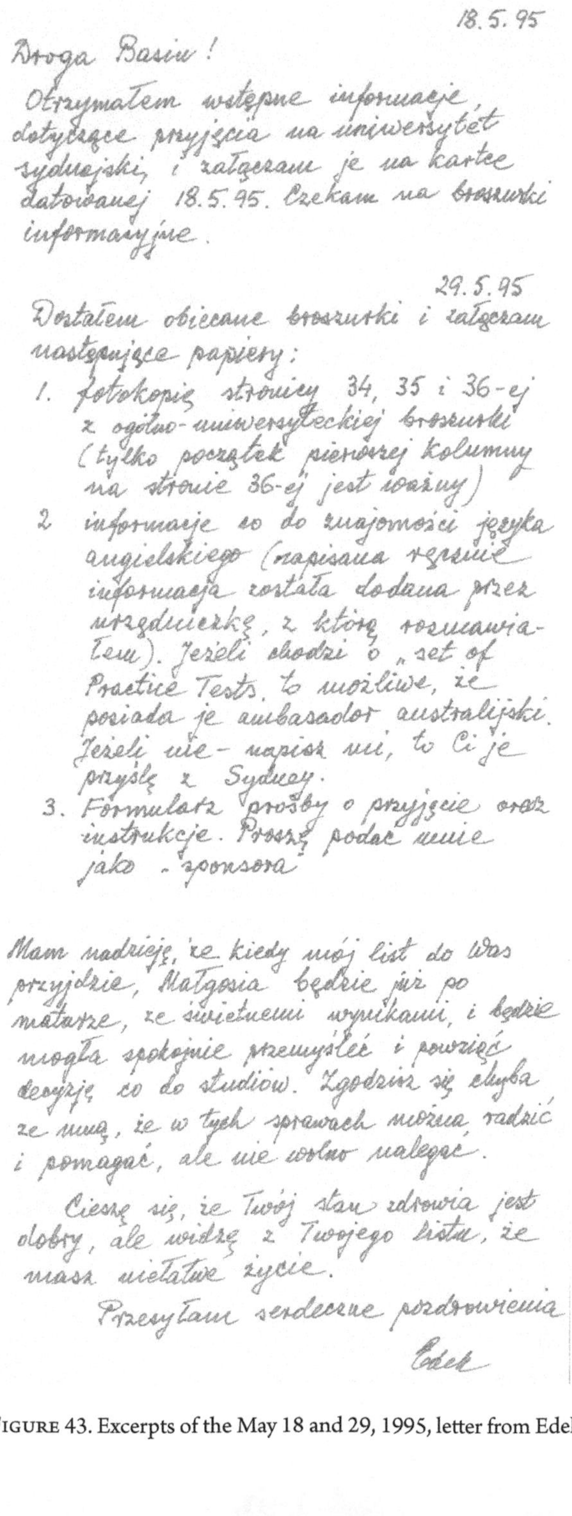

18.5.95

Droga Basiu!

Otrzymałem wstępne informacje dotyczące przyjęcia na uniwersytet sydnejski, i załączam je na kartce datowanej 18.5.95. Czekam na broszurki informacyjne.

29.5.95

Dostałem obiecane broszurki i załączam następujące papiery:

1. fotokopię stronicy 34, 35 i 36-ej z ogólno-uniwersyteckiej broszurki (tylko początek pierwszej kolumny na stronie 36-ej jest ważny)
2. informacje co do znajomości języka angielskiego (napisana ręcznie informacja została dodana przez urzędniczkę, z którą rozmawiałem). Jeżeli chodzi o „set of Practice Tests", to możliwe, że posiada je ambasador australijski. Jeżeli nie - napisz mi, to Ci je przyślę z Sydney.
3. Formularz prośby o przyjęcie oraz instrukcje. Proszę podać mnie jako „sponsora"

Mam nadzieję, że kiedy mój list do Was przyjdzie, Małgosia będzie już po maturze, ze świetnemi wynikami, i będzie mogła spokojnie przemyśleć i powziąć decyzję co do studiów. Zgodzisz się chyba ze mną, że w tych sprawach można radzić i pomagać, ale nie wolno nalegać.

Cieszę się, że Twój stan zdrowia jest dobry, ale widzę z Twojego listu, że masz niełatwe życie.

Przesyłam serdeczne pozdrowienia

Edek

FIGURE 43. Excerpts of the May 18 and 29, 1995, letter from Edek to Basia.

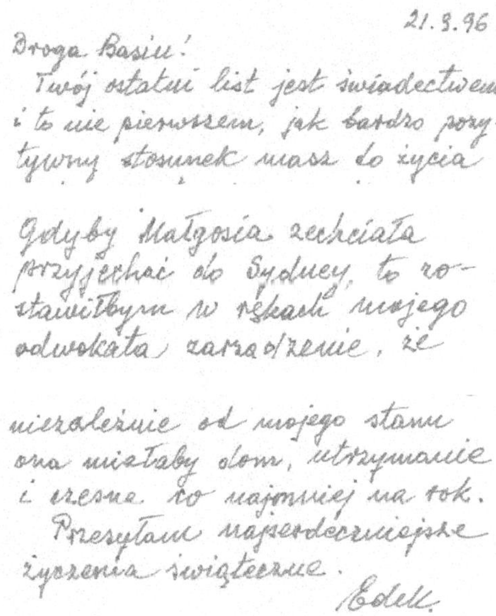

21.3.96

Droga Basiu!
Twój ostatni list jest świadectwem,
i to nie pierwszem, jak bardzo pozy-
tywny stosunek masz do życia

Gdyby Małgosia zechciała
przyjechać do Sydney, to zo-
stawiłbym w rękach mojego
adwokata zarządzenie, że

niezależnie od mojego stanu
ona miałaby dom, utrzymanie
i czesne co najmniej na rok.
Przesyłam najserdeczniejsze
życzenia świąteczne.
Edek.

Figure 44. Excerpts of the March 21, 1996, letter from Edek to Basia.

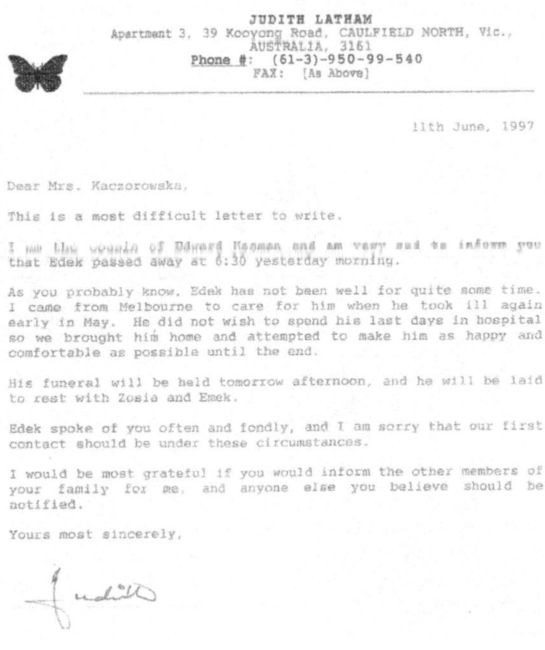

JUDITH LATHAM
Apartment 3, 39 Kooyong Road, CAULFIELD NORTH, Vic.,
AUSTRALIA, 3161
Phone #: (61-3)-950-99-540
FAX: [As Above]

11th June, 1997

Dear Mrs. Kaczorowska,

This is a most difficult letter to write.

I am the cousin of Edward Kagman and am very sad to inform you that Edek passed away at 6:30 yesterday morning.

As you probably know, Edek has not been well for quite some time. I came from Melbourne to care for him when he took ill again early in May. He did not wish to spend his last days in hospital so we brought him home and attempted to make him as happy and comfortable as possible until the end.

His funeral will be held tomorrow afternoon, and he will be laid to rest with Zosia and Emek.

Edek spoke of you often and fondly, and I am sorry that our first contact should be under these circumstances.

I would be most grateful if you would inform the other members of your family for me, and anyone else you believe should be notified.

Yours most sincerely,

Judith

Figure 45. June 11, 1997, letter from Edek's cousin, Judith Latham, in Australia, informing Basia that Edek passed away.

FIGURE 46. A member of the Einsatzgruppen is about to shoot a Jewish man sitting by a mass grave in 1942 in Winniza (formerly in the Polish-Lithuanian Commonwealth, later Ukraine); in the background are Wehrmacht soldiers and members of the Hitler Youth (top). A Jewish woman is attempting to protect a child with her own body just before they are fired upon with rifles at close range by Einsatzgruppen soldiers in Ivangorod (now Ivanhorod, Ukraine) in 1942 (bottom).

Figure 47. Jews from Tarnopol Voivodeship shot while facedown by the Einsatzgruppen in an open pit near Złoczów.

FIGURE 48. Auschwitz II-Birkenau (Brzezinka) concentration camp in May–June 1944: inmates heading towards the barracks (top); Jewish women and children, just unloaded from a new transport, walking towards the gas chamber (bottom).

FIGURE 49. Naked Jewish women wait in a line before their execution by the Ordnungspolizei (Order Police) (top). An Ordnungspolizei officer shoots Jewish women still alive after a mass execution of Jews from the Mizocz ghetto on October 14, 1942 (bottom).

References *

1. Marek Halter, *La force du Bien* [The power of Good] (Paris: Editions Robert Laffont, S. A., 1995); English version: *Stories of Deliverance: Speaking with Men and Women Who Rescued Jews from the Holocaust*, trans. Michael Bernard (New York: Carus Publishing Company, 1998), 34–35.
2. Zofia Sterner, The diary notes covering the period from September 4 to December 15, 1939 (in Polish).
3. Zofia Sterner, Two interviews on family history and activities during WWII, taped and transcribed by Andrzej Domański (son of Tadeusz Domański) in 1985 and 1986 (in Polish).
4. Zofia Sterner, Wacław Sterner, Barbara Sterner (Kaczarowska), Janina Dziarska, and Kazimierz Dziarski. Conversations with the author (Roman Dziarski), 1955–1977, 1994, 1996 (in Polish).
5. Wacław Sterner, *39–45, Chronicles of Terror*, https://www.zapisyterroru.pl/dlibra/publication/1242/edition/1227/content?navq=aHR0cDovL3d3dy56YXBpc3l0ZXJyb3J1LnBsL2RsaWJyYS9yZXN1bHRzP2FjdGlvbj1BZHZhbmNlZFNlYXJjaEFjdGlvbiZ0eXBlPS0zJnNlYXJjaF9hdHRpZDE9NjAmc2VhcmNoX3ZhbHVlMT1UZXh0JnA9Mg&navref=eWk7eTMgeWs7eTUgeWo7eTQ. Testimony as a

* All websites were accessed May 3–8, 2022.

witness before Judge Stanisław Rybiński for the Commission for the Investigation of German Crimes in Poland, Warsaw, April 2, 1946 (in Polish with English translation).
6. Wacław Sterner, *39–45, Chronicles of Terror*, https://www.zapisyterroru.pl/dlibra/publication/1243/edition/1228/content?navq=aHR0cDovL3d3dy56YXBpc3l0ZXJyb3J1LnBsL2RsaWJyYS9yZXN1bHRzP2FjdGlvbj1BZHZhbmNlZFNlYXJjaEFjdGlvbiZ0eXBlPS0zJnNlYXJjaF9hdHRpZDE9NjAmc2VhcmNoX3ZhbHVlMT1UZXh0JnA9Mg&navref=eWo7eTQgeW47eTggeWs7eTU. Testimony as a witness before Judge Halina Wereńko for the Commission for the Investigation of German Crimes in Poland, Warsaw, November 11, 1947 (in Polish).
7. Wacław Sterner, *39–45, Chronicles of Terror*, https://www.zapisyterroru.pl/dlibra/publication/712/edition/697/content?navq=aHR0cDovL3d3dy56YXBpc3l0ZXJyb3J1LnBsL2RsaWJyYS9yZXN1bHRzP2FjdGlvbj1BZHZhbmNlZFNlYXJjaEFjdGlvbiZ0eXBlPS0zJnNlYXJjaF9hdHRpZDE9NzAmc2VhcmNoX3ZhbHVlMT1QaG90b2dyYXBoJnA9MA&navref=dnk7dmoganM7amQgdno7dms. Testimony as a witness before Judge Halina Wereńko for the Commission for the Investigation of German Crimes in Poland, Warsaw, November 11, 1947 (in Polish with English translation).
8. Wacław Sterner, *Gefangeni i Dipisi* [Captured and Displaced] (Warsaw: Książka i Wiedza, 1979).
9. Wikipedia, s.v. "Invasion of Poland," https://en.wikipedia.org/wiki/Invasion_of_Poland.
10. Wikipedia, s.v. "Operation Tannenberg," https://en.wikipedia.org/wiki/Operation_Tannenberg.
11. Wikipedia, s.v. "Battle of Grunwald," https://en.wikipedia.org/wiki/Battle_of_Grunwald.
12. Wikipedia, s.v. "Molotov-Ribbentrop Pact," https://en.wikipedia.org/wiki/Molotov%E2%80%93Ribbentrop_Pact.
13. Wikipedia, s.v. "Soviet invasion of Poland," https://en.wikipedia.org/wiki/Soviet_invasion_of_Poland.
14. Wikipedia, s.v. "Einsatzgruppen," https://en.wikipedia.org/wiki/Einsatzgruppen.
15. Wikipedia, s.v. "Nazi crimes against the Polish nation," https://en.wikipedia.org/wiki/Nazi_crimes_against_the_Polish_nation.
16. Wikipedia, s.v. "Intelligenzaktion," https://en.wikipedia.org/wiki/Intelligenzaktion.

17. Wikipedia, s.v. "Generalplan Ost," https://en.wikipedia.org/wiki/Generalplan_Ost.
18. Wikipedia, s.v. "The Holocaust in Poland," https://en.wikipedia.org/wiki/The_Holocaust_in_Poland.
19. Kazimierz Iranek-Osmecki, *He Who Saves One Life: The Complete Documented Story of the Poles Who Struggled to Save Jews during World War Two* (New York: Crown Publishers, 1971), 19–29.
20. Wikipedia, s.v. "Warsaw Ghetto," https://en.wikipedia.org/wiki/Warsaw_Ghetto.
21. Ludwik Hirszfeld, *The Story of One Life* (New York: University of Rochester Press, 2010), 189.
22. Władysław Szpilman, *The Pianist: The Extraordinary True Story of One Man's Survival in Warsaw, 1939–1945* (New York: Picador USA, 1999), 13.
23. Jack Klajman, *Out of the Ghetto* (London: Vallentine Mitchell, 2000).
24. Szpilman, *The Pianist,* 17, 68, 69.
25. Bernard Goldstein, *Five Years in the Warsaw Ghetto* (Oakland, CA: AK Press, 2005), 68.
26. Szpilman, *The Pianist,* 74.
27. Ibid., 18.
28. Muzeum Historii Polski, "Protest!," https://polishfreedom.pl/en/protest-2/. Also see Wikipedia, s.v. "Protest!," https://en.wikipedia.org/wiki/Protest!
29. Wikipedia, s.v. "Warsaw Ghetto Uprising," https://en.wikipedia.org/wiki/Warsaw_Ghetto_Uprising.
30. Wikipedia, s.v. "Poniatowa concentration camp," https://en.wikipedia.org/wiki/Poniatowa_concentration_camp.
31. Wikipedia, s.v. "Polish resistance movement in World War II," https://en.wikipedia.org/wiki/Polish_resistance_movement_in_World_War_II.
32. Wikipedia, s.v. "Polish Underground State," https://en.wikipedia.org/wiki/Polish_Underground_State.
33. Wikipedia, s.v. "Katyń massacre," https://en.wikipedia.org/wiki/Katyn_massacre.
34. Wikipedia, s.v. "Warsaw Uprising," https://en.wikipedia.org/wiki/Warsaw_Uprising.
35. Wikipedia, s.v. "Wola massacre," https://en.wikipedia.org/wiki/Wola_massacre.
36. Wikipedia, s.v. "Ochota massacre," https://en.wikipedia.org/wiki/Ochota_massacre.

37. Wikipedia, s.v. "Witold Pilecki," https://en.wikipedia.org/wiki/Witold_Pilecki.
38. Wikipedia, s.v. "Timeline of Jewish-Polish history," https://en.wikipedia.org/wiki/Timeline_of_Jewish-Polish_history.
39. Wikipedia, s.v. "History of the Jews in Poland," https://en.wikipedia.org/wiki/History_of_the_Jews_in_Poland.
40. Halter, *La force du Bien*, 5–297.
41. Wikipedia, s.v. "Statute of Kalisz," https://en.wikipedia.org/wiki/Statute_of_Kalisz.
42. Wikipedia, s.v. "Blood libel," https://en.wikipedia.org/wiki/Blood_libel.
43. Iranek-Osmecki, *He Who Saves One Life*, 3–4.
44. Wikipedia, s.v. "Warsaw Confederation," https://en.wikipedia.org/wiki/Warsaw_Confederation.
45. Wikipedia, s.v. "Paradisus Judaeorum," https://en.wikipedia.org/wiki/Paradisus_Judaeorum.
46. Eva Hoffman, *Shtetl: The Life and Death of a Small Town and the World of Polish Jews* (Boston: Houghton Mifflin Harcourt, 1997), 26–72.
47. Wikipedia, s.v. "Council of Four Lands," https://en.wikipedia.org/wiki/Council_of_Four_Lands.
48. Wikipedia, s.v. "Deluge (history)," https://en.wikipedia.org/wiki/Deluge_(history).
49. Wikipedia, s.v. "Constitution of 3 May 1791," https://en.wikipedia.org/wiki/Constitution_of_3_May_1791.
50. Wikipedia, s.v. "Second Polish Republic," https://en.wikipedia.org/wiki/Second_Polish_Republic.
51. Hoffman, *Shtetl*, 110–120.
52. Wikipedia, s.v. "History of the Jews in 20th-century Poland," https://en.wikipedia.org/wiki/History_of_the_Jews_in_20th-century_Poland.
53. Iranek-Osmecki, *He Who Saves One Life*, 6–10.
54. Wikipedia, s.v. "General Jewish Labour Bund," https://en.wikipedia.org/wiki/General_Jewish_Labour_Bund.
55. Hoffman, *Shtetl*, 159–200.
56. Maria Ciesielska, *The Doctors of the Warsaw Ghetto* (Boston: Academic Studies Press, 2022), 7–8.
57. Hoffman, *Shtetl*, 256.
58. Ibid., 189.
59. Iranek-Osmecki, *He Who Saves One Life*, 10–12.
60. Wikipedia, s.v. "National Radical Camp," https://en.wikipedia.org/wiki/National_Radical_Camp.

61. Hirszfeld, *The Story of One Life*, 160–162.
62. Wikipedia, s.v. "August Hlond," https://en.wikipedia.org/wiki/August_Hlond.
63. Rafael F. Scharf, *Poland, What Have I To Do With Thee . . . Essays without Prejudice* (London: Vallentine Mitchell, 2002), 30, 60, 73, 74, 90, 104, 105.
64. Emmanuel Ringelblum, *Polish-Jewish Relations during the Second World War* (Evanston, IL: Northwestern University Press, 1992), 24.
65. Wikipedia, s.v. "30 January 1939 Reichstag speech," https://en.wikipedia.org/wiki/30_January_1939_Reichstag_speech.
66. Hoffman, *Shtetl*, 6.
67. Eva Hoffman, introduction to *Shtetl* [documentary], by Marian Marzynski, PBS, https://www.pbs.org/wgbh/pages/frontline/shtetl/reflections/.
68. Wikipedia, s.v. "Final Solution," https://en.wikipedia.org/wiki/Final_Solution.
69. Wikipedia, s.v. "Operation Reinhard," https://en.wikipedia.org/wiki/Operation_Reinhard.
70. Wikipedia, s.v. "The Holocaust," https://en.wikipedia.org/wiki/The_Holocaust.
71. Hoffman, *Shtetl*, 246.
72. Ringelblum, *Polish–Jewish Relations during the Second World War*, 247–248.
73. Mordekhai Tenenbaum-Tamaroff, "Dapim min hadelekah, Bet lohamei hageta'ot, hakibbuts hameuhad, 1947," in *The Neighbors Respond: The Controversy over the Jedwabne Massacre in Poland*, ed. Antony Polonsky and Joanna B. Michlic, 49–50 (Princeton: Princeton University Press, 2004) and in Antony Polonsky, "Poles, Jews and the Problems of a Divided Memory," *Ab Imperio* 2 (2004): 129, DOI:10.1353/imp.2004.0064.
74. Władysław Bartoszewski and Zofia Lewin, eds. *Righteous Among Nations: How Poles Helped the Jews, 1939–1945* (London: Earlscourt Publications, 1969).
75. Iranek-Osmecki, *He Who Saves One Life*, 19–297.
76. Hoffman, *Shtetl*, 201–240.
77. Joseph Kermish, introduction to *Polish-Jewish Relations during the Second World War*, by Emmanuel Ringelblum (Evanston, IL: Northwestern University Press, 1992), vii-xxxix.
78. Ringelblum, *Polish-Jewish Relations during the Second World War*, 100–155.
79. Goldstein, *Five Years in the Warsaw Ghetto*, 138–162.
80. Gunnar S. Paulsson, *Secret City: The Hidden Jews of Warsaw, 1940–1945* (New Haven and London: Yale University Press, 2002), 138–164.

81. Nechama Tec, *When Light Pierced the Darkness: Christian Rescue of Jews in Nazi-Occupied Poland* (New York: Oxford University Press, 1986), 27–51, 70–109.
82. Nechama Tec, *Dry Tears: The Story of a Lost Childhood* (New York: Oxford University Press, 1984).
83. Kermish, introduction, xxviii.
84. Ringelblum, *Polish-Jewish Relations during the Second World War*, 50–53.
85. Goldstein, *Five Years in the Warsaw Ghetto*, 43–45.
86. Ringelblum, *Polish-Jewish Relations during the Second World War*, 198.
87. Joseph Kermish, postscript to ibid., 307.
88. Hirszfeld, *The Story of One Life*, 285.
89. Tec, *When Light Pierced the Darkness*, 102–103.
90. Ibid., 99–112.
91. Paulsson, *Secret City*, 243.
92. Wikipedia, s.v. "Szczuczyn pogrom," https://en.wikipedia.org/wiki/Szczuczyn_pogrom.
93. Wikipedia, s.v. "Wąsosz pogrom," https://en.wikipedia.org/wiki/Wąsosz_pogrom.
94. Wikipedia, s.v. "Radziłów pogrom," https://en.wikipedia.org/wiki/Radziłów_pogrom.
95. Wikipedia, s.v. "Jedwabne pogrom," https://en.wikipedia.org/wiki/Jedwabne_pogrom.
96. Hoffman, *Shtetl*, 210.
97. Iranek-Osmecki, *He Who Saves One Life*, 67.
98. Peter Hayes, *Why? Explaining the Holocaust* (New York: W. W. Norton & Co., 2017), 249.
99. Joshua D. Zimmerman, "The Polish Underground Home Army (AK) and the Jews: What Postwar Jewish Testimonies and Wartime Documents Reveal," *East European Politics and Societies and Cultures* 34, no. 1 (2020): 194–220, https://journals.sagepub.com/doi/10.1177/0888325419844816.
100. Hayes, *Why? Explaining the Holocaust*, 250–252.
101. Zimmerman, "The Polish Underground Home Army (AK) and the Jews": 206.
102. Wikipedia, s.v. "Sobibor extermination camp," https://en.wikipedia.org/wiki/Sobibor_extermination_camp); and the United States Holocaust Memorial Museum Holocaust Encyclopedia, s.v. "Sobibor Uprising," https://encyclopedia.ushmm.org/content/en/article/sobibor-uprising.

103. Alina Skibińska and Jerzy Mazurek, "'Barwy Białe' w drodze na pomoc walczącej Warszawie. Zbrodnie AK na Żydach." *Zagłada Żydów. Studia i Materiały*, no. 7 (2011): 422–465, https://doi.org/10.32927/zzsim.798/.
104. Paulsson, *Secret City*, 173–183, 235.
105. Hayes, *Why? Explaining the Holocaust*, 240–258.
106. Krzysztof Persak, "Jedwabne before the Court. Poland's Justice and the Jedwabne Massacre—Investigations and Court Proceedings, 1947–1974," *East European Politics and Societies* 25, no. 3 (2011): 410–432.
107. Jan Grabowski, *Hunt for the Jews: Betrayal and Murder in German-Occupied Poland* (Bloomington & Indianapolis, IN: Indiana University Press, 2013).
108. Iranek-Osmecki, *He Who Saves One Life*, 250–253.
109. See footnote 41 by Joseph Kermish and Shmuel Krakowski, in Ringelblum, *Polish-Jewish Relations during the Second World War*, 223–235; and Kermish, postscript, in ibid, 309.
110. Bartoszewski and Lewin, *Righteous Among Nations*, xvi-lxxxvii.
111. Polish Center for Holocaust Research, http://www.holocaustresearch.pl/?l=a&lang=en; Centrum Badań nad Zagładą Żydów, https://ifispan.pl/socjologia/zespol-badan-nad-zaglada-zydow/; Jewish Historical Institute - Żydowski Instytut Historyczny, https://www.jhi.pl/; and Mordechai Anielewicz Centre for the Study and Teaching of the History and Culture of Jews in Poland, http://en.ihuw.pl/institute/about/departments/anielewicz-centre.
112. Iranek-Osmecki, *He Who Saves One Life*, 263–280.
113. Tec, *When Light Pierced the Darkness*, 64–69.
114. Iranek-Osmecki, *He Who Saves One Life*, 119–121.
115. Bartoszewski and Lewin, *Righteous Among Nations*, 116–120.
116. Ringelblum, *Polish-Jewish Relations during the Second World War*, 79, 83.
117. Wikipedia, s.v. "Raczyński's Note," https://en.wikipedia.org/wiki/Raczyński's_Note.
118. Wikipedia, s.v. "The Mass Extermination of Jews in German Occupied Poland," https://en.wikipedia.org/wiki/The_Mass_Extermination_of_Jews_in_German_Occupied_Poland.
119. Bartoszewski and Lewin, *Righteous Among Nations*, xxxvii-xliv.
120. Wikipedia, s.v. "Auschwitz concentration camp," https://en.wikipedia.org/wiki/Auschwitz_concentration_camp.
121. Bartoszewski and Lewin, *Righteous Among Nations*, 527–542.

122. Wikipedia, s.v. "Jan Karski," https://en.wikipedia.org/wiki/Jan_Karski.
123. Iranek-Osmecki, *He Who Saves One Life*, 182–185, 197–209.
124. Wikipedia, s.v. "Szmul Zygielbojm," https://en.wikipedia.org/wiki/Szmul_Zygielbojm.
125. Iranek-Osmecki, *He Who Saves One Life*, 215–217.
126. Joshua D. Zimmerman, "The Polish Underground Press and the Jews: The Holocaust in the Pages of the Home Army's *Biuletyn Informacyjny*, 1940–1943," in *Warsaw. The Jewish Metropolis: Essays in Honor of the 75th Birthday of Antony Polonsky*, ed. Glenn Dynner and Francois Guesnet (Leiden and Boston: Brill, 2015), 539–561 (quotes on 439, 440, 445, 455, 460–464).
127. Iranek-Osmecki, *He Who Saves One Life*, 139–143.
128. Wikipedia, s.v. "Żegota," https://en.wikipedia.org/wiki/Żegota.
129. Iranek-Osmecki, *He Who Saves One Life*, 236–244.
130. See Wikipedia, s.v. "Żegota" and Iranek-Osmecki, *He Who Saves One Life*, 236–244: $50,000 + 37,400,000 złotys = approx. $7.48 million at 1940 exchange rate for Polish złoty: 5 złotys = $1 (1 RM [Reichsmark] = 2 złotys, $1 = 2.5 RM [Reichsmark]); see Wikipedia, s.v. "Polish złoty," https://en.wikipedia.org/wiki/Polish_złoty#Exchange_rates. At 1943–1944 exchange rates, estimates vary: from $3.8 million (at half of the 1940 value of złoty) to $5 million (see Wikipedia, s.v. "The Holocaust in Poland").
131. Kermish and Krakowski, footnote 29, 213–214.
132. Iranek-Osmecki, *He Who Saves One Life*, 79–86, 151–160.
133. Ringelblum, *Polish-Jewish Relations during the Second World War*, 172–174.
134. Bartoszewski and Lewin, *Righteous Among Nations*, xxvii.
135. Iranek-Osmecki, *He Who Saves One Life*, 160–168.
136. Bartoszewski and Lewin, *Righteous Among Nations*, 148–152, 555–585.
137. Ringelblum, *Polish-Jewish Relations during the Second World War*, 179–181.
138. Iranek-Osmecki, *He Who Saves One Life*, 166–168.
139. Ringelblum, *Polish-Jewish Relations during the Second World War*, 186–188.
140. Iranek-Osmecki, *He Who Saves One Life*, 254–259.
141. Bartoszewski and Lewin, *Righteous Among Nations*, lxix-lxxi.
142. Wikipedia, s.v. "Rescue of Jews by Poles during the Holocaust," https://en.wikipedia.org/wiki/Rescue_of_Jews_by_Poles_during_the_Holocaust.

143. Zimmerman, "The Polish Underground Home Army (AK) and the Jews": 194, 195.
144. Joshua D. Zimmerman, *The Polish Underground and the Jews, 1939–1945* (New York: Cambridge University Press, 2015).
145. Tec, *When Light Pierced the Darkness*, 138.
146. Ibid., 137–149.
147. Ewa Kurek, *Your Life Is Worth Mine: How Polish Nuns Saved Hundreds of Jewish Children in German-Occupied Poland, 1939–1945* (New York: Hippocrene Books, 1997), 39–110.
148. Ibid., 99, 102.
149. Paulsson, *Secret City*, 241.
150. Emmanuel Ringelblum, *Notes from the Warsaw Ghetto: The Journal of Emmanuel Ringelblum* (New York: ibooks, 2006), 336–338.
151. Kurek, *Your Life Is Worth Mine*, 34–38.
152. Ringelblum, *Polish-Jewish Relations during the Second World War*, 150–151.
153. Kurek, *Your Life Is Worth Mine*, 216–217.
154. Iranek-Osmecki, *He Who Saves One Life*, 119–133.
155. Bartoszewski and Lewin, *Righteous Among Nations*, 1–611.
156. Tec, *When Light Pierced the Darkness*, 27–149.
157. Bartoszewski and Lewin, *Righteous Among Nations*, 41–62.
158. Tilar J. Mazzeo, *Irena's Children: The Extraordinary Story of the Woman Who Saved 2,500 Children from the Warsaw Ghetto* (New York: Gallery Books, 2017).
159. Wikipedia, s.v. "Irena Sendler," https://en.wikipedia.org/wiki/Irena_Sendler.
160. Wikipedia, s.v. "Polish Righteous Among the Nations," https://en.wikipedia.org/wiki/Polish_Righteous_Among_the_Nations.
161. Antonina Żabińska, *Ludzie i Zwierzęta* [People and Animals] (Kraków: Wydawnictwo Literackie, 2017).
162. Diane Ackerman, *The Zookeeper's Wife* (New York: W. W. Norton & Company, 2008).
163. Wikipedia, s.v. "Antonina Żabińska," https://en.wikipedia.org/wiki/Antonina_Żabińska.
164. Wikipedia, s.v. "Jan Żabiński," https://en.wikipedia.org/wiki/Jan_Żabiński.
165. Tec, *When Light Pierced the Darkness*, 101–102.
166. Eva Fogelman, *Conscience & Courage: Rescuers of Jews During the Holocaust* (New York: Anchor-Doubleday, 1994).

167. Wikipedia, s.v. "Righteous Among the Nations," https://en.wikipedia.org/wiki/Righteous_Among_the_Nations.
168. Kurek, *Your Life Is Worth Mine*, 216—interview with rabbi David Kahane.
169. Wikipedia, s.v. "World War II casualties of Poland," https://en.wikipedia.org/wiki/World_War_II_casualties_of_Poland.
170. Szymon Datner, *Las Sprawiedliwych* [The Forest of the Righteous] (Warsaw: Książka i Wiedza, 1968), 5, 86.
171. Bartoszewski and Lewin, *Righteous Among Nations*, xviii.
172. Hayes, *Why? Explaining the Holocaust*, 226–227.
173. Paulsson, *Secret City*, 231–248.
174. Ibid., 230.
175. Hayes, *Why? Explaining the Holocaust*, 114–137.
176. Bartoszewski and Lewin, *Righteous Among Nations*, xxv.
177. Goldstein, *Five Years in the Warsaw Ghetto*, 94.
178. Ibid., 96, 101–102.
179. Iranek-Osmecki, *He Who Saves One Life*, 83.
180. Ibid., 70–71.
181. Tec, *When Light Pierced the Darkness*, xxvi.
182. Ringelblum, *Notes from the Warsaw Ghetto*, 310, 326, 330.
183. Wolf Biermann, epilogue to *The Pianist*, by Władysław Szpilman, 214.
184. Ringelblum, *Notes from the Warsaw Ghetto*, 341–344.
185. Goldstein, *Five Years in the Warsaw Ghetto*, 158–159.
186. Paulsson, *Secret City*, 80–82, 233.
187. Ibid., 55–96, 231–241.
188. Hirszfeld, *The Story of One Life*, 327–328.
189. Paulsson, *Secret City*, 233.
190. Goldstein, *Five Years in the Warsaw Ghetto*, 153.
191. Paulsson, *Secret City*, 235.
192. Ibid., 234.
193. Tec, *When Light Pierced the Darkness*, 80.
194. Paulsson, *Secret City*, 138–141.
195. Wikipedia, s.v. "Hotel Polski," https://en.wikipedia.org/wiki/Hotel_Polski.
196. Paulsson, *Secret City*, 1, 231.
197. Kermish, postscript, 312.
198. Bartoszewski and Lewin, *Righteous Among Nations*, xlviii.
199. United States Holocaust Memorial Museum Holocaust Encyclopedia, s.v. "Warsaw," https://encyclopedia.ushmm.org/content/en/article/warsaw.

200. Havi Dreifuss, *Changing Perspectives on Polish-Jewish Relations During the Holocaust* (Jerusalem: Yad Vashem, 2012) 47, 49.
201. Joseph L. Lichten, foreword to *He Who Saves One Life*, by Kazimierz Iranek-Osmecki, x.
202. Paulsson, *Secret City*, 248.
203. Grabowski, *Hunt for the Jews*, 137, 138, 172, 173.
204. Tomasz Frydel, "Judenjagd. Reassessing the Role of Ordinary Poles as Perpetrators in the Holocaust," in *Perpetrators and Perpetration of Mass Violence Action; Motivations and Dynamics*, ed. Timothy Williams and Susanne Buckley-Zistel (New York: Routledge, 2018), 187–203.
205. Agnieszka Wierzcholska, "Helping, Denouncing, and Profiteering: A Process-Oriented Approach to Jewish-Gentile Relations in Occupied Poland from a Micro-Historical Perspective," *Holocaust Studies*, 23, no. 1–2 (2017): 34–58, DOI: 10.1080/17504902.2016.1209842.
206. Tomasz Frydel, "Ordinary Men?," in *Collaboration in Eastern Europe during the Second World War and the Holocaust*, ed. Peter Black, Béla Rásky, and Marianne Windsperger (Hamburg: New Academic Press, 2019), 69–125.
207. Eva Hoffman, *After Such Knowledge: Memory, History, and the Legacy of the Holocaust* (New York: Public Affairs, 2004), 214.
208. Hoffman, *Shtetl*, 244–245.
209. Grabowski, *Hunt for the Jews*, 5.
210. Wikipedia, s.v. "Anti-Jewish violence in Poland, 1944–1946," https://en.wikipedia.org/wiki/Anti-Jewish_violence_in_Poland,_1944–1946.
211. Wikipedia, s.v. "Kielce pogrom," https://en.wikipedia.org/wiki/Kielce_pogrom.
212. Doris L. Bergen, *War and Genocide: A Concise History of the Holocaust* (New York: Rowman & Littlefield Publishers and Barnes & Noble, 2007), 118–119.
213. Hayes, *Why? Explaining the Holocaust*, 256–257.
214. Leora Tec, The Neshoma Project, https://neshomaproject.org/ and Bridge to Poland, https://bridgetopoland.com/.
215. POLIN-Virtual Shtetl, https://sztetl.org.pl/en.
216. Hirszfeld, *The Story of One Life*, 318.
217. Hoffman, *Shtetl*, 247.
218. Tec, *When Light Pierced the Darkness*, 63.

219. Hayes, *Why? Explaining the Holocaust*, 328.
220. Szymon Datner, "German Nazi Crimes against Jews Who Escaped from the Ghettoes. 'Legal' Threats and Ordinances Regarding Jews and the Poles Who Helped Them," *Jewish Historical Institute Bulletin*, no. 75 (1970): 22, http://muzhp.pl/files/upload/aktualnosci/szymon_datner.pdf.
221. Jacek Leociak and Anna Goc, "Liczenie, które boli" [Counting that hurts], *Tygodnik Powszechny*, March 6, 2016, https://www.tygodnikpowszechny.pl/liczenie-ktore-boli-32667.
222. Wikipedia, s.v. "Jan Grabowski," https://en.wikipedia.org/wiki/Jan_Grabowski.
223. Wikipedia, s.v. "Jan T. Gross," https://en.wikipedia.org/wiki/Jan_T._Gross.
224. Paul Lungen, "University of Ottawa Holocaust Historian Sues Polish Group for Libel," *Canadian Jewish News*, November 22, 2018, https://thecjn.ca/news/canada/university-of-ottawa-holocaust-historian-sues-polish-group-for-libel/.
225. Ofer Aderet, "Historian May Face Charges in Poland for Writing That Poles Killed Jews in World War II," *Haaretz*, October 30, 2016, https://www.haaretz.com/world-news/europe/2016–10-30/ty-article/.premium/historian-may-face-charges-for-writing-that-poles-killed-jews-in-wwii/0000017f-e33f-d9aa-afff-fb7f45010000.
226. Szymon Datner estimates that one hundred thousand Jews who escaped from the ghettos in Poland during WWII did not survive (Datner, "German Nazi Crimes against Jews Who Escaped from the Ghettoes": 22). Jacek Leociak estimates that one hundred thousand to 130,000 Jews who escaped from the ghettos were missing at the end of the war and likely did not survive (Leociak and Goc, "Liczenie, które boli"). Jan Grabowski and Jan T. Gross posit that Poles could have saved one hundred thousand to two hundred thousand Jews, but instead killed them or through betrayal collaborated in their murders (Wikipedia, s.v. "Jan Grabowski"; Wikipedia, s.v. "Jan T. Gross"; Paul. "University of Ottawa Holocaust historian sues Polish group for libel"; Aderet, "Historian May Face Charges in Poland for Writing That Poles Killed Jews in World War II,"). The number two hundred thousand is based on the assumption that 250,000 Jews escaped from the ghettos, fifty thousand survived, and thus two hundred thousand were killed by

Poles or with their help (Grabowski, *Hunt for the Jews,* 172). This number seems exaggerated because it assumes that 10% of Jews escaped from the ghettos and that Poles killed or collaborated in the murders of all those who escaped and did not survive. But Leociak and Goc point out that it is not possible to determine the fate of all the Jews who escaped from the ghettos or the causes of their deaths, and to what extent Poles contributed to their deaths (Leociak and Goc, "Liczenie, które boli").

Historians emphasize that because there are no exact data, it is not possible to precisely determine the numbers of victims and survivors, especially the numbers of Jews saved, denounced, or killed by Poles. However, estimates are important to roughly assess the scale of this help and the atrocities. Approximately 2.5 million Jews were in German-occupied Poland in 1942 before the start of the great deportations. About half (1.3 million) lived in cities with ghettos of over twenty thousand Jews (Wikipedia, s.v. "List of Jewish ghettos in German-occupied Poland", https://en.wikipedia.org/wiki/List_of_Jewish_ghettos_in_German-occupied_Poland), and the other half (approximately 1.2 million) lived in small towns and villages.

Recent more detailed research from eight counties (in Polish *powiaty*: Bielski, Biłgorajski, Bocheński, Dąbrowski, Dębicki, Łukowski, Miechowski, Węgrowski, and Złoczowski; in: Grabowski, *Hunt for the Jews,* 15, 28, 60, 61, 137, 138, 172, 173; and Barbara Engelking and Jan Grabowski, eds., *Dalej jest noc. Losy Żydów w wybranych powiatach okupowanej Polski,* Warszawa: Stowarzyszenie Centrum Badań nad Zagładą Żydów, 2018, vol. I, 30, 36, 118, 124, 337, 367, 369, 485, 486, 587-592, vol. II, 208-211, 450, 512, 559, 746-754) allows somewhat more accurate estimates. These data and estimates indicate a 10% median escape rate from the ghettos (with a range of 4%–13%) and a 22% median survival rate of the escapees (with a range of 12%–47%). The escape rates from the ghettos in some cities were somewhat lower: 6.1% in Warsaw (twenty-eight thousand Jews escaped out of 460,000; Paulsson, *Secret City,* 231-248), but probably around 10% in other cities, for example, approximately 9.5% in Łódź (twenty thousand out of 210,000; many of whom fled before the establishment of the ghetto, because Łódź was incorporated into the Third Reich territory, and the ghetto was then separated from the rest of the city and difficult to escape from; Wikipedia, s.v. "Łódź Ghetto", https://en.wikipedia.org/wiki/Łódź_Ghetto). However, the survival rates of Jewish escapees in the cities were higher than in the villages and small towns; for example, in Warsaw, it was from 30% (Dreifuss, *Changing Perspectives on Polish-Jewish Relations During the Holocaust,* 47, 49) to 41% (Paulsson, *Secret City,* 230-248), i.e., approximately 35% on average.

If we assume a 10% escape rate from all the ghettos (that is 250 thousand Jews) and a range of survival rates of those who escaped – from 22% in villages and small towns to 35% in cities – this range yields approximately 55 thousand to 87 thousand Jews who survived and 163 thousand to 195 thousand who perished. The above-cited studies in eight rural counties (Grabowski, *Hunt for the Jews,* 15, 28, 60, 61, 137, 138, 172, 173; and Engelking and Grabowski, *Dalej jest noc,* vol. I, 30, 36, 118, 124, 337, 367, 369, 485, 486, 587-592, vol. II, 208-211, 450, 512, 559, 746-754) also estimated that a median of 47% (range 26%–82%) of Jews who escaped from the ghettos and perished while hiding among Poles were either killed by Poles (23%) or denounced and killed by the Germans (24%). Thus, this rough estimate of the number of Jewish deaths for which Poles were responsible (26%–82% of 163–195 thousand) is 43–160 thousand.

But had more or most Poles been willing to help and had they not denounced Jews or their helpers, many more Jews would have escaped from the ghettos and survived the war. However, knowing Hitler's maniacal hatred of Jews and other "inferior races," the Nazis would have either implemented other ways of finding Jews or executed their next plan, the *Generalplan Ost* (Wikipedia, s.v. "Generalplan Ost"), to eliminate ethnic Poles and all the remaining Jews hiding among them. All these and other similar estimates are either educated guesses based on incomplete data and many assumptions or highly hypothetical speculations. Thus, the actual numbers of Jews who would have survived had all Poles offered them all possible help are unknown, but one likely estimate is at least forty thousand to one hundred sixty thousand or more.

227. Jan T. Gross, *Neighbors: The Destruction of Jewish Community in Jedwabne, Poland* (Princeton: Princeton University Press, 2001, and Penguin Books, 2002).

228. Polonsky and Michlic, *The Neighbors Respond.*
229. Bogdan Białek, Jan Tomasz Gross, and Adam Michnik, *Po Sąsiadach* [After the Neighbors] (Kielce: Stowarzyszenie im. Jana Karskiego, 2022).
230. Anna Bikont, afterword to ibid., 78.
231. Szpilman, *The Pianist,* 21.
232. Jerzy Jedlicki, "How to Grapple with the Perplexing Legacy, Polityka, 10 February 2001," in Polonsky and Michlic, *The Neighbors Respond,* 239–240.
233. Ringelblum, *Polish-Jewish Relations during the Second World War,* 226–245.
234. Paulsson, *Secret City,* 1.
235. Wikipedia, s.v. "Atomic bombings of Hiroshima and Nagasaki," https://en.wikipedia.org/wiki/Atomic_bombings_of_Hiroshima_and_Nagasaki.
236. Wikipedia, s.v. "World War II casualties," https://en.wikipedia.org/wiki/World_War_II_casualties.
237. Scharf, *Poland, What Have I To Do With Thee?,* 103.
238. Wikipedia, s.v. "Nuremburg trials," https://en.wikipedia.org/wiki/Nuremberg_trials.
239. Hayes, *Why? Explaining the Holocaust,* 306–311.
240. Gabriel N. Finder and Alexander V. Prusin, *Justice Behind the Iron Curtin: Nazis on Trial in Communist Poland* (Toronto: University of Toronto Press, 2018).
241. Hayes, *Why? Explaining the Holocaust,* 36–72, 334.
242. Ibid., 340.
243. Ibid., 334.
244. Daniel Tilles, "'Death to Jews' Chanted at Torchlit Far-Right March in Polish City," *Notes from Poland,* November 12, 2021, https://notesfrompoland.com/2021/11/12/death-to-jews-chanted-at-torchlit-far-right-march-in-polish-city/. Ben Cohen, "Cries of 'Death to the Jews!' Ring Out at Angry Demonstration in Poland as Far-Right Agitators Burn 'Symbol of Tolerance,'" *Algemeiner,* November 12, 2021, https://www.algemeiner.com/2021/11/12/cries-of-death-to-the-jews-ring-out-at-angry-demonstration-in-poland-as-far-right-agitators-burn-symbol-of-tolerance/. Vanessa Gera, "Poland Arrests 3 in Connection to Antisemitic Demonstration" *Associated Press,* November 15, 2021,

https://apnews.com/article/europe-poland-arrests-race-and-ethnicity-racial-injustice-e75a79c42f9363c291f3c7a2a3be97de.

245. Wikipedia, s.v. "Nazi Party," https://en.wikipedia.org/wiki/Nazi_Party.
246. Wikipedia, s.v. "German resistance to Nazism," https://en.wikipedia.org/wiki/German_resistance_to_Nazism.
247. Christopher R. Browning, *Ordinary Men: Reserve Police Battalion 101 and the Final Solution in Poland* (New York: Harper Collins, 2017).

List of Figures

Figure 1. Pre-World War II Europe.

Figure 2. Pre-World War II Poland. The cities, towns, and villages featured in the story are indicated with black triangles; the border between the German and the Soviet occupation zones from October 1939 to June 1941 is shown by black dots. After the German invasion of the Soviet Union on June 22, 1941, the entire territory of Poland fell under German occupation.

Figure 3. The narrator, Zofia (Zochna) Sterner (1943), and Wacław (Wacek) Sterner (1930s), Zofia's husband.

Figure 4. Zofia and Wacek Sterner on vacation in the Carpathian Mountains in Poland before WWII, late 1930s.

Figure 5. Basia—Barbara Sterner, daughter of Zofia and Wacek Sterner—in Warsaw, 1943.

Figure 6. Tadeusz Domański, Zofia Sterner's brother, with Zofia in Warsaw, early 1940s.

Figure 7. Tadeusz, Zofia, and Wacek (from left to right) in Warsaw, 1933.

Figure 8. The Domański family in Warsaw, c. 1916: Anna (nee Szczerek, June 23, 1877–December 26, 1957) and Józef (1863–April 5, 1941) with children (from left to right): Zofia (Zochna), Janina (Niusia, later Dziarska), and Tadeusz.

FIGURE 9. Niusia (Janina Dziarska) and Kazio (Kazimierz Dziarski), her husband, c. 1939.

FIGURE 10. Niusia and Kazio on vacation in the Mazovia region in Poland before WWII, late 1930s.

FIGURE 11. Kazio (top, the first on the left, middle row) with other Polish officers in his unit in Wiesendangen on November 28, 1941; and on a street in the Zürich area in 1942 (bottom, Kazio in the middle).

FIGURE 12. The Dziarski family in Warsaw in 1906: Wiktoria (nee Kacprzak, died February 7, 1943) and Michał Andrzej Dziarski (c. 1873–March 5, 1924) with their children (from left to right: Maria [Mancia, February 1, 1906–Feb 1945]; Anna [later Barczewska, c. 1892–July 12, 1930]; Jadwiga [Jadzia, c. 1903–c. 1908]; Janina [Janka, later Urbańska, c. 1894–c.1965]; and Eugeniusz [Gienio, December 17, 1896–December 4, 1972]). Kazio and Zofia [later Winiarska] were not born yet.

FIGURE 13. Zosia and Edek Kosman in Vaucluse, Australia, November 1988.

FIGURE 14. The First Battle of Tannenberg of 1410, also known as the Battle of Grunwald, painted by Jan Matejko, after which Hitler's Operation Tannenberg was named.

FIGURE 15. Twelve-year-old Kazimiera Mika cries over the body of her fourteen-year-old sister Anna killed by machine gun fire from a low-flying Luftwaffe plane in a field near Warsaw on September 13, 1939; no military targets were there, just a few women working in the field.

FIGURE 16. Public execution of twenty-five prominent Polish citizens in front of the Municipal Museum in the Market Square of Bydgoszcz on September 9, 1939; to terrorize the remaining population, the Nazis displayed the bodies for six hours (top). Execution of civilians by Einsatzgruppen in Kórnik on October 20, 1939 (bottom).

FIGURE 17. Polish civilians wearing blindfolds photographed just before their execution by Einsatzgruppen soldiers in Palmiry forest near Warsaw in 1940. In Palmiry, about seventeen hundred Poles were murdered in secret executions between December 7, 1939 and July 17, 1941.

FIGURE 18. Mass execution of fifty-six Polish civilians in Bochnia near Kraków on December 18, 1939 (top) and public execution of Polish civilians in Kraków on June 26, 1942 (bottom).

FIGURE 19. Magirus-Deutz gas van near Chełmno used by the Nazis for suffocation of civilians (top). A teenage boy stands beside his murdered family shortly before his own murder by the Einsatzgruppen in Zborów near Lwów (Polish part of Ukraine before WWII) on July 5, 1941 (bottom).

FIGURE 20. Polish girls in the Nazi labor camp in Dzierżązna near Zgierz (1942–1943).

FIGURE 21. Current view of the house on 27 Szustra Street (currently Dąbrowskiego Street) in the Mokotów district in Warsaw, where Niusia's apartment #3 containing her dental office was located and where Jews led out from the ghetto by Zofia found refuge.

FIGURE 22. Destitute and dying Jewish children on the streets in the Warsaw Ghetto (January–August 1941).

FIGURE 23. A young unconscious woman dying on the street in the Warsaw Ghetto (top); and dead bodies collected daily from the streets in the Warsaw Ghetto on a wagon for transport to a mass grave (bottom), September 19, 1941.

FIGURE 24. *Łapanka* in Warsaw in 1939.

FIGURE 25. Two starving children with a nurse in a hospital in the Warsaw Ghetto (1942).

FIGURE 26. Jews awaiting deportation at the *Umschlagplatz* in the Warsaw Ghetto (top); and Jews from the Warsaw Ghetto being loaded onto cattle train cars for transport to Treblinka death camp (bottom), 1942–43.

FIGURE 27. Jewish mothers and children surrendering after the defeat of the Warsaw Ghetto Uprising in 1943 (top) and being escorted to the *Umschlagplatz* (bottom).

FIGURE 28. Jewish resistance members captured by the SS during the Warsaw Ghetto Uprising in 1943 (top). Jews pulled from a bunker by the German troops in the Warsaw Ghetto Uprising in 1943 (bottom).

FIGURE 29. Katyń massacre—a mass grave of Polish military officers and upper-class civilians murdered by the Soviet NKVD in April and May 1940.

FIGURE 30. Polish Resistance fighters from the Warsaw Uprising in August to October 1944, including young teenage fighters (bottom).

FIGURE 31. German anti-tank gun (top) and Luftwaffe Stuka bombing the city (bottom) during the Warsaw Uprising (1944).

FIGURE 32. End of the Warsaw Uprising: Polish resistance fighter coming out of a sewer tunnel is taken prisoner (top); Polish resistance prisoners marching out of Warsaw on October 5, 1944 (bottom).

FIGURE 33. Wacek Sterner's tag from the prisoner-of-war camp in Sandbostel, Germany, with his prisoner's number 224676 (1944–1945).

FIGURE 34. People of Wola leaving the city after the Warsaw Uprising in 1944.

protect a child with her own body just before they are fired upon with rifles at close range by Einsatzgruppen soldiers in Ivangorod (now Ivanhorod, Ukraine) in 1942 (bottom).

FIGURE 47. Jews from Tarnopol Voivodeship shot while facedown by the Einsatzgruppen in an open pit near Złoczów.

FIGURE 48. Auschwitz II-Birkenau (Brzezinka) concentration camp in May–June 1944: inmates heading towards the barracks (top); Jewish women and children, just unloaded from a new transport, walking towards the gas chamber (bottom).

FIGURE 49. Naked Jewish women wait in a line before their execution by the Ordnungspolizei (Order Police) (top). An Ordnungspolizei officer shoots Jewish women still alive after a mass execution of Jews from the Mizocz ghetto on October 14, 1942 (bottom).

Figure Credits

FIGURE 1. https://thefutureofeuropes.fandom.com/wiki/Maps_for_Mappers/Historical_Maps?file=1936_AD.png.

FIGURE 2. https://commons.wikimedia.org/wiki/File:Rzeczpospolita_1923.png.

FIGURES 3–13, 21, 33, 36, 39–45. Author's family collection.

FIGURE 14. https://commons.wikimedia.org/wiki/File:Jan_Matejko,_Bitwa_pod_Grunwaldem.jpg.

FIGURE 15. https://commons.wikimedia.org/wiki/File:Polish_victim_of_German_Luftwaffe_action_1939.jpg

FIGURE 16. https://commons.wikimedia.org/wiki/File:Bydgoszcz-rozstrzelanie_zakładników_9.09.1939.jpg; https://commons.wikimedia.org/wiki/File:Bundesarchiv_Bild_146–1968-034–19A,_Exekution_von_polnischen_Geiseln.jpg.

FIGURE 17. https://commons.wikimedia.org/wiki/File:Palmiry_before_execution.jpg; https://commons.wikimedia.org/wiki/File:Palmiry_ostatnia_droga.jpeg.

FIGURE 18. https://commons.wikimedia.org/wiki/File:The_Bochnia_massacre_German-occupied_Poland_1939.jpg; https://commons.wikimedia.org/wiki/File:WWII_Krakow_-_04.jpg

FIGURE 19. https://commons.wikimedia.org/wiki/File:Destroyed_Magirus-Deutz_furniture_transport_van_Kolno_Poland_1945.jpg; https://commons.wikimedia.org/wiki/File:Bundesarchiv_Bild_183-A0706–0018-030,_Ukraine,_ermordete_Familie.jpg.

FIGURE 20. https://commons.wikimedia.org/wiki/File:Polish_children_in_Nazi-German_labor_camp_in_Dzierżązna.jpg.

FIGURE 22. United States Holocaust Memorial Museum, courtesy of Rafael Scharf, https://collections.ushmm.org/search/catalog/pa1074129; https://commons.wikimedia.org/wiki/File:Homeless_children_Warsaw_Ghetto.jpg.

FIGURE 23. United States Holocaust Memorial Museum, courtesy of Guenther Schwarberg, https://collections.ushmm.org/search/catalog/pa2441; https://collections.ushmm.org/search/catalog/pa2773.

FIGURE 24. https://commons.wikimedia.org/wiki/File:Łapanka.jpg.

FIGURE 25. United States Holocaust Memorial Museum, https://collections.ushmm.org/search/catalog/pa1039046. Courtesy of Emil Apfelbaum, ed., "Maladie de famine: recherches cliniques sur la famine executees dans le ghetto de Varsovie en 1942" [The Disease of Hunger: Clinical Research on Starvation Undertaken in the Warsaw Ghetto in 1942], American Joint Distribution Committee.

FIGURE 26. https://commons.wikimedia.org/wiki/File:Umschlagplatz_Warsaw_Ghetto_01.jpg; https://commons.wikimedia.org/wiki/File:Umschlagplatz_loading.jpg.

FIGURE 27. https://en.wikipedia.org/wiki/File:Stroop_Report_-_Warsaw_Ghetto_Uprising_BW.jpg; https://commons.wikimedia.org/wiki/File:Stroop_Report_-_Warsaw_Ghetto_Uprising_10.jpg.

FIGURE 28. https://commons.wikimedia.org/wiki/File:Stroop_Report_-_Warsaw_Ghetto_Uprising_08.jpg; https://commons.wikimedia.org/wiki/File:Stroop_Report_-_Warsaw_Ghetto_Uprising_11.jpg.

FIGURE 29. https://commons.wikimedia.org/wiki/File:Katyn_Massacre_-_Mass_Graves_2.jpg

FIGURE 30. https://commons.wikimedia.org/wiki/File:Warsaw_Uprising_by_Chrzanowski_-_Henio_Roma_-_14828.jpg; https://commons.wikimedia.org/wiki/File:Polish_Boy_Scouts_fighting_in_the_Warsaw_Uprising.jpg.

FIGURE 31. https://commons.wikimedia.org/wiki/File:Powstanie_warszawskie_walki_na_placu_Teatralnym.jpg; https://commons.wikimedia.org/wiki/File:Warsaw_Uprising_stuka_ju-87_bombing_Old_Town.jpg.

FIGURE 32. https://commons.wikimedia.org/wiki/File:Bundesarchiv_Bild_146-1994-054-30,_Warschauer_Aufstand,_polnischer_Soldat.jpg; https://commons.wikimedia.org/wiki/File:Warsaw_Uprising_Surrender-_5_of_October_1944.jpg.

FIGURE 34. https://commons.wikimedia.org/wiki/File:Bundesarchiv_Bild_101I-695-0423-13,_Warschauer_Aufstand,_*flüchtende*_Zivilisten.jpg.

FIGURE 35. https://commons.wikimedia.org/wiki/File:Pruszkow_Transit_Camp_women_and_children.jpg.

FIGURE 37. https://commons.wikimedia.org/wiki/File:Polish_civilians_murdered_by_German-SS-troops_in_Warsaw_Uprising_Warsaw_August_1944.jpg; https://commons.wikimedia.org/wiki/File:Palenie_zwłok_przez_Verbrennungskommando.jpg.

FIGURE 38. https://commons.wikimedia.org/wiki/File:Kings_Castle_Square,_Warsaw,_1945.jpg; https://commons.wikimedia.org/wiki/File:Warsaw_Ghetto_after_WWII_04.jpg; https://commons.wikimedia.org/wiki/File:Warsaw_Ghetto_destroyed_by_Germans,_1945.jpg.

FIGURE 46. https://commons.wikimedia.org/wiki/File:The_last_Jew_in_Vinnitsa,_1941.jpg; https://en.wikipedia.org/wiki/File:Einsatzgruppen_murder_Jews_in_Ivanhorod,_Ukraine,_1942.jpg.

FIGURE 47. https://commons.wikimedia.org/wiki/File:Nazi_Holocaust_by_bullets_-_Jewish_mass_grave_near_Zolochiv,_west_Ukraine.jpg.

FIGURE 48. https://commons.wikimedia.org/wiki/File:Birkenau_Inmates_heading_towards_the_barracks_in_the_camp.jpg; https://commons.wikimedia.org/wiki/File:Birkenau_a_group_of_Jews_walking_towards_the_gas_chambers_and_crematoria.jpg.

FIGURE 49. https://commons.wikimedia.org/wiki/File:Naked_Jewish_women_wait_in_a_line_before_their_execution_by_Ukrainian_auxiliary_police.jpg; https://commons.wikimedia.org/wiki/File:German_officer_executes_Jewish_women_who_survived_a_mass_shooting_outside_the_Mizocz_ghetto,_14_October_1942.jpg.

FRONT COVER. https://commons.wikimedia.org/wiki/File:Umschlagplatz_Warsaw_Ghetto_01.jpg.

Index

T

Printed in the USA
CPSIA information can be obtained
at www.ICGtesting.com
JSHW021522110324
58997JS00004B/194

9 798887 191980